Modern Critical Views

Modern Critical Views

Modern Critical Views

RALPH ELLISON

Edited and with an introduction by
Harold Bloom
Sterling Professor of the Humanities
Yale University

CHELSEA HOUSE PUBLISHERS
New York ◇ Philadelphia

© 1986 by Chelsea House Publishers, a division
of Main Line Book Co.

Introduction © 1986 by Harold Bloom

Printed and bound in the United States of America

10   9   8   7   6   5   4   3   2

∞ The paper used in this publication meets the minimum re-
quirements of the American National Standard for Permanence of
Paper for Printed Library Materials, Z39.48–1984.

Library of Congress Cataloging-in-Publication Data
Ralph Ellison.
    (Modern critical views)
    Bibliography: p.
    Includes index.
    1. Ellison, Ralph—Criticism and interpretation.
I. Bloom, Harold.   II. Series.
PS3555.L625Z87   1986   813'.54   86-9691
ISBN 0-87754-710-6

Contents

Editor's Note

This book gathers together eleven representative essays upon the literary achievement of Ralph Ellison, the author of *Invisible Man,* a novel that to many critics seems the finest work of American fiction between William Faulkner and Thomas Pynchon. The essays are reprinted here in the chronological order of their individual publication. I am grateful to Henry Finder for his assistance in locating the essays in this volume.

The editor's introduction explores some analogues between Ellison and Pynchon, and then centers upon the Invisible Man's antithetical relations both to Rinehart the Runner and Reverend, and to Ras the Exhorter and Destroyer. R. W. B. Lewis begins the chronological sequence of criticism with a moving review of Ellison's essays, *Shadow and Act,* which he interprets as the author's real autobiography, as distinguished from the symbolic version in *Invisible Man.*

In the first of the many exegeses of *Invisible Man* included in this volume Jonathan Baumbach associates Ellison and Faulkner as examples of remarkabl verbal energy sometimes marred by oratorical excess. Allen Guttmann reads th novel as accurate prophecy of an augmenting American social nightmare, whi... Tony Tanner, centering upon what he terms "the music of invisibility," emphasizes the complexities of the book's crucial image of hibernation.

A similar emphasis informs Robert B. Stepto's analysis, which brilliantly works through the dialectic of "literacy and hibernation" in the novel. Susan L. Blake, exploring the incorporation of folklore, ritual, and myth in all of Ellison's major fiction, concludes that by working in the larger contexts of Western literary and mythic tradition, Ellison has, paradoxically, exchanged "the self-definition of the folk for the definition of the masters," turning ritual into rationalization. Ellison's Emersonian stance as a contemporary man of letters is evoked by Charles T. Davis in an account of the literary and personal friendships between Ellison, Richard Wright, and James Baldwin. In contrast to Blake, Davis finds *Invisible Man* "a personal odyssey that leads to the discovery of a rich black folk

heritage, which accompanies the acquisition of a psychological equilibrium
. . . almost sufficient to face a chaotic and often senseless world."

  We move to contemporary modes of criticism in the final essays of this
volume, starting with the analysis of creativity and commerce in the Trueblood
episode by Houston A. Baker, Jr. Michael G. Cooke sensitively explores the
images of creative solitude as modes of self-realization in Ellison, while Douglas
Robinson provides a highly suggestive critique of the Jonah motif as a vital, anti-
apocalyptic element in *Invisible Man*. In a previously unpublished essay, Berndt
Ostendorf concludes this volume with a comprehensive examination of the ways
in which anthropology, Modernism, and jazz interact in framing and mapping
Ellison's writing.

Introduction

More than a third of a century after its original publication (1952), Ralph Ellison's *Invisible Man* is fully confirmed as an American Classic. I remember reading *Invisible Man* when it first appeared, and joining in the enthusiastic reception of the book. A number of readings since have caused the novel to seem richer, and rereading it now brings no temptation to dissent from the general verdict. One can prophesy that *Invisible Man* will be judged, some day, as the principal work of American fiction between Faulkner's major phase and *Gravity's Rainbow* by Pynchon. Only West's *Miss Lonelyhearts*, of all the novels between Faulkner and Pynchon, rivals *Invisible Man* as an eminent instance of the American imagination in narrative, and West's scope is specialized and narrow, however intense in its superbly negative exuberance.

Rereading *Invisible Man*, the exuberance of the tale and the strength of its nameless narrator seem to me far less negative than they did back in 1952. I agree with Douglas Robinson that Ellison gave us a Book of Jonah in descent from *Moby-Dick*, and so I agree also with Robinson's argument against R.W. B. Lewis's distinguished and influential contention that *Invisible Man* is an apocalyptic work. Ellison's novel is the narrator's book, and not the book of Rinehart or of Ras the Exhorter, and the narrator goes underground only as Jonah does, to come up again, in order to live as a narrator. Like Jonah, like the Ancient Mariner of Coleridge, like Melville's Ishmael, and even like Job, the narrator escapes apocalpyse and returns to tell us his story.

When we first meet the narrator, he is living an underground existence that seems to have suggested to Pynchon the grand invention of the story of Byron the Light Bulb in *Gravity's Rainbow* (I owe this allusive link to Pamela Schirmeister). Byron the Bulb's war against the System which insists that he burn out is a precisely apocalyptic transumption of the Invisible Man's struggle against Monopolated Light & Power:

1

That is why I fight my battle with Monopolated Light & Power. The deeper reason, I mean: It allows me to feel my vital aliveness. I also fight them for taking so much of my money before I learned to protect myself. In my hole in the basement there are exactly 1,369 lights. I've wired the entire ceiling, every inch of it. And not with fluorescent bulbs, but with the older, more-expensive-to-operate kind, the filament type. An act of sabotage, you know. I've already begun to wire the wall. A junk man I know, a man of vision, has supplied me with wire and sockets. Nothing, storm or flood, must get in the way of our need for light and ever more and brighter light. The truth is the light and light is the truth. When I finish all four walls, then I'll start on the floor. Just how that will go, I don't know. Yet when you have lived invisible as long as I have you develop a certain ingenuity. I'll solve the problem. And maybe I'll invent a gadget to place my coffee pot on the fire while I lie in bed, and even invent a gadget to warm my bed—like the fellow I saw in one of the picture magazines who made himself a gadget to warm his shoes! Though invisible, I am in the great American tradition of tinkers. That makes me kin to Ford, Edison and Franklin. Call me, since I have a theory and a concept, a "thinker-tinker." Yes, I'll warm my shoes; they need it, they're usually full of holes. I'll do that and more.

Even Pynchon must have envied those 1,369 lights, all of them old-fashioned filaments if none of them an immortal Byron the Bulb. Ellison's Invisible Man is another ancestor of all those heroic schlemiels who constitute Pynchon's hopeless preterites, the Counterforce of Tyrone Slothrop, Roger Mexico, poor Byron the Bulb, and the other Gnostic sparks of light who flash on amidst the broken vessels of the Zone. As befits his great namesake Emerson, Ellison is both pragmatist and transcendentalist, a combination that in Pynchon falls downwards and outwards into entropy and paranoia. It is a perplexing irony that Ellison's narrator ends with a prophecy that Ellison himself has been unable to fulfill (*Invisible Man* being his first and last novel) but that Pynchon has inherited:

Yes, but what *is* the next phase? How often have I tried to find it! Over and over again I've gone up above to seek it out. For, like almost everyone else in our country, I started out with my share of optimism. I believed in hard work and progress and action, but now, after first being "for" society and then "against" it, I assign myself no rank or any limit, and such an attitude is very much against the trend of the times. But my world has become one of infinite possibilities. What a phrase—still it's a good phrase and a good view of life, and a man shouldn't accept any other; that much I've learned underground. Until some gang succeeds in putting the world in a strait-jacket, its definition is possibility. Step outside the narrow borders of what men call reality and you step into chaos—ask Rinehart, he's a master of it—or imagination. That too I've learned in the cellar, and not by deadening my sense of perception; I'm invisible, not blind.

Pynchon has stepped, of course, into both chaos and imagination, but his chaos is the apocalyptic Zone where we may yet live again (if we live), and his imagination is his Kabbalistic vision that he calls "sado-anarchism." The step beyond *Invisible Man* is one that Ellison is too humane and too humanistic to have taken. Pynchon, chronicler of the Counterforce but hardly its prophet, gives us the Invisible Man a generation later in the image of Rocketman, the sublimely inane Slothrop, who is literally scattered into more than invisibility in the Zone, and who may have been sighted for a final time as a fleeting photograph on the record jacket of a rock band.

II

The antinomies between which Ellison's narrator moves are Rinehart (more an image than a man) and the poignant figure of Ras the Exhorter, very much a man, indeed the most sympathetic personality in the novel, more so even than the martyred Tod Clifton. Driven mad by white oppression and brutality, Ras becomes Ras the Destroyer, at once Ahab and Moby-Dick, and is silenced by his own spear, slung back at him by the narrator, an Ishmael turned avenger in self-defense. But Ras, though he suffers Ahab's fate, is no Ahab, and his remains an uncanny prophecy to blacks and whites alike. Clifton speaks the truth when he observes: "But it's on the inside that Ras is strong. On the inside he's dangerous." Ras speaks the dangerous eloquence of justified indignation and despair:

Ras struck his thighs with his fists. "*Me* crazy, mahn? You call *me* crazy? Look at you two and look at me—is this *sanity?* Standing here in three shades of blackness! Three black men fighting in the street because of the white enslaver? Is that sanity? Is that consciousness, scientific understahnding? Is that the modern black mahn of the twentieth century? Hell, mahn! Is it self-respect—black against black? What they give you to betray—their women? You fall for that?"

"Let's go," I said, listening and remembering and suddenly alive in the dark with the horror of the battle royal, but Clifton looked at Ras with a tight, fascinated expression, pulling away from me.

"Let's go," I repeated. He stood there, looking.

"Sure, you go," Ras said, "but not him. You contahminated but he the real black mahn. In Africa this mahn be a chief, a black king! Here they say he rape them godahm women with no blood in their veins. I bet this mahn can't beat them off with baseball bat—shit! What kind of foolishness is it? Kick him ass from cradle to grave then call him *brother*? Does it make mahthematics? Is it logic? Look at him, mahn; open your eyes," he said to me. "I look like that I rock the blahsted world! They know about me in Japan, India—all the colored countries. Youth! Intelligence! The mahn's a natural prince! Where is your eyes? Where your self-respect? Working for them dahm people? Their days is numbered, the time is almost here and you fooling 'round like this was the nineteenth century. I don't understand you. Am I ignorant? Answer me, mahn!"

If Ras is the imagination ruined by apocalyptic expansiveness, verging upon Pynchonean paranoia, then the image of Rinehart is chaos come again, but chaos verging upon an entropy that negates any new origin out of which a fresh creation might come. Rinehart is visibility personified, a moving shadow identified by and identical with what he wears: dark glasses, in particular, interpreted by the narrator as the Pauline "through a glass, darkly," and a white hat. If Ras is both Exhorter and Destroyer, Rinehart is both numbers runner and the Reverend B. P. Rinehart, Spiritual Technologist, who makes the Seen Unseen and tells us to Behold the Invisible. The narrator, gazing into Rinehart's church, experiences a true defeat, subtler than any Ras could hope to inflict:

Then the door opened and I looked past their heads into a small crowded room of men and women sitting in folding chairs, to the front where a slender woman in a rusty black robe played passionate boogie-woogie on an upright piano along with a young man wearing a skull cap who struck righteous riffs from an electric guitar which was connected to an amplifier that hung from the ceiling above a gleaming white and gold pulpit. A man in an elegant red cardinal's robe and a high lace collar stood resting against an enormous Bible and now began to lead a hard-driving hymn which the congregation shouted in the unknown tongue. And back and high on the wall above him there arched the words in letters of gold:

LET THERE BE LIGHT!

The whole scene quivered vague and mysterious in the green light, then the door closed and the sound muted down.

It was too much for me. I removed my glasses and tucked the white hat carefully beneath my arm and walked away. Can it be, I thought, can it actually be? And I knew that it was. I had heard of it before but I'd never come so close. Still, could he be all of them: Rine the runner and Rine the gambler and Rine the briber and Rine the lover and Rinehart the Reverend? Could he himself be both rind and heart? What is real anyway? But how could I doubt it? He was a broad man, a man of parts who got around. Rinehart the rounder. It was true as I was true. His world was possibility and he knew it. He was years ahead of me and I was a fool. I must have been crazy and blind. The world in which we lived was without boundaries. A vast seething, hot world of fluidity, and Rine the rascal was at home. Perhaps *only* Rine the rascal was at home in it. It was unbelievable, but perhaps only the unbelievable could be believed. Perhaps the truth was always a lie.

In some sense, Rinehart's truth which was always a lie becomes the dominant influence upon the narrator. It not only drives him underground, but it confirms his obsession with illumination, his parodistic reliance upon 1,369 lights. Rinehart is the authentic dweller in possibility, which Emily Dickinson called a fairer house than prose, being as it is superior of windows, more numerous of doors. Harlem or black existence is again either chaos or imagination, the possibility of Rinehart or the increasingly furious possibility of Ras the Destroyer.

The narrator, though, is finally the only authentic American, black or white, because he follows *the* American Religion, which is Emersonian Self-Reliance. He insists upon himself, refuses to go on imitating his false fathers, and evades both Rinehart and Ras. True, he is the Emersonian driven underground, but he will emerge more Emersonian than ever, insisting that he has become Representative Man:

Who knows but that, on the lower frequencies, I speak for you?

The Invisible Man says that he is frightened by this truth, and so are we. What is more frightening, for us and for him, is truer now than it was a third of a century ago, and is even more Emersonian. We have learned that, on the higher frequencies, Ellison speaks for us.

R. W. B. LEWIS

Ellison's Essays

Shadow and Act contains Ralph Ellison's real autobiography — in the form of essays and interviews — as distinguished from the symbolic version given in his splendid novel of 1952, *Invisible Man*. Some of the twenty-odd items in it were written as early as 1942, and not all of them have been published before. One or two were rejected by liberal periodicals, apparently because Ellison insisted on saying that Negro American life was not everywhere as hellish or as inert or as devastated by hatred and self-hatred as it was sometimes alleged; it is not unlikely that liberal criticism will be equally impatient with this new book. Most of the pieces, were, however, written after *Invisible Man* and in part are a consequence of it. They may even help to explain the long gap of time between Ellison's first novel and its much awaited successor. There have been other theories about this delay: for example, an obituary notice by Le Roi Jones who, in a recent summary of the supposedly lethal effect of America upon its Negro writers, referred to Ellison as "silenced and fidgeting away in some college." But he has not been silent, much less silenced — by white America or anything else. The experiences of writing *Invisible Man* and of vaulting on his first try "over the parochial limits of most Negro fiction" (as Richard G. Stern says in an interview), and, as a result, of being written about as a literary and sociological phenomenon, combined with sheer compositional difficulties, seem to have driven Ellison to search out the truths of his own past. Inquiring into his experience, his literary and musical education, Ellison has come up with a number of clues to the fantastic fate of trying to be at the same time a writer, a Negro, an American, and a human being.

From *The New York Review of Books* (January 28, 1965). © 1965 by Nyrev, Inc.

It is hard at the best of times to be even two of those things; the attempt to be all four must be called gallant. For even those among us who consent to Negroes being accepted as human beings, don't really want them to be writers. We want them to be warriors, and wounded warriors at that; with their creative talents enlisted in the (great and real) struggle for racial justice. This is our curious contemporary device for keeping the Negro in his place, which, when it is not on the actual battlefield, is thought to be in some immitigable psychological hell. When a Negro like Ellison says, "Why, this is not *altogether* hell, after all," and then goes on to talk about the role and responsibility of the writer, his remarks are resented as mere aestheticism, or worse, as a kind of betrayal. A good many pages of *Shadow and Act* describe Ellison's patient effort to explain the organic relation between his personal sense of life, his racial and national identity, and his chosen artistic vocation: to explain, not how he sought to escape or deny his Negro-ness by fleeing into the color-less domain of art, but how it has been essentially *as* a writer that he managed to discover what it means for him to be a Negro American and a human being. It is obviously a tough point to get across.

Ellison works towards that point from several directions and in various modes. In interviews with Richard Stern and the editors of the *Paris Review,* he reflects on the origins of *Invisible Man,* on the devious craft of fiction, and on the usual failure of dialogue between Negro writer and white reader. In an exchange with Stanley Edgar Hyman he argues for the "specificity" of literary works, including his own, and questions the value of "archetype-hunting," especially since, with Negro writing, it tends to reimpose the stereotypes Negroes are most anxious to shake off. On the question of a "Negro culture," Ellison rejects the notion of African antecedents. "I know of no valid demonstration," he says, "that culture is transmitted through the genes . . . The American Negro people is North American in origin . . . its spiritual outlook is basically Protestant, its system of kinship is Western, its time and historical sense are American." In essays on twentieth-century fiction and on Stephen Crane, and in a speech in 1953 accepting the National Book Award, Ellison evinces just that outlook and sense of kinship; though, as I'll suggest, in beguilingly specialized terms.

It is above all in an autobiographical lecture called "Hidden Name and Complex Fate," and in a long reply to an essay by Irving Howe, that Ellison confronts these intertwining issues with full intellectual and imaginative authority. Elsewhere the book's central argument is at times spotty and groping, and once in a while gummy; but these two pieces have an assurance and a truth that are bound to unsettle and dismay all those whose minds have grown rigid with the fixed concept of the American Negro as trapped agony incarnate.

The Oklahoma of Ellison's childhood had joined the Union long after the Emancipation, and hence had no tradition of slavery except for the ancestral memories brought into it by the descendants of slaves. Even those memories were effectively diverse; for while "slavery was a most vicious system and those who endured and survived it a tough people," Ellison observes, a person born into slavery might look forward to becoming "a coachman, a teamster, a cook, the best damned steward on the Mississippi, the best jockey in Kentucky, a butler, a farmer, a stud, or, hopefully, a free man!" In Oklahoma, there was segregation, to be sure, though perhaps less thirty years ago than now; but there was always a certain amount of elbowroom. The experience of precarious freedom within carefully defined limits made Ellison aware of a similar phenomenon in the music of the southwestern jazzmen of the day. Their music expressed for him "the freedom lying within the restrictions of their musical traditions as within the limitations of their social background." The sense of that twofold possibility —artistic and social—remained with Ellison when he moved on later to the deep South and then to New York City. He is aware that Oklahoma was not Harlem: that is just his point. His point, too, is that Harlem—particularly Harlem as currently imagined—is not Oklahoma; and that there is a variety that adds spice and vigor and even a sort of battered enjoyment to American Negro life, and that those qualities should be added to the anguish and the appalling humiliations in any account of it.

There were separate but equal moviehouses back in Oklahoma, standing shoulder to shoulder and entered from the same doorway. But, Ellison remarks dryly, "I went to the movies to see pictures, not to be with whites." He also went to the library. Ellison seems to have known what every aspiring writer has to know: that his apprenticeship can take place only in literature. In "Black Boys and Native Sons," Irving Howe, while admiring *Invisible Man,* accused Ellison of forgetting the urgencies of the Negro cause in the interests of mere "literature," and of failing in particular to continue along the savage polemical path mapped out by Richard Wright. In reply, Ellison argues that, quite apart from the frozen inaccuracy of Howe's and Wright's appraisal of the Negro situation, Negro writers do not and cannot descend from Negroes, but from writers. "James Baldwin," he goes on, "is the product not of a Negro storefront church but of the library, and the same is true of me." It is depressing to realize that this is a daring statement. (But it is the kind of insight that distinguishes a genuine writer.)

As a novelist, Ellison was drawn to the novels of Dostoevsky and Conrad, and much more to those of Malraux (though not, oddly enough, to Silone, with whom he has much in common, attempting, like Silone, to convert political violence into poetry, from the periphery of the culture into which he is moving).

But as a Negro American writer, he was drawn to the classical period of American literature — and exactly because he found there "the conception of the Negro as the symbol of Man." I am not quite convinced that slavery and the Negro were as central to the imaginations of Whitman, Emerson, Thoreau, Melville, and Mark Twain as Ellison makes out. But his reading of these writers, like Eliot's Protestant American reading of Donne and Dante, is the critical paraphrase by which every authentic writer creates a new literary tradition for himself, to suit his artistic needs and abilities. Melville and Mark Twain and other writers showed Ellison how to give shape to his subject: that is, to his experience, as a Negro in modern America. Drawing on earlier treatments of the Negro as the symbol of Man, Ellison found ways not only to articulate, but to universalize his own complex identity — and to celebrate its pain-wracked, eternally wondering and comical nature. Writers after Mark Twain have been mainly useful to him because of their technical skills; for, except in the novels of Faulkner, Ellison finds that "the human Negro" has to a large extent disappeared from American fiction, has been replaced by Jim Crow (whose late arrival in fiction Ellison describes in a manner similar to C. Vann Woodward's account of the belated rise of Jim Crow in historic fact).

Ellison had originally expected to make a career in music, as a composer of symphonies and as a jazz trumpeter. He abandoned the notion, but almost a third of *Shadow and Action* consists of luxuriantly written and affectionate recollections of jazzmen and singers of blues and spirituals. There is also a review of Le Roi Jones's book, *Blues People,* in which Ellison contends characteristically that, by treating his subject sociologically, Jones failed to see that music was what slaves had instead of freedom and that, later, the blues were what Negroes had instead of religion. In both epochs, he suggests, music was the vehicle by which an otherwise powerless black people could profoundly influence, could indeed enthrall or counterenslave, the white people. This section of Ellison's book contains the least intimidating, because the most unpretentious and humane, descriptions of Negro musical expression that I have read. And when Ellison defines the blues as the "chronicle of personal catastrophe expressed lyrically," and as "an impulse to keep the painful details and episodes of a brutal experience alive in one's aching consciousness . . . and to transcend it, not by the consolations of philosophy but by squeezing from it a near-tragic, near-comic lyricism" — he makes the same connection between art and experience, that he makes in the essays on literature and his autobiographical memoir. One can also make out a fairly exact summary of the themes of *Invisible Man*.

This may be the worst possible moment for an attempt at dialogue between or about Negroes and whites in America. But Ellison's demonstration of his identity had a singular effect upon me. The more he invoked the phrase "Negro

American," the more I found myself mumbling to myself the phrase "white American" — not in pride nor shame, but with a shock of recognition. Ellison's identity, because of the power and wisdom and stubborn sanity of its pronouncement, serves to limit mine, to establish its boundaries and focus *its* intermixing elements. No experience is more to be cherished; for Ellison is not only a self-identifier but the source of self-definition in others. At just that point, a falsely conceived integration (the melting of indistinguishable persons) ceases, and the dialogue can begin.

JONATHAN BAUMBACH

Nightmare of a Native Son

Who knows but that, on the lower frequencies, I speak for you?
—*Invisible Man*

I hesitate to call Ralph Ellison's *Invisible Man* a Negro novel, though of course it is written by a Negro and is centrally concerned with the experiences of a Negro. The appellation is not so much inaccurate as it is misleading. A novelist treating the invisibility and phantasmagoria of the Negro's life in this "democracy" is, if he tells the truth, necessarily writing a very special kind of book. Yet if his novel is interesting only because of its specialness, he has not violated the surface of his subject; he has not, after all, been serious. Despite the differences in their external concerns, Ellison has more in common as a novelist with Joyce, Melville, Camus, Kafka, West, and Faulkner than he does with other serious Negro writers like James Baldwin and Richard Wright. To concentrate on the idiom of a serious novel, no matter how distinctive its peculiarities, is to depreciate it, to minimize the universality of its implications. Though the protagonist of *Invisible Man* is a southern Negro, he is, in Ellison's rendering, profoundly all of us.

Despite its obvious social implications, Ellison's novel is a modern gothic a Candide-like picaresque set in a dimly familiar nightmare landscape called the United States. Like *The Catcher in the Rye, A Member of the Wedding,* and *The Adventures of Augie March,* Ellison's novel chronicles a series of initiatory experiences through which its naive hero learns, to his disillusion and horror, the way of the world. However, unlike these other novels of passage, *Invisible Man* takes place, for the most part, in the uncharted spaces between the conscious and the unconscious, in the semilit darkness where nightmare verges on reality

From *Five Black Writers: Essays on Wright, Ellison, Baldwin, Hughes, and Le Roi Jones.*
© 1970 by New York University. New York University Press, 1970. Originally entitled "Nightmare of a Native Son: *Invisible Man* by Ralph Ellison."

and the external world has all the aspects of a disturbing dream. Refracted by satire, at times, cartooned, Ellison's world is at once surreal and real, comic and tragic, grotesque and normal — our world viewed in its essentials rather than its externals.

The Negro's life in our white land and time is, as Ellison knows it, a relentless unreality, unreal in that the Negro as a group is loved, hated, persecuted, feared, and envied, while as an individual he is unfelt, unheard, unseen — to all intents and purposes invisible. The narrator, who is also the novel's central participant, never identifies himself by name. Though he experiences several changes of identity in the course of the novel, Ellison's hero exists to the reader as a man without an identity, an invisible "I." In taking on a succession of identities, the invisible hero undergoes an increasingly intense succession of disillusioning experiences, each one paralleling and anticipating the one following it. The hero's final loss of illusion forces him underground into the coffin (and womb) of the earth to be either finally buried or finally reborn.

The narrator's grandfather, whom he resembles (identity is one of the major concerns of the novel), is the first to define the terms of existence for him. An apparently meek man all his life, on his deathbed the grandfather reveals:

> Son, after I'm gone I want you to keep up the good fight. I never told you, but our life is a war and I have been a traitor all my born days, a spy in the enemy's country ever since I give up my gun back in the Reconstruction. Live with your head in the lion's mouth. I want you to overcome 'em with yesses, undermine 'em with grins, agree 'em to death and destruction, let 'em swoller you till they vomit or bust wide open.

Though at the time he understands his grandfather's ambiguous creed only imperfectly, the hero recognizes that it is somehow his heritage. In a sense, the old man's code of acquiescent resistance is an involved justification of his nonresistance; it is a parody on itself, yet the possibility always remains that it is, in some profound, mysterious way, a meaningful ethic. On a succession of occasions, the hero applies his grandfather's advice, "agreeing 'em to death," in order to understand its import through discovering its efficacy. On each occasion, however, it is he, not "'em," who is victimized. Consequently, the hero suffers a sense of guilt — not for having compromised himself but for failing somehow to effect his grandfather's ends. Ironically, he also feels guilty for deceiving the white "enemy," though he has "agreed them" not to death or destruction, only to renewed complacency. For example:

> When I was praised for my conduct I felt a guilt that in some way I was doing something that was really against the wishes of the white

folks, that if they had understood they would have desired me to act just the opposite, that I should have been sulky and mean, and that really would have been what they wanted, even though they were fooled and thought they wanted me to act as I did.

The hero's cynical obsequiousness has self-destructive consequences. Having delivered a high school graduation speech advocating humility as the essence of progress, he is invited to deliver his agreeable oration to a meeting of the town's leading white citizens. Before he is allowed to speak, however, he is subjected to a series of brutal degradations, which teach him, in effect, the horror of the humility he advocates. In this episode, the first of his initiatory experiences, the invisible man's role is symbolically prophesied. The hero, along with nine other Negro boys, is put into a prize ring, then is blindfolded and coerced into battling his compatriots. Duped by the whites, the Negro unwittingly fights himself; his potency, which the white man envies and fears, is mocked and turned against him to satisfy the brutal whims of his persecutor. That the bout is preceded by a nude, blond belly dancer whom the boys are forced to watch suggests the prurience underlying the victimizer's treatment of his victim. The degrading prizefight, a demonstration of potency to titillate the impotent, in which the Negro boys blindly flail one another to entertain the sexually aroused stag audience, parallels the riot in Harlem at the end of the novel, which is induced by another institution of white civilization, the Brotherhood (a fictional guise for the Communist party). Once again Negro fights against Negro (Ras the Destroyer against the hero), although this time it is for the sake of "Brotherhood," a euphemism for the same inhumanity. In both cases, the Negro unwittingly performs the obscene demands of his enemy. In magnification, Harlem is the prize ring where the Negroes, blindfolded this time by demagoguery, flail at each other with misdirected violence. The context has changed from South to North, from white citizens to the Brotherhood, from a hired ballroom to all of Harlem, but the implication remains the same: the Negro is victimized by having his potency turned against himself by his impotent persecutor.

After the boxing match, what appears to be gold is placed on a rug in the center of the room and the boys are told to scramble for their rewards. The hero reacts: "I trembled with excitement, forgetting my pain. I would get the gold and the bills, I thought. I would use both hands. I would throw my body against the boys nearest me to block them from the gold."

He is, on the rug as in the boxing ring, degraded by self-interest. Though his reaction is unpleasant, it is, given the provocation, the normal, calculable one. He has been tempted and, unaware of any practicable ethical alternative, has succumbed in innocence. When the temptation recurs in more complex guises later in the novel and Ellison's nameless hero as adult falls victim to his self-interest, he is, despite his larger moral purposes, culpable and must assume responsibility for the terrible consequences of his deeds. In each of the various analogous episodes, the hero is torn between his implicit commitment to his grandfather's position — subversive acquiescence — and his will to identify — the primal instinct of self-assertion. Both commitments dictate pragmatic, as opposed to purely ethical, action, with, inevitably, immoral and impractical consequences. The rug becomes electrified, the gold coins turn out to be brass — a means, like the bout, of mocking the Negro's envied potency. That the fight and electrification follow in sequence the naked belly dancer in the course of an evening of stag entertainment for tired white businessmen indicates the obscene prurience behind the white citizen's hatred of the Negro. By debasing and manipulating the Negro's potency, the white mutes its threat and at the same time experiences it vicariously. It is in all a mordant evocation, satiric in its rendering and frightening in its implications. The white man's fascination with the Negro as a source of power (potency) is another of the thematic threads that holds together what might otherwise be a picaresque succession of disparate episodes. The ballroom humiliation serves as a gloss on the following scene, in which the hero is expelled from the Negro state college for, ironically, the consequence of his obedience to a white trustee.

The president of the Negro college, Dr. Bledsoe (all of Ellison's names characterize their bearers), entrusts the hero, up to then a model student, with the responsibility of chauffeuring a philantropic white trustee, Mr. Norton, on a tour of the manicured country surrounding the campus. Driving aimlessly — or perhaps with more aim than he knows — the hero suddenly discovers that he has taken the trustee to the backwoods homestead of Jim Trueblood, the area's black sheep, an "unenlightened" Negro whose sharecropper existence (and incestuous, child-producing accident with his daughter) is a source of continued embarrassment to the "progressive" community of the college. The hero would like to leave, but Norton, curiously fascinated by the fact that Trueblood has committed incest (and survived), insists on talking with the sharecropper. At Norton's prodding, Trueblood tells his story, an extended and graphically detailed account of how he was induced by a dream into having physical relations with his daughter. The story itself is a masterpiece of narrative invention and perhaps the single most brilliant scene in the novel.

As Trueblood finishes his story, we discover in a moment of ironic revelation that the bloodless Norton is a kind of euphemistic alter ego — a secret sharer — of the atavistic Trueblood. Earlier, while being driven deeper into the backwoods country — the reality behind the ivy league facade of the college — Norton had rhapsodized to the narrator about the unearthly charms of his own daughter, for whose death he feels unaccountably guilty:

> Her beauty was a well-spring of purest water-of-life, and to look
> upon her was to drink and drink and drink again. . . . She was
> rare, a perfect creation, a work of purest art. . . . I found it dif-
> ficult to believe her my own. . . . I have never forgiven myself.
> Everything I've done since her passing has been a monument to her
> memory.

Trueblood, then, has committed the very sin that Norton has, in the dark places
of his spirit, impotently coveted. Upon hearing Trueblood's story, Norton participates vicariously in his experience, has his own quiescent desires fulfilled while
exempted, since Trueblood has acted for him, from the stigma of the act.
Underlying Norton's recurrent platitude that "the Negro is my fate" (he means
that they are his potency) is the same prurience that motivates the sadism of the
white citizens in the preceding scene. However, in an ironic way, Trueblood *is*
Norton's fate. When Trueblood finishes his story, Norton feels compelled to pay
him, as the white citizens reward the Negro boxers, in exchange for, in a double
sense, having performed for him. When Norton (who exists here really as idea
rather than character) leaves Trueblood's farm, he is exhausted and colorless, as
if he had in fact just committed incest with his own daughter.

Having exposed Norton to the horror of his own philantropic motives, after
a further misadventure among inmates of a Negro insane asylum, the hero is expelled from school by Bledsoe because "any act that endangered the continuity
of the dream is an act of treason." The boy, sensing his innocence, feels haunted
by his grandfather's curse. Through Ellison's surrealistic rendering, we sense the
nightmare reality of the hero's experience (as we do not with Norton's comparable nightmare):

> How had I come to this? I had kept unswervingly to the path before
> me, had tried to be exactly what I was expected to be, had done ex-
> actly what I was expected to do—yet, instead of winning the ex-
> pected reward, here I was stumbling along, holding on desperately
> to one of my eyes in order to keep from bursting out my brain against
> some familiar object swerved into my path by my distorted vision.
> And now to drive me wild I felt suddenly that my grandfather was
> hovering over me, grinning triumphantly out of the dark.

Accepting responsibility for the sins of his innocence, the hero goes to New
York, armed with several letters of "identification" which Bledsoe has addressed
to various trustees for the ostensible purpose of finding him a job. When the
hero discovers that the letters have been written "to hope him to death, and
keep him running," that the renowned Negro educator Bledsoe has betrayed

him treacherously, has in effect ordered him killed as an almost gratuitous display of power, he experiences a moment of terrible disillusion. At the same time he senses that this betrayal is in some way a reenactment of the past: "Twenty-five years seemed to have lapsed between his handing me the letter and my grasping its message. I could not believe it, yet I had a feeling that it all had happened before. I rubbed my eyes, and they felt sandy as though all the fluids had suddenly dried."

In a way, it *has* happened before; for Bledsoe's act of victimization (the beating of Negro by Negro) is analogous to the punishment the hero received in the prize ring at the hands of the largest of the other Negro boys. Bledsoe's deceit, like its analog, is motivated by the desire to ingratiate himself with the white society which dispenses rewards — which provides, or so he believes, the source of his power.

As one episode parallels another, each vignette in itself has allegorical extensions. Employed by Liberty Paints, a factory "the size of a small city," the narrator is ordered to put ten drops of "black dope" into buckets of optic white paint in order, he is told, to make it whiter. The mixing of the black into the white is, of course, symbolic: the ten drops are analogous to the ten boys in the prize ring, and in each case the white becomes whiter by absorbing the Negro's virility, by using the black to increase the strength of the white. Yet the name "optic white" suggests it is all some kind of visual illusion. When the black dope runs out, the hero as apprentice paint mixer is ordered by his boss, "the terrible Mr. Kimbro," to replace it, without being told which of seven possible vats has the right substance. Left to his own discretion, the hero chooses the wrong black liquid, concentrated paint remover, which makes the white paint transparent and grayish; this act symbolizes the implicit threat of Negro potency left to its own devices. The paint-mixing scene is paralleled by the violence of the insane Negro veterans at the bar (the Golden Day) in which they beat their white attendant Supercargo into grayness and terrorize the already depleted Norton. It anticipates the antiwhite violence of Ras the exhorter-turned-destroyer, the only alternative to invisibility the white man has left the Negro.

Yet there is the illusion of another alternative: when the narrator adds the black drops to the paint which already contains the black remover, though the mixture appears gray to him, it passes for white in Kimbro's eyes. This is, in symbol, the role of subterfuge and infiltration — his grandfather's legacy and curse.

> I looked at the painted slab. It appeared the same: a gray tinge glowed through the whiteness, and Kimbro had failed to detect it. I stared for a minute, wondering if I were seeing things, inspected another and another. All were the same, a brilliant white diffused with gray.

I closed my eyes for a moment and looked again and still no change.
Well, I thought as long as he's satisfied.

Kimbro permits the gray-tinged paint to be shipped out and the hero wonders whether, after all, he has been the deceiver or the deceived. He suspects, when Kimbro dismisses him, that he somehow has been the dupe. That the paint passes for white in Kimbro's eyes suggests that the black with which it was mixed was, like the hero's existence, to all intents and purposes, invisible.

Essentially invisible, the narrator undergoes a succession of superficial changes of identity—in a sense, changes of mask—each entailing a symbolic, though illusory, death and rebirth. Knocked unconscious by the explosion of a machine which makes the base of a white paint, a machine that he was unable to control, the hero is placed in another machine, a coffin-like electrified box, in order to be "started again." The shock treatments surrealistically rendered recall the electrification from the rug, however magnified in intensity. Like most of the episodes in the novel, it is on the surface a comic scene, though in its implications (lobotomy and castration) it is a singularly unpleasant nightmare. The hero's first awareness upon awakening is that he is enclosed in a glass box with an electric cap attached to his head, a combination coffin-womb and electrocutor. When he is blasted with a charge of electricity, he instinctively screams in agonized protest, only to be told in response as if he were indeed a piece of equipment," 'Hush goddamit . . . We're trying to get you started again. Now shut up!' " After a while he is unable to remember who he is or whether he has in fact existed before his present moment of consciousness: "My mind was blank, as though I'd just begun to live." Like the charged rug, though considerably more cruel, the shock treatments are intended to neutralize him, in effect to castrate him. In his moments of confused consciousness he hears two voices arguing over the proper method to treat his case. One is in favor of surgery, the other in favor of the machine.

> "The machine will produce the results of a prefrontal lobotomy without the negative effect of the knife," the voice said. "You see, instead of severing the prefrontal lobe, a single lobe, that is, we apply pressure in the proper degrees to the major centers of nerve control—our concept is Gestalt—and the result is as complete a change of personality as you'll find in your famous fairy-tale cases of criminals transformed into amiable fellows after all that bloody business of a brain operation. And what's more," the voice went on triumphantly, "the patient is both physically and neurally whole."
> "But what of his psychology?"
> "Absolutely of no importance!" the voice said. "The patient will

live as he has to live, with absolute integrity. Who could ask more? He'll experience no major conflict of motives, and what is even better, society will suffer no traumata on his account."

There was a pause. A pen scratched upon paper. Then, "Why not castration doctor?" a voice asked waggishly, causing me to start, a pain tearing through me.

"There goes your love of blood again," the first voice laughed. "What's that definition of a surgeon, 'A butcher with a bad conscience'?"

They laughed.

I quote this passage at length to suggest the high-voltage charge of Ellison's satire, capable at once of being mordantly comic and profoundly terrifying. The clinical attitude of the psychologist ("society will suffer no traumata on his account") suggests the northern white position toward the Negro, as opposed to the butcher-surgeon who represents the more overtly violent southern position. The ends of both, however, are approximately the same — emasculation; the difference is essentially one of means.

The narrator is, in this scene, almost visibly invisible, discussed impersonally in his presence as if he were not there. When he is unable to recall his name, his mother's name, any form of his identity, any form of his past, the doctors seem pleased and deliver him from the machine, the only mother he knows.

I felt a tug at my belly and looked down to see one of the physicians pull the cord which was attached to the stomach node, jerking me forward. . . .

"Get the shears," he said. "Let's not waste time."

"Sure," the other said. "Let's not waste time."

I recoiled inwardly as though the cord were part of me. Then they had it free and the nurse clipped through the belly band and removed the heavy node.

In describing the birth from the machine, Ellison suggests through evocation that it is also a kind of castration. Insofar as it leaves the hero without the potency of self, it is, in implication, just that.

Aside from the Prologue and parts of the Epilogue, which have an enlightened madness all their own, the experience of the machine birth is the least realistic, the most surrealistic, in the novel. And this brings us to what I think is the novel's crucial flaw, its inconsistency of method, its often violent transformations from a kind of detailed surface realism in which probability is limited to the context of ordinary, everyday experiences to an allegorical world of almost endless imaginative possibilities. Often the shift is dramatically effective, as when the

hero and Norton enter the insane world of the Golden Day (here the truth is illuminated by a nominal madman who has the insane virtue of pure sight) and
Norton is forced into a frightening moment of self-recognition. On other occasions, the visional shifts jar us away from the novel's amazing world into an
awareness of the ingenuity of its creator. Since Ellison is at once prodigiously
talented and prodigiously reckless, *Invisible Man* is astonishingly good at its
best. By the same token the book is uneven; on occasion it is very bad as only
very good novels can be. Given the nature of his vision, Ellison's world seems
real or alive — when it is surrealistically distorted, and for the most part made-
up or abstract — when it imitates the real world. Largely recounted in the manner
of traditional realism, the hero's adventures in the Brotherhood up until the
Harlem riot constitute the least interesting section of the novel.

In joining the Brotherhood, the narator gives up his past to assume a new
identity or rather new nonidentity, Brother _____. Because of his remarkable
speech-making abilities, as well as his conscious ambition to be some kind of
savior, he becomes one of the leading figures of the Harlem Brotherhood. Finally, his controversial activities make it necessary for him to disguise himself in
order to get through Harlem safely. Brother _____'s disguise — dark glasses and
a wide-brimmed hat — which he has hoped would make him inconspicuous in
Harlem, creates for him still another identity, which is, in effect, just a new
aspect of nonidentity. Wearing the hat and glasses, Brother _____ is unrecog-
nized as his Brotherhood self, but is mistaken for a man named Rinehart, a
charlatan of incredible diversification. Rinehart, whose identities include
numbers runner, police briber, lover, pimp, and Reverend, is, the hero discovers, a kind of alter ego to his invisibility. If you are no one, you are at the
same time potentially everyone. The hero has disguised himself in order to avoid
the consequences of his acts and instead finds himself held responsible for
Rinehart's inordinate sins — for all sins — which are, in the Dostoevskian sense,
his own. When the Brotherhood's theoretician Hambro informs the hero that,
with the alteration of the larger plan, his role has changed from exhorter to
pacifier, he senses his likeness to his dazzling alter ego:

> ". . . Besides I'd feel like Rinehart. . . ." It slipped out and he
> looked at me.
>   "Like who?"
>   "Like a charlatan," I said.
>   Hambro laughed. "I thought you learned about that, Brother."
>   I looked at him quickly. "Learned what?"
>   "That it's impossible *not* to take advantage of the people."
>   "That's Rinehartism — cynicism. . . ."

In following the dictates of the Brotherhood, the hero has hurt, he discovers to his pain, the very people he has intended to help. Without benefit of glasses and hat, he has been a Rinehart in disguise all the time. He has been, paradoxically, an unwitting cynic. Duped by his self-conscious, romantic ambitions to be another Booker T. Washington, the hero has let the Brotherhood use him for their cynical "historic" purposes. As a Brotherhood agent, he demagogically incites the Harlem Negroes to potential action only to leave them prey to the misdirected violence of Ras, their violence ultimately turned, like that of the boys in the prize ring, against themselves. With awareness comes responsibility, and the hero recognizes that he alone must bear the guilt for the Brotherhood's betrayal of the Negro. The ramifications of his awful responsibility are manifested generally in the hellish Harlem riot at the end of the novel and particularly in the disillusion and death of the most admirable of the Brotherhood, Tod Clifton (the name suggests a kind of Promethean entrapment), whose career prophesies and parallels that of the hero.

Earlier in the novel, Ras, after sparing Tod's life, has exhorted his adversary to leave the Brotherhood and join his racist movement (a fictionalized version of the Black Muslims). Their confrontation, an objectification of the hero's interior struggle, anticipates Tod's defection from the Brotherhood.

> "Come with us, mahn. We build a glorious movement of black people. *Black people!* What do they do, give you money? who wahnt the damn stuff? Their money bleed black blood, mahn. It's unclean! Taking their money is shit, mahn. Money without dignity—that's *bahd* shit!"
>
> Clifton lunged toward him. I held him, shaking my head. "Come on, the man's crazy," I said, pulling on his arm.
>
> Ras struck his thighs with his fists. "Me crazy, mahn? You call me crazy? Look at you two and look at me—is this sanity? Standing here in three shades of blackness! Three black men fighting in the street because of the white enslaver? Is that sanity? Is that consciousness, scientific understanding? Is that the modern black mahn of the twentieth century? Hell, mahn! Is it self-respect—black against black? What they give you to betray—their women? You fall for that?"
>
> "Let's go," I repeated. He stood there, looking.
>
> "Sure, you go," Ras said, "but not him. You contahminated but he the real black mahn. In Africa this mahn be a chief, a black king!"

In this eloquent scene, Clifton finally rejects Ras, but he is undeniably moved by his enemy's crude exhortation. Ras—the name suggests an amalgam of race and rash — is a fanatic, but given his basic premise, that the white man is the Negro's natural enemy, his arguments are not easily refutable. Unable to answer Ras, Clifton, out of a sense of shame or guilt, knocks the Exhorter down, committing an act of Rasian violence. The punch is an acknowledgment, a communion, an act of love. As they leave, the hero discovers that Clifton has tears in his eyes. Clifton says, referring to Ras, " 'That poor misguided son of a bitch.' 'He thinks a lot of you, too,' I said."

Clifton is sympathetic to Ras's motives, but he is nevertheless too civilized to accept his methods. The Brotherhood, then, with its cant of "historic necessity," represents to Clifton the enlightened alternative to racist violence through which the Negro can effect his protest. Entrapped by the Brotherhood through the commitment imposed by his integrity, Clifton becomes, even more than the narrator, a victim of the Brotherhood's betrayal. Like the implicit suicide of Conrad's Lord Jim, Clifton's death (he provokes a policeman into shooting him) is a sacrifice to a culpability too egregious to be redeemed in any other way, and, at the same time, a final if gratuitous act of heroism. In giving himself up to be murdered, Clifton takes on the whole responsibility for the Brotherhood's betrayal of the Negro. If by his sacrifice he does not redeem the hero from his own culpability, he at least through his example sets up the possibility of Brother _____'s redemption. If the various characters with whom the "invisible" hero is confronted represent possible states of being, Clifton symbolizes the nearest thing to an idea.

Clifton's death, because it permits the hero to organize the Negroes around a common cause (the narrator's funeral oration is a magnificent parody of Anthony's), is potentially an agent of good, for Clifton can be considered in a meaningful sense a sacrifice. However, even that is denied him. At the last minute the Brotherhood withdraws its support from the hero, and, left to their own devices and the exhortation of Ras, the aroused Negroes perform arbitrary acts of plunder and violence. That Clifton's death initiates the Harlem riots, which serve the Brotherhood's new purpose of pacifying the Negro by exhausting his hate-charged energies in meaningless self-conflict, is a last terrible mockery of his decent intentions.

In hawking the chauvinistic "Sambo dolls" which dance at the tug of an invisible string, Clifton was not so much mocking the Brotherhood's attitude toward the Negro as he was parodying himself. His own comment about Ras suggests in a way the impulse of his nihilistic act:

"I don't know," he said. "I suppose sometimes a man *has* to plunge outside history. . . ."
"What?"

> "Plunge outside, turn his back. . . . . Otherwise, he might kill
> somebody, go nuts."

Deceived by the bogus historians of the Brotherhood, Clifton has "plunged outside history," though in punching the white policeman he demonstrated that he
had not quite "turned his back." As an alternative to violent reprisal — Clifton
was an essentially gentle man racked by rage — he became a heckler of the
Brotherhood, of the Negro, of the white man's treatment of the Negro, of
himself, of the universe. Though he is one of the few noble characters in
Ellison's world, his destruction is less than tragic. A man of tragic stature, Clifton is a captive participant in an absurd world which derogates him and mocks
the significance of his death as it did his life. Clifton's sacrificial act, its intention
perverted, is mostly invisible. The others of the Brotherhood — Wrestrum (rest
room), Tobitt (two bit), Jack (money, masturbation) — who in their commitment to "science" have become as dehumanized and corrupt as those they op-
pose, survive the shift in tactical policy.

When the hero discovers that it is through him that the Brotherhood has
betrayed Clifton, he feels responsible for his friend's death. Earlier, in outrage
he spat at one of Clifton's dancing puppets, knocking it "lifeless," performing
symbolically what the policeman does actually — the murder of Clifton. When
the hero knocks over the doll, an outsider laughs at what he thinks is the likeness
between the spitter and the spat-on doll. Just as Clifton in selling the obscene
doll has been mocking himself, the hero in spitting at the doll has been attack-
ing himself as well as Clifton, though without benefit of awareness. Only after
his showdown with the Brotherhood, and even then incompletely, does the hero
become aware that he has been performing all along as if he were, in life size,
the dancing puppet doll.

At his moment of greatest self-awareness, the hero suffers his most intense
sense of guilt. Watching two nuns in the subway (one black, one white), he
remembers a ritual verse he had once heard.

> Bread and wine,
> Bread and wine,
>   Your cross ain't nearly so
> Heavy as mine.

The rhyme comes to him as an automatic response, its singsong at first over-
riding its sense. Momentarily, almost without awareness, as the pain of wound
travels from flesh to brain, he comes to assume its implications. As he watches
some Negroes maltreat a white shopkeeper, he experiences a terrible revelation:

> A pressure of guilt came over me. I stood on the edge of the walk
> watching the crowd threatening to attack the man until a policeman

appeared and dispersed them. And although I knew no one could do much about it, I felt responsible. All our work had been very little, no great change had been made. And it was all my fault. I'd been so fascinated by the motion that I'd forgotten to measure what it was bringing forth. I'd been asleep, dreaming.

A sleepwalker in a world never real enough for him to believe in, the hero experiences a succession of awakenings, only to find himself participating in still another level of nightmare. In accepting Clifton's role as martyr-saint, in taking on the responsibility for all of Harlem, all of Brotherhood, in extension, *all*, he succeeds only in setting himself up for a final, self-destroying victimization. Aware of the futility of all his past acts and, in implication, all acts in the absurd context of his world, the hero commits an act of meaningless violence. Entrapped by a situation for which he is at least partly responsible, with his neck quite literally at stake (Ras wants to hang him), he impales the demonic innocent, Ras, through the jaw with his own spear.

That Jack, the leader of the Brotherhood, has one eye (as earlier the euphemistic preacher Barbee is revealed as blind) is symbolic of the distorted perspective of the Brotherhood's "scientifically objective view" of society, in which the human being is a casual puppet in the service of the "historic" strings that manipulate him. Clifton makes only *paper* Negroes dance; it is Jack and Tobitt who treat flesh and blood Negroes as if they were puppet Sambo dolls. (By having Clifton charge a "brotherly two bits" for the puppet dolls, Ellison, through suggestion, transfers the onus of traitor to Tobitt and in extension to the Brotherhood itself.) When the hero discovers that the Brotherhood has betrayed him, he consciously resolves to impersonate the puppet doll he has so long mimicked unwittingly—to, as his grandfather advised, "overcome 'em with yeses . . . agree 'em to death and destruction." For all his Rinehartian machinations, he manages, however, only to abet the scheme of the Brotherhood.

Seeking redemption from his compounded guilt, he is sucked into the maelstrom of the Harlem riot for which he suffers a sense of limitless, unreclaimable responsibility. He realizes that "By pretending to agree I had indeed agreed, had made myself responsible for that huddled form lighted by flame and gunfire in the street, and all others whom now the night was making ripe for death." The flaming buildings and streets, the burnt tar stench, the black figures moving shadowlike through the eerily illumined night become an evocation of Hell, a mirror for the hero's raging interior guilt. At the center of the riot—at the very seat of Hell—he experiences the deaths of his various corrupted identities, shedding the false skins to get at the pure invisibility underneath. As Ras approaches, the hero searches for his "Rineharts," his dark glasses, only to "see the crushed lenses fall to the street. 'Rinehart, I thought, Rinehart!' " as if he had just witnessed Rinehart himself—his Rinehart self—collapse in death before him. To propitiate Ras and stop the riots, the hero disavows allegiance to the Brotherhood, killing in effect his Brotherhood self. But as he is invisible, he is unheard, his words as always not communicating his meanings. Struck by the absurdity of the demonic Ras on horseback, of the senseless pillage and murder around him, and, after all, of existence itself, the hero is for the moment willing to relinquish his life if it will make the white man see him and consequently see himself. But the example of Clifton's meaningless sacrifice dissuades him. The hero, faced with death, decides that it is "better to live out one's own absurdity than to die for that of others, whether for Ras's or Jack's." When in self-protection he impales Ras, who is in a sense the deepest of his identities, he experiences the illusion of death and rebirth: "It was as though for a moment I had surrendered my life and begun to live again."

Newly baptized by an exploded water main, like the birth from the machine, a somewhat illusory (and comic) resurrection, the hero seeks to return to Mary, his ex-landlady, who has become a symbolic mother to him. But as he is unable to imitate Christ, he is unable to reach Mary. Instead, chased by two white looters, he falls through an open manhole. Unable to find the exit to his coffinlike cell, he burns various papers of his past (high school diploma, Sambo doll, Brotherhood card) for torches to light his way out, only to discover in a moment of terrible realization that the Jacks and Nortons have left him no exit, that without his paper symbols he has no past and consequently no home, no identity. With this knowledge he relaxes in the carrion comfort of his dank hole, having returned at last to the womb of the earth. It is, as he puts it, a "death alive," from which emergence will be rebirth, his victimization transcended, his guilt perhaps purged, his soul if possible redeemed. A nonparticipant in existence, an invisible man by choice, the hero continues to live in his private cellar, which he has illumined by 1,369 lights (a symbolic attempt at transcending his invisibility—at seeing himself), the electricity supplied gratuitously in spite of themselves by Monopolated Light & Power. As the whites had mocked his potency and used it for their own ends, he is now paying them back in kind. Though he is protected from the pain of disillusion while isolated from the brutal, absurd world he hates and, in spite of himself, loves, the hero plans some day to emerge into the outside world because, a son of God and man, one of us, he is willing to believe that "even the invisible victim is responsible for the fate of all."

Much of the experience in Ellison's novel is externally imposed; that is, each scene, through alllusive reference, is made to carry a burden of implication beyond that generated by its particular experience. Consequently the weight of the novel, its profound moral seriousness, resides primarily in conception rather than rendering. Given the problem of transforming large abstractions into evocative experiences, Ellison is nevertheless able more often than not to create occasions resonant enough to accommodate his allegorical purposes. Finally, one senses that the novel, for all its picaresque variety of incident, has curiously static quality. This is not because the episodes are the same or even similar—on the contrary, one is compelled to admire the range and resourcefulness of Ellison's imaginative constructions—but because they are all extensions of the same externally imposed idea; they all *mean* approximately the same thing.

Like so many of our serious writers, Ellison is not prolific. It took him, by his own testimony, some seven years to write *Invisible Man*, and now eleven years after its publication his second novel is still not completed. If Ellison's reputation had to rest, as it does at the time of this writing, on his one impressive if uneven novel, *Invisible Man* is, I suspect, vital and profound enough to survive its faults—to endure the erosions of time. As a satirist and surrealist, Ellison excels among his contemporaries and can bear comparison with his mentors— Kafka, Joyce, and Faulkner. As a realist, he is less adept: talky, didactic, even at times, if the term is possible for so otherwise exciting a writer, tedious. For all that, Ellison has written a major novel, perhaps one of the three or four most considerable American novels of the past two decades.

An excerpt from his forthcoming novel, "And Hickman Arrives," published in the first issue of *The Noble Savage*, exhibits some of the same evangelical rhetoric that gives *Invisible Man* its terrible impact. Still it is idle from a fifty-page fragment to prophesy what kind of novel it will make. Moreover, "And Hickman Arrives" has many of the damaging excesses of the first novel. Ellison has a penchant for letting good things go on past their maximum effectiveness. Yet his excesses are also his strength; like Faulkner before him, Ellison is a writer of amazing verbal energy and at his best he creates experiences that touch our deepest selves, that haunt us with the suffocating wisdom of nightmare. American novelists have often had a predilection for large, protracted books, as if great length were a virtue in itself. Ellison is no exception. However, he is one of the few novelists on the scene today who seems capable of producing a large, serious novel, justified by the size of its experience and the depth of its informing intelligence. On the lowest (and highest) frequencies, he speaks for us.

ALLEN GUTTMANN

American Nightmare

With every manifestation of black discontent, Ralph Ellison's novel *Invisible Man* seems more prophetic, rings truer when sounded by our sense of American society at the present moment. Drawing imaginatively from the symbolic arsenal of literary Modernism, Ellison has written more realistically than Richard Wright. About the many lives of American Negroes, he tells us more than Gunnar Myrdal and a great deal more than Franz Fanon. It is not that the medium guarantees the message; surrealism, as a literary mode, is in no way superior to realism. It is simply that Ellison, on the basis of a single novel, can be called a great writer.

Although Ellison has often maintained that his study of modern writers is what made possible the transformation into art of his experience as a Negro, his familiarity with the *surréalisme* propounded by André Breton has not been established. Nonetheless, Breton's argument that surrealism draws its images directly from the unconscious mind, in the manner of a dream, is relevant to a discussion of *Invisible Man.*

The most dreamlike moments are the most significant, the most dramatic. The action is broken into a sequence of dreams, each more memorable than the prosy narrative that connects them. In an interview conducted by the *Paris Review,* Ellison commented, "I despise concreteness in writing, but when reality is deranged in fiction, one must worry about the seams." The seams still show, like the incongruities of a dream or of a myth, but they are as quickly forgotten.

The first page of the Prologue explicates the title: "I am invisible, understand, simply because people refuse to see me." The narrator, nameless throughout,

From *American Dreams, American Nightmare.* © 1970 by Southern Illinois University Press. Originally entitled "Focus on Ralph Ellison's *Invisible Man:* American Nightmare."

is a man "of substance, of flesh and bone, fiber and liquids." *His* invisibility is a function of *their* blindness (and blindness is undoubtedly one of the most basic and obvious metaphors of the novel). The precision of the title's vagueness is important — *Invisible Man,* without the definite article. This particular invisible man is one of many, not all of whom are Negroes. As Ellison insists in the introduction to *Shadow and Act* and in his *Harper's* essay, "A Very Stern Discipline," his intention was to write as a man who is also a Negro. The Prologue plays with the narrator's color when he writes that he's not "a spook like those who haunted Edgar Allan Poe," but the narrator wants "to put invisibility down in black and white" because invisibility can be white as well as black.

Accordingly, the epigraphs are nicely paired. The first is from *Benito Cereno:* " 'You are saved,' cried Captain Delano, more and more astonished and pained; 'you are saved: what has cast such a shadow upon you?' " In the unquoted reply, Benito Cereno answers, "The Negro." Neither of Melville's characters was able to *see* the manhood of Babo (the slave who led the mutiny against Benito Cereno). The second epigraph, taken from Eliot's *Family Reunion,* reminds the reader that white men can also be invisible. To miss this is — in a metaphor from the *Harper's* essay — "to allow the single tree of race to obscure our view of the magic forest of art." In the present political crisis, the point needs to be made, but once made, it can be dropped.

The narrator is a Negro and the forms and stuff of his invisibility (if we can speak so) are part and parcel of the experience of Negroes in the United States, created from their defeats and humiliations, their humor, their ecstasy, their language, their culture. In his odyssey, the narrator acts out the stages of Negro history from the Emancipation to the present.

The first stage is apparent acquiescence, but chapter 1 is deceptive. The narrator's grandfather had given him some deathbed advice: "I want you to overcome 'em with yeses, undermine 'em with grins, agree 'em to death and destruction, let 'em swoller you till they vomit or bust wide open." These words, periodically remembered, seem like the answer, initially shunned, which must finally be accepted, but when the narrator *does* act upon these words, the result is a tragicomic holocaust, the race riot described in chapter 25. At first, however, the narrator puzzles over his grandfather's advice and follows the strategy of Booker T. Washington, whose Atlanta Address of 1895 is alluded to in the handfinger metaphor of the second paragraph and quoted in the narrator's valedictory speech. He says of himself, "I visualized myself as a potential Booker T. Washington." He believes in the myth of Horatio Alger, in the American Dream — and sees the American flag obscenely tattooed on the belly of the soft-thighed dancer whom "the most important men of the town" use to tantalize Negro youths. The initial chapter's progression from the dancer to the "battle-royal" of the blindfolded Negro boxers to the electrified rug to the narrator's Washingtonian speech is a nightmare of humiliation made more horrid by the narrator's delight, after this descent into Hell, in receiving a scholarship to the state college for Negroes. (This and other episodes are related to Dante's descent, alluded to in the Prologue.)

Whether or not Alabama really resembles the Waste Land, the opening section of chapter 2 is an unmistakably Eliotic pastiche of broken fountain, dead grass, sunken rock, and dry winds. The college itself is very like Tuskegee, at least in its situation. (Ellison himself studied music at Tuskegee.) The Founder is drawn from Booker T. Washington, whose rhetoric the narrator continues to accept.

Allowed to chauffeur Mr. Norton, a white trustee, he foolishly fulfills Norton's repressed desires. He takes him to see Trueblood, a Negro who had done what Norton has longed to do, a man who has committed incest with his own daughter. From Trueblood's farm, the narrator goes to the ironically named roadhouse, the Golden Day, where transcendentalism is a mob of maniacs, a collection of the Ids who overwhelm Supercargo, their keeper, their superego. This nightmare, like the others, has its comic aspect. Brushing Norton's white hair, the prostitutes reverse racial stereotypes: "Girl, don't you know that all these rich ole white men got monkey glands and billy goat balls? These ole bastards don't never git enough."

Returning with great difficulty to the school, the narrator learns that Bledsoe, the director, is no Trueblood. He is rather a Machiavellian who sees the world as a "power set-up. . . . But I've made my place in it and I'll have every Negro in the country hanging on tree limbs by morning if it means staying where I am." The confrontation of cynicism and innocence follows the marvelously rhetorical speech of Homer A. Barbee, the preacher whose web of sentiment and exhortation is ripped to shreds by the brutal reality of Bledsoe.

Dismissed from school, the narrator retains his innocence. He heads for New York, "not a city of realities, but of dreams," and is too naive to open the "letters of introduction" given him by Bledsoe. Still convinced that the white man's ethic of success fits the black man's condition, he is his own Procrustes. The hunt for a job is tiresome reading, but it leads to the satire of the interview with young Mr. Emerson, a homosexual who urges the narrator to meet him at Club Calamus (clearly an allusion to Whitman), who pants to be Huckleberry Finn with this apparently delectable Jim. In what must be a burst of mingled pity and lust, Emerson shows the narrator one of the letters of introduction. It is, of course, a condemnation, another betrayal of innocence and trust.

The next stage is a comedy of colors, in which things look whiter when black is added, in which the Government is the chief purchaser of "Optic White," made by Liberty Paints, used for monuments and other symbols of inauthentic authority. This chapter too is another descent into the Underworld, where aged Lucius Brockway runs the complicated machinery that makes the whitewash possible. The fantasy ends in a fight and an explosion, in a death followed by a rebirth.

The rebirth is simply the renaissance of illusion. The badly injured narrator is now victimized by modern technology as applied by bureaucratic organization. More concretely, he is strapped and wired and electrically shocked by company doctors who see him only as an object. (The electrical shocks are also a reminder of the rug in chapter 1.) He is eventually released to stumble along Lenox Avenue, until he is rescued by Mary Rambo, an Aunt Jemima figure who offers sanctuary rather than a possible identity. She is, in a sense, his Calypso (with no sexual transactions implied).

On his way to the next stage of the sequence, the narrator encounters an aged, unashamedly Negro yam-vendor. The episode is hysterically allusive with hints of Ben Franklin's self-celebrated entry into Philadelphia. The narrator gobbles yams because he *likes* them, and the scene contrasts with the breakfast eaten when he first arrived in New York, the breakfast at which he shunned Southern foods as "an act of discipline." Now he eats defiantly: "I no longer had to worry about who saw me or about what was proper. To hell with all that." He imagines Bledsoe confronted by chitterlings: "Bledsoe, you're a shameless chitterling eater! I accuse you of relishing hog bowels!" Buying more yams because he's a "serious yam eater," he proclaims, "I yam what I am!" Whether this is an echo of the voice on Mount Sinai or a quotation from Popeye the Sailor Man, or both or neither, is left to the reader. But the marvelous moment is followed by a letdown. The third yam is frostbitten — identity isn't that easy to come by.

Then, without intending to, the narrator whose dreams of heroism led only to disgrace becomes a hero. Finding a crowd already angered by an eviction in progress, he speaks to calm them, and incites them to action, for which he is complimented by a strange man and a strange woman, members of the Brotherhood (which is, of course, a Marxist group remarkably like the Communist Party to which Ellison had at one time been attracted).

For the narrator, as for Richard Wright and many other Negro intellectuals, political activity in cooperation with radical whites seemed a likely answer, at least for the moment. The narrator receives a new name from Brother Jack, a new role, and a new identity. He discovers that people treat him not equally but preferentially. Men admire him, women offer themselves to him. But, in gathering the Brotherhood at a building called the Chthonian, Ellison implies that this too is a descent into the Underworld. Brotherhood is illusory. Success breeds envy. Brother Jack, with the aid of the aptly named Brother Wrestrum, soon turns against his protégé. Because of his leadership in Harlem, the narrator is sent downtown to speak on the Woman Question.

He turns exile to advantage. He finds that he is an effective speaker, but for the wrong reasons. "'Brotherhood, darling,' she said, gripping my biceps with her little hands. 'Teach me, talk to me. . . .'" She hears tom-toms in his voice. While the narrator spreads the gospel of brotherhood in this ancient way, hard-won political gains are lost.

He is recalled and returned to Harlem, where he discovers the degradation of Tod Clifton, the only Negro leader, within the Brotherhood, with abilities remotely near his own. Clifton has become a street-corner merchant of Sambo dolls, obscene little paper symbols of loss of identity. Upset perhaps by the narrator's angry reaction (he spits on the doll), Clifton loses his head and strikes a policeman. The policeman kills him. As Harlem approaches detonation, the narrator attempts to defuse the situation through funereal ritual — procession, drums, orations.

He learns, when the Brotherhood gathers, that he has misinterpreted History. "Under your leadership, a traitorous merchant of vile instruments of anti-Negro, anti-minority racist bigotry has received the funeral of a hero." When he answers that he acted on his personal responsibility, he is derided — as he was in the first chapter derided and threatened when he spoke, accidentally, of social equality rather than of social responsibility. The Brotherhood is as cynical as Dr. Bledsoe. "We do not shape our policies to the mistaken and infantile notions of the man in the street. Our job is not to *ask* them what they think but to *tell* them." During this encounter, Brother Jack's glass eye tumbles out — eerie symbol of the reiterated theme of blindness.

After the meeting, the narrator wanders the streets of Harlem. When followers of a black nationalist leader, Ras the Exhorter, pursue him, he buys himself dark glasses and a hat — and attains still another identity, that of the man of disguises. Now he is mistaken for Rinehart, the numbers-racketeer, the lover, the cynic, the zoot-suited joker, the ghetto-based reincarnation of Melville's Confidence Man. Rinehart's world "was possibility and he knew it. . . . A vast seething, hot world of fluidity, and Rine the rascal was at home in it." Dropping the Hegelian-Marxist notion of freedom as the recognition of necessity, the narrator defines freedom as the recognition of possibility. Now his blindness is ended. Now he will recognize his invisibility and use it to deceive others. "They want a machine? Very well, I'd become a supersensitive confirmer of their misconceptions." But this solution too is a dream.

The narrator conforms to expectations and, as he knew it would, Harlem explodes. It is a Walpurgisnacht through which he moves. "The moon was high now and before me the shattered glass glittered in the street like the water of a flooded river upon the surface of which I ran as in a dream." He joins the looters, leaves them, sees Ras the Exhorter, now become "Ras the Destroyer upon a great black horse." Suddenly the narrator realizes that he's been duped again—the Brotherhood *wanted* the riot for the martyrs it produced, for its demonstration of the "error" of premature violence.

Ras is not ready to accept the Prodigal Son. He flings his spear at him, misses, sets his men on him. The narrator flings the weapon back, spears Ras through both cheeks, and flees. He finds safety underground, first in a coal-chute, where blackness is disguise, where he symbolically burns the deceptive documents and papers he had lugged through his career in the briefcase given him by his high school principal. Like Theseus, he finds his way out, but he stays underground, builds himself the well-lighted hole described in the Prologue.

In the Epilogue, he takes up the affirmative images of the Prologue; he *seems* to remain faithful to the American Dream which most white Americans have betrayed. He ponders his grandfather's advice (and the rhetoric becomes excessively Faulknerian): "Did he [grandfather] mean to affirm the principle, which they [the whites] themselves had dreamed into being out of the chaos and darkness of the feudal past, and which they had violated and compromised to the point of absurdity even in their own corrupt minds? Or did he mean that we had to take the responsibility for all of it, for the men as well as the principle, because we were the heirs who must use the principle, because no other fitted our needs? Not for the power or for the vindication, but because we, with the given circumstances of our origin, could only thus find transcendence?" The principle, the dream, is unquestioned throughout a long paragraph of questions. The assumption is that the unrealized American Dream is not an impossible one.

He repeats, "My world has become one of infinite possibilities." He applies Whitman's rhetoric to the theory of cultural pluralism: "America is woven of many strands; I would recognize them and let it so remain. . . . Our fate is to become one, and yet many—This is not prophecy, but description." These affirmations are supported by the metaphor of hibernation, defined, in the Prologue, as "a covert preparation for a more overt action." In the Prologue, the narrator compares himself to a bear and the bear to the "Easter chick." Now, in the Epilogue, he announces that the hibernation is over: "I must shake off the old skin and come up for breath." But he smells a stench which might be "the smell either of death or of spring—I hope of spring. But don't let me trick you, there *is* a death in the smell of spring." Like the Whitman of "When Lilacs Last in the Dooryard Bloom'd," he seems to realize that spring and winter are reciprocals, that winter is a prerequisite for spring just as death is a prerequisite for rebirth. He is a chastened and illusionless man who prepares now to emerge to play his "socially responsible role."

Or is he? The narrator's ingenuousness has survived so many disillusionments that we are reluctant, as readers, to believe in his final affirmation. He has cried "Wolf!" so often (or "Sheep!") that the reader is liable to respond with the skepticism lacking in the narrator. Marcus Klein comments on this problem: "There is a constant increase of wattage, but what is to be seen remains the same," i.e., the acceptance of invisibility, the determination to use this invisibility for some unspecified but socially responsible purpose.

What is the role the narrator now must play? By universalizing the significance of the adventures ("Who knows but that, on the lower frequencies, I speak for you?"), Ellison has put himself in the position of a man maintaining — if he ends affirmatively — that solutions exist for problems which are political, social, and psychological rather than literary. The Epilogue concerns the narrator's state of mind, but it includes an implicit judgment of the State of the Nation.

Given the present State of the Nation, it is hard not to read the conclusion as ironic. Perception n must be as illusory as perception $n\text{-}1$. But we know, from external evidence, that Ellison did *not* mean irony. In his *Paris Review* interview he says: "In my novel the narrator's development is one through blackness to light; that is, from ignorance to enlightenment: invisibility to visibility. He leaves the South and goes North; this, as you will notice in reading Negro folk tales, is always the road to freedom — the movement upward. You have the same thing again when he leaves his underground cave for the open." The scheme, taken from Kenneth Burke, is tripartite — purpose, passion, perception. It is the smoke and ashes of burned cities that make the Epilogue seem ironic when it is not.

The relation of a novel to its cultural context resembles the narrator's room, with its 1,369 lights lit by current stolen from Monopolated Light & Power. Novels — and especially *this* novel — draw much of their power from the context to which they indirectly refer. Good novels, in turn, illuminate the society in which they are written. But Ellison's context has changed, or has seemed to change. A statistically obvious *improvement* in the situation of American Negroes has been accompanied by a great sense (in many) of deprivation and frustration. The unparalleled (in America) openness of the present conflicts between blacks and whites has made the novel seem prophetic in its nightmares and innocent in its small measure of optimism.

But perhaps it is useful to consider a contrary proposition. If the narrator has, like Trueblood, looked into chaos and survived, if he really has descended to the Underworld and returned, then — perhaps — his affirmations are a clue to the labyrinth of American society in the sixties. Ellison may not be our Theseus, but there are other writers on the loose, doomsayers, who resemble Minotaurs.

TONY TANNER

The Music of Invisibility

*Could this compulsion to put invisibility down in black and white be thus
an urge to make music of invisibility?*

—*Invisible Man*

In the introduction to his essays *(Shadow and Act)*, Ralph Ellison, recalling
the circumstances of his youth, stresses the significance of the fact that while
Oklahoman jazz musicians were developing "a freer, more complex and driving
form of jazz, my friends and I were exploring an idea of human versatility and
possibility which went against the barbs or over the palings of almost every
fence which those who controlled social and political power had erected to
restrict our roles in the life of the country." The fact that these musicians working with "tradition, imagination and the sounds and emotions around them,"
could create something new which was both free yet recognizably formed (this
is the essence of improvisation) was clearly of the first importance for Ralph
Ellison; the ideas of versatility and possibility which he and his friends were exploring provide the ultimate subject matter, and nourish the style, of his one
novel to date, *Invisible Man,* a novel which in many ways is seminal for subsequent American fiction. His title may owe something to H. G. Wells's novel
The Invisible Man, for the alienated Griffin in Well's novel also comes to
realize "what a helpless absurdity an Invisible Man was—in a cold and dirty
climate and a crowded, civilized city" and there is a very suggestive scene in
which he tries to assemble an identity, which is at the same time a disguise,
from the wigs, masks, artificial noses, and clothes of Omniums, the large Lon-
don Store. It would not be surprising if Well's potentially very probing little

From *City of Words: American Fiction 1950–1970.* © 1971 by Tony Tanner. Harper and
Row, 1971.

novel about the ambiguity involved in achieving social "identity" had stayed in Ellison's extremely literate memory. But if it did so it would be because Ellison's experience as a Negro had taught him a profounder sort of invisibility than any chemically induced vanishing trick. As the narrator says in the opening paragraph, it is as though he lives surrounded by mirrors of distorting glass, so that other people do not see him but only his surroundings, or reflections of themselves, or their fantasies. It is an aspect of recent American fiction that work coming from members of so-called minority groups has proved to be relevant and applicable to the situation of people not sharing their immediate racial experience or, as it may be, sexual inclination; and *Invisible Man,* so far from being limited to an expression of an anguish and injustice experienced peculiarly by Negroes, is quite simply the most profound novel about American identity written since the war.

The book begins and ends in a small underground room, situated significantly in a "border area." It is there that the unnamed narrator — unnamed because invisible on the social surface — is arranging his memories, structuring his experiences, creating his life. It is important to bear this in mind since the book is not only an account of events but quite as importantly about what the consciousness of the narrator has managed to make of those events, how it has managed to change because of them. His little room is flooded with the light from 1,369 light bulbs, run by free current drained off from the Monopolated Light & Power Company. It is an echo of Hemingway's "clean, well-lighted place" but with many significant differences. The narrator has had experience of electricity before. As a child he had been engaged in one of those grotesque entertainments in which white Southerners make negro youths fight among themselves for coins which they are then invited to pick up from an electrified rug. The narrator discovers that if he is careful he can contain the electricity, but then he is thrown bodily on to the rug by white men who persist in shouting misleading cues and directions. The agony is intense and it seems that a century will pass before he can roll free.

The whole experience is an early paradigm of the treatment he is to receive all through his adult life. Later in life he is given electric shock "treatment" which is intended to have the effect of a prefrontal lobotomy without actually cutting into the brain. The white doctor explains his technique, describing how they apply pressure to the centres of nerve control — "our concept is Gestalt." This implies that simply by applying the appropriate pressures they can alter the way a man reads reality, another device for that monitoring of consciousness which is so abhorrent to the American hero. And the electricity is important here. It can be seen as the indispensable force by which society warms and lights its way. That power can be also used to make cruel sport of the individual, to condition him, make him jump to the whim of the man at the controls. The question is, can the narrator find a way to "contain" this power, to use it without being its helpless victim or its ruthless exerciser?

The first time he finds himself in opposition to the existing authorities, Dr. Bledsoe, who runs the Uncle Tom-like State College for negroes in the South, tells him, "This is a power set-up son, and I'm at the controls." The moral would seem to be—control or be controlled; as when, later in his life, he sees two pictures of bullfighting in a bar in one of which the matador gracefully dominates the bull while in the second he is being tossed on the black bull's horns. There is a black powerhouse close to the white buildings of the college, and while the notion of black power which has since emerged in America is not entirely irrelevant here, Ellison is making the much more profound point that power is what keeps society going at all levels; the lights in the library and the chapel, the machines in the factory and the hospital all derive from the morally neutral force of electricity. Morality starts when man diverts this power to specific ends. The experience of the narrator is that it is usually used for the more or less cynical manipulation of individuals. Yet electricity is also a source of light, and the achievement of the narrator must be to find a way out of the power setup altogether (for to be a controller is more pernicious than to be one who is controlled) and tap some of that power for his own private purpose—to "illuminate the blackness of my invisibility," to become aware of his own form.

The odyssey which the narrator, with the aid of his 1,369 light bulbs, looks back on takes place on many levels. His travelling is geographic, social, historical, and philosophical. In an early dream he finds inside his briefcase an envelope which contains an endless recession of smaller envelopes, the last of which contains the simple message "Keep This Nigger-Boy Running." It is only at the end when he finally burns all the contents of his real briefcase that he can start to control his own momentum. Up to that point his movements are really controlled from without, just like the people in the New York streets who to him seem to walk as though they were directed by "some unseen control." The pattern of his life is one of constraint and eviction; he is alternately cramped and dispossessed. This is true of his experience in the college, the factory, the hospital, the Party. What he discovers is that every institution is bent on processing and programming the individual in a certain way; yet if a man does not have a place in any of the social structures the danger is that he might fall into chaos.

At his college, in the chapel everybody seems to have eyes of robots and faces like frozen masks (i.e. "fixed" in rigid roles), and the blind preacher telling them "the way" inaugurates a theme of the blindness or warped vision of all the creatures of the given structures of society, whether leaders or led—a point underlined when Brother Jack's glass eye falls out. References to dolls, actors, masks, dummies, and so on, proliferate throughout, and before the narrator is startled or pushed out of his first given role—at the state college—he too is described, by a man of accredited perceptions, as a "'mechanical man.'" The speaker is addressing Mr Norton, a trustee of the college, whom he aptly calls "'a trustee of consciousness.'" He is making the point that such institutions turn out automata, who accept the rigid and restraining role imposed on them as true identity, and defer to the white man's version of reality.

The point about all the representatives of social power that the narrator encounters—teacher, preacher, doctor, factory owner, Party member, whatever—is that they all seek to control reality and they believe that they can run it according to their plan. To this extent one can say that they have a mechanizing attitude towards reality, and it is no accident that the narrator is constantly getting involved with literal machines (in the factory, the hospital, etc.) as well as with what one might call the mechanizers of consciousness, the servants of church, college or Party. On the other hand there is the point that these institutions, these people at the social controls, do seem to give the individual a role, a place in the scheme of things. At one stage the narrator is enthusiastic about the Party, because it gives the world a meaningful shape and himself an important role in it: "everything could be controlled by our science. Life was all pattern and discipline."

The alternative to the servile docility and rigid regulations of the state college would seem to be the utter chaos of the Golden Day Saloon, which with its fighting and drinking and debauchery seems to be in continuous rehearsal for "the end of the world," as one mad participant proclaims it (see R. W. B. Lewis's fine essay "Days of Wrath and Laughter" for a discussion of the apocalyptic hints in the novel). It may be more real, more authentic than the fabricated performances in the chapel at the college, but in its utterly shapeless confusion it offers no opportunities for self-development or self-discovery. Society does indeed impose false surfaces on things; a point well made at the paint factory where the narrator has to mix in a black constituent which nevertheless produces a dazzling "Optic White" paint used for government buildings. It reminds the narrator of the white painted buildings of the campus; it also reminds him that the Golden Day had once been painted white but that now it was all flaking away. The fact that the paint is called Liberty Paint in conjunction with the suggestion that it is at least in part an optical illusion (the narrator can see a grey in the white which his overseer ignores or cannot detect) is a fairly clear irony; we are in fact "caught" in the official version of reality—the painted surfaces—maintained by the constituted authorities. On the other hand, if you strip all the false paint away you are likely to be confronted with the merely chaotic "truth" of the Golden Day. In the same way, the mechanizers and controllers of reality turn people into automata and manipulable dummies; but can a man achieve any visible shape or role if he refuses to join any of the existing patterns?

This is indeed the narrator's problem. When he is about to be sent away from the college he feels that he is losing the only identity that he has ever known. At this stage he equates a stable niche in the social structure with an identity, and for a long time his quest is for some defining and recognized employment. The matter of the letters from Bledsoe is instructive; they are supposed to be helping him find a job which might enable him to return to his higher education, whereas in fact they are treacherously advancing Bledsoe's scheme of keeping him as far away from college as possible. He feels all along that he is playing a part in some incomprehensible "scheme," but it is only when the younger Emerson shows him one of the letters that he begins to understand. "Everyone seemed to have some plan for me, and beneath that some more secret plan." It is an essential part of his education that he should come to realize that "everybody wanted to use you for some purpose" and that the way they recognize you, on and in their own terms, is not to be confused with your identity.

After his accident in the factory he undergoes what is in effect a process of rebirth—not organically but electrically. From his fall into the lake of heavy water and on to his coming to consciousness with a completely blank mind in a small glass-and-nickel box, and his subsequent struggle to get out, it reads like a mechanized parody of the birth process. The electrical treatment has temporarily erased his earlier consciousness and he cannot say who he is or what his name is. His only concern is to get out of the machine without electrocuting himself. "I wanted freedom, not destruction . . . I could no more escape than I could think of my identity. Perhaps, I thought, the two things are involved with each other. When I discover who I am, I'll be free." This, coming nearly halfway through the book, is a crucial turning point. The machine is every system by which other people want to manipulate him and regulate his actions. In much the same way the Party gives him a new identity and tries to reprogramme him for its ends. The narrator is not a nihilist—he does not wish to smash the machine, knowing that he will probably be destroyed with it—but he wants to find some sort of freedom from the interlocking systems which make up society, and he realizes that it will have to be mainly an inner freedom. At the end he can look back and see that the individuals from various professions or parties who had sought to direct and use him "were very much the same, each attempting to force his picture of reality upon me and neither giving a hoot in hell for how things looked to me." This is why he wants to be free of all parties, all partial

pictures, all the imposed and imprisoning constructs of society. This urge will
bring him to a second rebirth near the end—this time a private, self-managed
one. But before coming to that we should consider some of the advice and
examples he has received from figures who are not on the side of the system-
makers, not enlisted among the controllers.

His grandfather on his deathbed has given the advice to "overcome 'em
with yeses," and only by the end can the narrator see a possible hidden meaning
in this exhortation. Before he leaves for New York, the vet in the Golden Day
advises him that, once there, he should play the game without believing it: he
explains that he will be "hidden right out in the open" because "they" will not
expect him to know anything and therefore will not be able to see him. When
asked by the narrator who "they" refers to, he answers, "Why the same *they* we
always mean, the white folks, authority, the gods, fate, circumstances—the
force that pulls your strings until you refuse to be pulled any more." Three further things he says to the narrator are of particular importance. He tells him that
much of his freedom will have to be "symbolic" — a deeper truth perhaps than he
knows for the boy who will ultimately find his freedom in the symbols called
words. He says, "Be your own father, young man," an Oedipal echo (picking up
the description we have already had of the narrator standing where three roads
converge) and a warning to the boy that he will have to create an identity, not
rely on assuming one already waiting for him. Thirdly, he bids him remember
that the world is "possibility." And this anticipates the narrator's encounter with
Rinehart which is perhaps the most important "epiphany" in the book.

Before this encounter there is the decisive incident connected with Tod
Clifton, the narrator's friend who suddenly drops all Party work and makes himself into a sort of parody Negro. Tod becomes a street-hawker in Harlem, mon-
gering self-mocking black dolls. He is duly killed, as his name forwarns us, by a
policeman—the cause of his death being described as "resisting reality." It is
Tod who, after a bitter encounter with the black fanatic Ras, speculates that, "I
suppose sometimes a man *has* to plunge outside history." History is the temporal dimension of the social structure, its emerging shape, as well as being the
accumulation of memories which weigh on us. It is everything that has condi-
tioned society and the individual within it. History we could say is the visible
part of society's progress or change, the fraction that shows above the surface. It
is worth stressing this because we often see the narrator entering, or falling into,
or retreating to, dark subterranean places. It is in a subway, looking at some
sharply dressed black boys, that the narrator has his vision of the significance of
all those anonymous people who play no part in history, the transitory ones who
will never be classified, too silent to be recorded, too ambiguous to be caught
"the most ambiguous words." "What if history was gambler . . . What if

history was not a reasonable citizen, but a madman full of paranoid guile and these boys his agents, his big surprise? For they were outside . . . running and dodging the forces of history instead of making a dominating stand." If history is a gambler—and truth tends to come in underground places in this book—then all those people up on the surface who regard it as a manipulable machine are wrong. Up there they "distort" people in the interests of some abstract "design"; they force people into tight little boxes, just as Tod is literally trapped in the ultimate confinement of the coffin. Having seen this much the narrator is effectively through with all parties of the surface. It remains for him to see whether there is any alternative mode of life.

This is when he encounters Rinehart, or rather the phenomenon of Rinehart, since Rinehart is not a man to be met so much as a strategy to be made aware of. The narrator comes to "know" Rinehart by being mistaken for him when he adopts a safety disguise. After being taken for a number of contradictory Rineharts—from gambler to Reverend—the narrator suddenly understands and appreciates the significance of this figure. "His world was possibility and he knew it. He was years ahead of me and I was a fool. . . . The world in which we lived was without boundaries. A vast seething, hot world of fluidity, and Rine the rascal was at home. Perhaps *only* Rine the rascal was at home in it." The realization makes him feel as though he has just been released from a plaster cast; it suggests what life on the surface never suggested: "new freedom of movement." "You could actually make yourself anew. The notion was frightening, for now the world seemed to flow before my eyes. All boundaries down, freedom was not only the recognition of necessity, it was the recognition of possibility." This is as succinct an expression of the discovery earned in this book as one could wish for. But what follows is also important. "And sitting there trembling I caught a brief glimpse of the possibilities posed by Rinehart's multiple personalities and turned away." I stress this because although the narrator learns his most important lesson from the spectacle of Rinehart he does not wish to emulate him.

If we can simplify the structuring of reality implicit in the book for a moment, we could say that just as figures like Norton, Emerson, Bledsoe and Brother Jack are at home on the surface, which is the realm of social rigidification and the mechanistic manipulations of history; just so Rinehart is the figure most at home in the subterranean world, a fluid darkness flowing on underneath history and society, beneath their shaping powers. This lower realm clearly has its potencies and its truths. But a world of no boundaries, a world given over to "the merging fluidity of forms," which the narrator sees when he puts on his dark glasses, such a world can finally only be a chaos. And Ellison himself has made this point very clear in an interview. Rinehart's middle name is "Proteus" and Ellison intended something quite specific by his character.

Rinehart is my name for the personification of chaos. He is also intended to represent America and change. He has lived so long with chaos that he knows how to manipulate it. It is the old theme of *The Confidence Man*. He is a figure in a country with no solid past or stable class lines; therefore he is able to move about easily from one to the other.

To emulate Rinehart would be to submit to chaos. Rinehart, whose heart is in fact all rind, really represents the ultimate diffusion and loss of self; a freedom, indeed, which might easily turn into that nightmare of jelly. The narrator, attempting to discover or create his own identity, does not want to dissolve in fluidity. Yet if he rejects both the life-denying mechanical fixities of the surface operators, and the fluid adaptations and adaptive improvisations of a Rinehart, the question emerges—where can he go, what can he do?

Perhaps we can get nearer the answer if we ask, not where will he go, but how will he move? One thing he learns after all his experiences on different levels is that the prevailing notion that success involved rising *upward* is a lie used by society to dominate its members. "Not only could you travel upward toward success but you could travel downward as well; up *and* down, in retreat as well as in advance, crabways and crossways and around in a circle, meeting your old selves coming and going and perhaps all at the same time." This notion of movement is related to that "running and dodging" of the forces of history he had earlier discerned as a possibility. At the height of the Harlem riots the narrator finds himself running from all parties, but with the new realization that he no longer has to run either for or from the Jacks and Emersons and the Bledsoes and Nortons, "but only from their confusion, impatience, and refusal to recognize the beautiful absurdity of their American identity and mine." And just when it seems that he will be killed in the converging forces of that apocalyptic night (which, like the battle-royal he was involved in as a child, is in fact engineered by unscrupulous white people so that the rebels and rioters who think they are generating a scheme of their own are in fact fulfilling someone else's) the narrator falls down a hole into the dark chamber of his second rebirth.

First of all he has to burn all the papers in his briefcase to find his way out of the hole: those papers represent all the schemes and treacheries that his various controllers have planned for him. He is in fact burning up his past and all the false roles it has sought to trap him in. With the aid of the light from the flames, (i.e. he has learned something from this past experience) he enters another dimensionless room where he loses all sense of time. He has to go down a long dark passage and then he lies down in a state between waking and dreaming. Subsequently he has a dream of being castrated by a group consisting of all those who had sought to direct and control his previous life. But when he wakes, he is beyond them. "They were all up there somewhere, making a mess of the world. Well, let them, I was through and, in spite of the dream, I was whole." At this point he decides to take up residence underground and with this gesture of repudiation — a plague on both your houses — so characteristic of American literature, the book might well have ended. But there is an Epilogue, and in some ways this is the most important part of the book.

As was noted, while writing the book the narrator has been living underground and in a "border area." The point is worth remembering because throughout his life he has been striving to avoid being forced into either of the two extremes of life-style exemplified by Emerson's and Jack's surface New York and Rinehart's Harlem. "I don't belong to anything," he cries at one point. To be able to exist in a border area is to resist being wholly drawn into one or the other, to secure a bit of private freedom on the edge. And what he has been doing in his refuge of secret illumination is best suggested by a sentence he remembers from his school teacher, talking about *A Portrait of the Artist as a Young Man*. "Stephen's problem, like ours, was not actually one of creating the uncreated conscience of his race, but of creating the *uncreated features of his face*." The narrator has discovered what many American heroes have discovered, that he is not free to reorganize and order the world, but he can at least exercise the freedom to arrange and name his perceptions of the world. He cannot perhaps assert and define himself in action, but sometimes at least he can assert and create himself in some private space not in the grip of historical forces. While running and dodging in the outside world, the hero may be evolving and discovering and defining his true features in his inner world, like this narrator. His most important affirmation may be, not of any pattern in the outside world, but of the patterning power of his own mind.

This is not the artist as hero so much as the hero out of dire necessity having to become an artist. For it is only in the "symbolic" freedom of lexical space that he can both find and be himself. In writing his book the narrator has created his face. He is aware of the paradox involved in the compulsion "to put invisibility down in black and white" — the phrase pointing nicely both to the black and white which make up the legibility of print, and the patterning of symbolic black and white which in the book itself is one of his main strategies for rendering his experience visible. But in the pursuit of this paradox lies his only freedom. He tells the story of a yokel who beat a prizefighter against all the odds because he simply stepped "inside of his opponent's sense of time." Just so the narrator can step out of other people's times and schemes, but only by creating his own in his writing. He has a memory or dream of asking his mother to define freedom and she answers, "I guess now it ain't nothing but knowing how to say what I got up in my head." This is the freedom which the narrator achieves in the act of seeking it in his writing.

But the problem remains of "the next step." He had every reason for going underground: "my problem was that I always tried to go in everyone's way but my own," which meant that he had never been master of his own direction, and "to lose your direction is to lose your face." He has gone into hibernation in his cellar to find direction and face. But he makes another discovery there. "I couldn't be still even in hibernation. Because, damn it, there's the mind, the *mind*. It wouldn't let me rest." Here indeed we find a conflict of urges shared by many American heroes—the desire to hibernate (celebrated definitively in Washington Irving's tale of Rip Van Winkle—one of the first American "outsiders"!), and the inability to remain still in hibernation. Ellison's narrator speaks both of his "craving for tranquillity, for peace and quiet," and of the "ache" to "convince yourself that you do exist in the real world." The difficulty here is that if you remain in hibernation you are likely to stagnate in unseen inertia; but if you rejoin the shared reality of the surface you are going to be forced into role playing.

Ellison's narrator defends the value of hibernation as a covert preparation for some subsequent action, but after writing his book he is still wrestling with the problem of defining the nature of that ensuing action. "Yes, but what *is* the next phase?" In hibernation you can become visible to yourself, but to remain in hibernation indefinitely is simply to die. So at the end the narrator says, "the old fascination with playing a role returns, and I'm drawn upward again," and ends his book with the confession that perhaps "I've overstayed my hibernation, since there's a possibility that even an invisible man has a socially responsible role to play." At the same time there is the recognition that "up above there's an increasing passion to make men conform to a pattern." What the narrator seeks is a way of rejoining the reality of the surface without being forced into another man's pattern or made to play a role to fit an alien scheme. In this he is only one of many recent American heroes who seek some other alternative to the twin "deaths" of total inertia and diffusion into role playing. It is as though they are bound to oscillate between the reality-starvation involved in complete ego-autonomy, as defined by David Rapaport, and the loss of ego-autonomy involved in the other-directed behaviour of Erving Goffman's hollow role players (see appendix 5). Confronting this problem—sometimes an impasse—is one of the main subjects of recent American fiction. No wonder the Invisible Man says he has "become acquainted with ambivalence."

We could say then that the Invisible Man, like many after him, is seeking a new way of being in reality. We do not see him rejoin the surface; again like many after him, he leaves us with a verbal definition of the nature of his resolve.

He has learned a whole new way of looking at reality and his relation to it. As he now sees it "my world has become one of infinite possibilities" and "life is to be lived, not controlled." What he also recognizes, and this is crucial, is that he too is imposing a pattern on reality by writing the book. Of course, his motive is different and it is the sort of pattern which clarifies and extends his own consciousness rather than one which cramps and limits someone else. But it is important to keep the fact in mind: "the mind that has conceived a plan of living must never lose sight of the chaos against which that pattern was conceived. That goes for societies as well as for individuals."

He is including here a recognition of the fact that even to perceive reality is to organize it in a certain way in one's consciousness — that too is a Gestalt principle. This is another reason why the novel is so preoccupied with eyesight and the problems involved in the fact that we live at the intersections of endlessly different paths of vision. Without some patterning we cannot even experience reality, let alone participate in it. What he has learned is that it is always dangerous to start to confuse your own particular patterning with reality itself. From that point of view reality *is* chaos, and we live only in the patterns we derive from it or impose on it. But if you live too long in any one pattern you are likely to become completely sealed off from all contact with reality — like those people D. H. Lawrence describes as living under an umbrella.

> Man must wrap himself in a vision, make a house of apparent form and stability, fixity. In his terror of chaos he begins by putting up an umbrella between himself and the everlasting whirl. Then he paints the underside of his umbrella like a firmament. . . . Man fixes some wonderful erection of his own between himself and the wild chaos, and gradually goes bleached and stifled under his parasol. Then comes a poet, enemy of convention, and makes a slit in the umbrella; and lo! the glimpse of chaos is a vision, a window to the sun.

Ellison's narrator has made this discovery in his own way for himself. What he also recognizes is that his book, too, like any work of art, is a "fixity" of "apparent form." A glimpse of chaos is also a glimpse of the Golden Day: to achieve any sense of ongoing identity man needs those houses and umbrellas. Consciousness depends on architecture. What is important is not to forget the fluidity in which it stands.

When he has only been in New York for a short time, the Invisible Man meets a man pushing a cart loaded down with thousands of abandoned blueprints and scrapped plans for houses and buildings. As the man says, "Folks is always making plans and changing 'em." The narrator in his naivety says, "but

that's a mistake. You have to stick to the plan," and the man answers, "you kinda young, daddy-o." It is a little parable in passing. Human beings are inve-
terate planners, but plans are just so many clues for arranging which ultimately
go to the scrap heap. What the narrator has to learn is that there are bound to be
plans, but that any one plan you get involved in may well involve some falsification or constriction of your essential self. He drops out of all plans for a while
to draw up his own. But once drawn up that too has to be left behind, as it were.
The highest aspiration would seem to be not to get trapped in any one plan,
while recognizing that to achieve any identity is to be involved in plans. One
could envisage for the narrator a continuing life of moving in and out of plans;
like the rest of us oscillating between chaos and pattern but much more aware of
it than most. In that awareness lies a measure of his freedom.

In this connection his final comment that he is sloughing off his old skin is
an important metaphor. For "skin," read "plan of any kind." And just as the
narrator sheds skins, so Ellison himself "sheds" styles, an example of what I
meant when I said that the activity of the American hero was often an analogue
of the activity of his author. Ellison is quite explicit about this. In the interview
referred to he describes how he deliberately changed the style of the book as the
narrator moved from the South to the North and from thence into a more private territory; at first it is more naturalistic, then expressionistic, and finally surrealistic, each modulation intended to express both the state of mind of the narrator and the society he is involved in. As the hero manages to extract himself
from a series of fixed environments, so the author manifests a comparable sup-
pleness by avoiding getting trapped in one style.

Another statement from Ellison makes this very clear and helps to explain
the extraordinary proliferation—and sometimes convulsion—of styles which is
so especially characteristic of recent American fiction (it is seldom indeed one
finds a serious writer committing himself to the sort of naturalism which earlier
American writers had helped to develop). Naturalism, Ellison maintains, tends
to lead writers to despair, and it fails to confront the diversity of America. Instead, he says,

> I was to dream of a prose which was flexible, and swift, confronting
> the inequalities and brutalities of our society forthrightly, but yet
> thrusting forth its images of hope, human fraternity and individual
> self-realization. It would use the riches of our speech, the idiomatic
> expression and the rhetorical flourishes from past periods which are
> still alive among us.

He feels that it must be possible to write a kind of fiction which can arrive at relevant truths "with all the bright magic of a fairy tale." Ellison's prose in the novel

is heavily foregrounded, demonstrating quite deliberately an ability to draw on sources as disparate as Revelations, the blues, classical literature, Dante, Southern white rhetoric, Harlem slang, and so on. This should not be seen as a wildly eclectic attempt to import significance but rather as a delighted display of the resources of consciousness and imagination which he can bring to bear against the pressures of a changing environment. In such a way the American writer procures some verbal freedom from the conditioning forces which surround him.

Ellison has not at this time published another novel, although one called "And Hickman Arrives" has long been promised. Considering the wealth of *Invisible Man* one might wonder whether he had not put all his material into that one book. He has published a book of essays called *Shadow and Act,* however, and in these he is visibly concerned with the same basic themes and problems; whether reviewing books on the Negro question or peering back into his own past, he is always exploring the nature of his American identity and its relations with the reality around him. And like his fictional narrator he particularly resents those who would preempt his reality by defining it in their terms.

Both as a novelist and as an essayist, one of his primary aims in writing is to challenge any "patterning" of life — whether fictional, ideological or sociological —which is a falsification of existence as he has experienced it. Perhaps the best image Ellison has for the American writer is the one he takes from the story of Menelaus and Proteus. Eidothea's advice to Menelaus is to keep a firm hold on Proteus until, after all his changes of shape, he appears as himself, at which point he will reveal the name of the offended god and how they can make their way home without further interruption.

> For the novelist, Proteus stands for both America and the inheritance of illusion through which all men must fight to acheive reality. Our task then is always to challenge the apparent forms of reality . . . and to struggle with it until it reveals its mad, variimplicated chaos, its false faces, and on until it surrenders its insight, its truth.

What we should notice is that the Invisible Man does not emulate Proteus Rinehart any more than Ellison envisages the American writer capitulating to the Protean reality around him. In many recent American novels we will find the hero in quest of identity confronting a Protean figure whose quick metamorphoses seem to make him enviably well adapted to reality; but the hero seldom takes him for a model, no matter how much he may learn from him, for that way lies chaos, the nightmare jelly, the ultimate dissolution of self. No fixed patterns, then, but not a reversion to Protean fluidity either; instead a struggle with, a resistance to, both, conducted in some "border area" where author and hero alike attempt to create themselves and come into the meaning of their experience. In projecting his situation in these terms, or in this "Gestalt," Ellison was, to take up the last line of his novel, speaking albeit "on the lower frequencies" for more American writers than he can have realized.

ROBERT B. STEPTO

Literacy and Hibernation: *Ralph Ellison's* Invisible Man

I'm not blaming anyone for this state of affairs, mind you; nor merely crying mea culpa. *The fact is that you carry part of your sickness within you, at least I do as an invisible man. I carried my sickness and though for a long time I tried to place it in the outside world, the attempt to write it down shows me that at least half of it lay within me.*
— RALPH ELLISON, *Invisible Man*

Anochecí Enfermo   Amanecí bueno
(I went to bed sick. I woke up well.)
—JAY WRIGHT, *Dimensions of History*

As I have suggested [elsewhere], the Afro American pregenetic myth of the quest for freedom and literacy has occasioned two basic types of narrative expressions, the narratives of ascent and immersion. The classic ascent narrative launches an "enslaved" and semiliterate figure on a ritualized journey to a symbolic North; that journey is charted through spatial expressions of social structure, invariably systems of signs that the questing figure must read in order to be both increasingly literate and increasingly free. The ascent narrative conventionally ends with the questing figure situated in the least oppressive social structure afforded by the world of the narrative, and free in the sense that he or she has gained sufficient literacy to assume the mantle of an articulate survivor. As the phrase "articulate survivor" suggests, the hero or heroine of an ascent narrative must be willing to forsake familial or communal postures in the narrative's most oppressive social structure for a new posture in the least oppressive environment—at

From *From Behind the Veil: A Study of Afro-American Narrative.* © 1979 by the Board of Trustees of the University of Illinois. The University of Illinois Press, 1979.

best, one of solitude; at worst, one of alienation. This last feature of the ascent narrative unquestionably helps bring about the rise and development of an immersion narrative in the tradition, for the immersion narrative is fundamentally an expression of a ritualized journey into a symbolic South, in which the protagonist seeks those aspects of tribal literacy that ameliorate, if not obliterate, the conditions imposed by solitude. The conventional immersion narrative ends almost paradoxically, with the questing figure located in or near the narrative's most oppressive social structure but free in the sense that he has gained or regained sufficient tribal literacy to assume the mantle of an articulate kinsman. As the phrase "articulate kinsman" suggests, the hero or heroine of an immersion narrative must be willing to forsake highly individualized mobility in the narrative's least oppressive social structure for a posture of relative stasis in the most oppressive environment, a loss that is only occasionally assuaged by the newfound balms of group identity. (The argument is, of course, that these "shared epiphanies" were previously unavailable to the questing figure when he or she was adrift in a state of solitude.) When seen in this way, the primary features of the ascent and immersion narratives appear to call for an epiloging text that revoices the tradition's abiding tropes in such a way that answers to all of the following questions are attempted: Can a questing figure in a narrative occasioned by the pregeneric myth be both an articulate survivor *and* an articulate kinsman? Must all such quests in the narrative literature conclude as they began, in imposed configurations of social structure? And can the literary history of Afro-American narrative forms—which is, at root, the chronicle of a dialectic between ascent and immersion expressions—become, in and of itself, the basis for a narrative form?

The whole of *Invisible Man* is a grand attempt to answer these questions, but the burden of reply falls mainly upon the narrative's frame (its Prologue and Epilogue), rather than upon its tale. I do not wish to demean the tale, for it is a remarkable invention: it presents the spatial expressions of social structure as well as the nearly counterpointing rituals of ascent (to self-consciousness) and immersion (in group consciousness) which collectively contextualize and in some sense occasion the questing narrator's progress from muteness to speech, or formlessness to form. However, what is narratively new in *Invisible Man*, and what permits it to answer the above-cited questions, is not its depiction of a pilgrim's progress, but its brave assertion that there is a self and form to be discovered beyond the lockstep of linear movement within imposed definitions of reality. For this reason the inventive tale of the questing narrator's steady progression to voice and selfhood cannot stand alone as the *narrative* of Ellison's hero. The tale must be framed, and in that sense controlled, because progression as a protean literary form and progress as a protean cultural myth must be contextualized. *Invisible Man*'s success as a fresh narrative strategy depends upon its ability to formalize in art the "fiction" of history expounded primarily in its frame. To the extent that *Invisible Man*'s frame controls its tale, its hero may gloss his personal history, and art may impose upon event.

With all this in mind, we may proceed to examine certain aspects of *Invisible Man*'s frame. I would like to begin with the hero's hole itself, which, in the context of the tradition, is clearly a revoicing of the private ritual ground to which Du Bois's persona retreats after his ritual of immersion in the Black Belt. Despite the fact that these ritual grounds are situated differently — the prefiguring space is a "high Pisgah," while the epiloging space is a "warm hole" below ground — there are many similarities between the two constructions. In the first place, both spaces are discovered or achieved after several literal and figurative rail journeys that clearly revoice the primary episode of flight on the "freedom train." I refer here on one hand to Du Bois's various symbolic rides in that social structure-in-motion called the Jim Crow car, rides which prompt his vision and hope of *communitas* in this world, and on the other hand to the Invisible Man's equally conspicuous subway rides which establish the particular rhythm of immersion and ascent that guides him finally to see the people of Harlem ("They'd been there all along, but . . . I'd missed them . . . I'd been asleep") and to consider hibernation as a viable if transient state of being. In either case, the elevated study or the subterranean hole, the private space is a construction wherein the best thoughts occasioned by these travels may collect and linger — wherein physical motion is interrupted, and body and voice are at rest, but the mind travels on.

Another point of similarity involves each space's distance from those spatial expressions of social structure (the Black Belt or Harlem) in which major acquisitions of tribal literacy are accomplished. In *The Souls* Du Bois's study is high up on Atlanta hill, not engulfed in the "dull red hideousness" of rural Georgia. In *Invisible Man* the hero's "warm hole" is not in "the jungle of Harlem," but in a "border area" that is, as the hero admits, a grand spatial and historical joke: it is of Harlem as far as the utility company's "master meter" is concerned, but out of Harlem according to most other conventional measurements of American reality, because it is a basement section of "a building rented strictly to whites" that was "shut off" (reconstructed?) and "forgotten during the nineteenth century" (Reconstruction?). In either case, vertical distance — placement upon a different plane — accentuates the more apparent horizontal displacement between tribal space and private space. These distances force each questing narrator to fashion a rhetoric that earnestly seeks to minimize the distances and to portray the narrators as group-conscious as well as self-conscious figures.

Here, I think, the points of congruence between Du Bois's study and Invisible Man's hole are most pronounced; yet here we can also begin to see how Ellison's construction assumes its own integrity. When the Invisible Man speaks in the Epilogue of how his grandfather must have meant "the principle, that we were to affirm the principle on which the country was built and not the men, or at least not the men who did the violence" and also of how "we of all, we, most of all, had to affirm the principle . . . because we were older than they, in the sense of what it took to live in the world with others," he clearly restates in his own terms Du Bois's persona's claim that "we the darker ones come even now not altogether empty-handed: there are to-day no truer exponents of the pure human spirit of the Declaration of Independence than the American Negroes." Furthermore, both questing narrators seek to qualify or contextualize these assertions of race pride and responsibility by forwarding expressions of their abiding faith in the ideal of cultural pluralism. Certainly this is suggested when we recall the following passage from chapter 1 of *The Souls* (which is, for all intents and purposes, that narrative's prologue):

> Work, culture, liberty, — all these we need, not singly but together, not successively but together, each growing and aiding each, and all striving toward that vaster ideal that swims before the Negro people, the ideal of human brotherhood, gained through the unifying ideal of Race; The ideal of fostering and developing the traits and talents of the Negro, not in opposition to or contempt for other races, but rather in large conformity to the greater ideals of the American Republic.

and place beside it these ringing, epiloging words from *Invisible Man*:

> Whence all this passion toward conformity anyway? — diversity is the word. Let man keep his many parts and you'll have no tyrant states. . . . America is woven of many strands; I would recognize them and let it so remain. It's "winner take nothing" that is the great truth of our country. Life is to be lived, not controlled; and humanity is won by continuing to play in face of certain defeat. Our fate is to become one, and yet many — This is not prophecy, but description.

Amid the similarities there lies one profound discrepancy: Ellison's refusal to sustaintain Du Bois's Herderian overlay of racial idealism. Ellison discerns a quite substantial distinction in meaning and image between the prospect of ideal races conforming to a national ideal, and that of intact races interweaving to become a national fabric. That distinction has much to do with how he subsequently fashions his questing narrator as a group-conscious and self-conscious human being.

In *The Souls,* Du Bois's hero's group consciousness is distinctly racial in character. Ensconced in his study after his immersion journey and transported by the bits of ancient song wafting up from below, he becomes a weary traveler in a tribal song — an embodied and embodying voice or, in terms indebted to Ellison, a tribally visible man. The creation of this voice and visibility is central to *The Souls's* narrative strategy; it provides the rationale for Du Bois's refusal to formalize his first and last chapters as framing prologue and epilogue, even though they function largely this way in the narrative. Unlike Ellison, Du Bois is not after an expression of group consciousness that bursts beyond tribal boundaries. Therefore he need not situate his hero's private ritual ground outside the geography of his hero's tale any more than he already has. Here we must recall especially that Du Bois's final siting of his hero is occasioned in part by autobiographical impulses. Through generous reference to the "master" Sorrow Songs, Du Bois binds his narrative's resulting space and his narrator's resulting self to what has come before, and in that way seeks his own visibility in the events and images his narrative has recorded. The whole machinery of *The Souls* is geared for acts of unveiling (making *visible*) the soul of a race and of a man; it lacks the components for processing such subtleties as invisible articulate heroes residing outside History and Veil alike.

The final posture of Ellison's questing narrator may be clarified in the following terms. To begin with, the hero's hole is described in a formal frame removed from the tale. That frame is, in a sense, that hole, because Ellison is indeed after expressions of group consciousness and self-consciousness that respectively transcend tribal literacy and resist the infecting germs of heroic self-portraiture. The whole of the frame (or, if you will, the whole of the hole) proclaims that the narrative distinction to be drawn between tale and frame is a trope for other distinctions central to *Invisible Man*, including those between blindness and insight, sleepfulness and wakefulness, sickness and health, social structure and nonstructure, History and history, embodied voice and disembodied voice, and acts of speech and of writing. All this occasions a second and fresh rhetoric that is not found in the framing chapters of *The Souls*, but is prefigured instead by the "why do I write" passages in slave narratives, several examples of which were given earlier. The strategy behind Ellison's rhetoric is, however, quite different from that of the fugitive slaves. Ellison is less interested in having his hero authenticate his tale (or rather, its content) and more interested in having that tale de-valorized in such a way that the principles of living (which are, at base, principles of writing or artfulness) delineated in the frame may finally take hold and control the way in which the narrative as a whole is read.

"So why do I write," the Invisible Man asks rhetorically, and again and again in the final pages of the Epilogue his answers — brimming with references to release from lethargy, negation of "some of the anger and some of the bitterness," shaking off the old skin, springtime, and love — serve to minimize the distance between his private space and the "concrete, ornery, vile and sublimely wonderful" world in which, alas, the rest of us reside. Indeed, we sense that when he asks the question with which the narrative ends — "Who knows but that, on the lower frequencies, I speak for you?" — "for you" expresses that last distancing interval that remains before speech "to you." But finally it is writing or the experience of writing, and not speech, that shapes whatever group consciousness the Invisible

Man will bring in tow upon his return. Writing has taught him much about himself—indeed, it has made him a highly self-aware invisible man. But it has also taught him that his personal history is but an arc of the parabola of human history, and that his personal tale is but a finite particle in the infinity of tale-telling. According to Ellison's vision, what group-orients the Invisible Man and ends his hibernation is his marvelously robust desire to take another swing around that arc of what other men call reality, to tell, shape, and / or "lie" his tale anew. In this way, then, he becomes both an articulate survivor and an articulate kinsman.

Before we follow the Invisible Man to a realm beyond hibernation, the whys and wherefores of his writing while underground should be examined further. What interests me specifically is the apparent cause-and-effect relationship between the explicit emptying of the briefcase at the end of the tale and the implicit filling of pages during the term of hibernation, a sequence that revoices a feature of slave narratives such as Douglass's 1845 *Narrative*. The Douglass narrative tells us that, in 1835, Douglass and a few of his fellow slaves concocted an escape plan that depended mainly upon each slave's possessing a "protection" or "pass," allegedly written by "Master" William Hamilton but actually composed by Douglass himself. Such a pass granted each man "full liberty" to travel to Baltimore and spend the Easter holidays—celebrating, one assumes, the ancient Resurrection of the One, and the more recent ascent of at least another one. Unfortunately, the plan is thwarted, and each slave has to save his kin by "denying everything" and destroying his "forged" protection. But through telling the tale Douglass manages to inform us once again of the great bond between freedom and literacy, and also of the great power that comes with an ability not only to read a culture's signs (in this case, a sign that is truly a written document) but also to write them and, in that supreme way, manipulate them. In short, the *Narrative*'s escape episode is a primary trope for acts of authorial control over text and context.

The lesson advanced by Douglass's escape or "protection" episode is one of many which Ellison's narrator is destined to learn the hard way; indeed, his remarkable innocence and gullibility regarding these matters provide a major comic strain in the narrative's tale. The perpetual sight of our valiant hero doggedly lugging his briefcase around New York, and even risking life and limb in order to retrieve it from a burning Harlem tenement, is funny enough; but the heart of the joke has less to do with the Invisible Man's attachment to his briefcase than with what he has consciously and subconsciously gathered inside it. Our hero's tale is substantially that of how he accumulates a motley array of cultural signs, mostly written "protections" or "passes" (diplomas, letters of recommendation, slips of paper bearing new names, etc.) that supposedly identify him and grant him "full liberty" in the "real" world beyond "home." Ellison's double-edged joke is that none of these "protections" are worth more than the paper they're written on (they are indeed "paper protections"), and that all of them ironically "keep a nigger-boy running," but not on a path that would be recognizable to Douglass or any other self-willed hero with any control over his fate.

This is not to say that the non-written signs are without importance. On the contrary, part of Ellison's point is that Tarp's leg iron, Mary Rambo's "grinning darky" bank, Tod Clifton's sambo doll, and the Rinehart-like dark glasses and "high hat" are all cultural signs of a tribal sort. Our questing narrator thinks he knows how to read them, but he only knows or reads in a very limited way. Collectively, these non-written signs represent the Invisible Man's illiteracy vis-à-vis his tribe as much as the written signs betoken his illiteracy vis-à-vis the non-tribal social structures besetting him; his unwitting act of gathering both types of signs in one bulging briefcase finally occasions the demystification of the one type by the other. Once the Invisible Man *sees* this — once he comprehends that seemingly mute objects such as the dark glasses, hat, and leg iron are the only "protections" he possesses, and that the written documents from Bledsoe, Jack, and the rest are the only signs that may be *usefully* destroyed (here, burned to light his way) — he is ready to begin his life and tale again, or rather to *prepare* to begin again. The demystification and nearly simultaneous use and destruction of the cultural signs gathered in the briefcase during the tale occasion his removal to a fresh space, the "warm hole" of the narrative's frame.

All this suggests that the Invisible Man is finally free in his framing hole, and that that freedom is expressed most conspicuously by his nearly empty briefcase. But this is not completely true — nor is it in keeping with the full measure of the lesson learned from an innocent but almost deadly trafficking in false "protections." Perhaps the most profound lesson our hero learns when the once-precious "protections" are demystified is that they are worthless, not because of what they do or do not say, but because they are authenticating documents over which he has absolutely no authorial control. (They impose on him and his tale much as the competing authenticating texts of what guarantors often impose upon a fugitive slave's tale.) Seen in this light, the Invisible Man's frenzied movement and speech (his "sleepwalking" and "sleeptalking") in the narrative's tale are tropes for his total lack of control over that history or tale, and his relative stasis in the narrative's frame (pointedly, his "wakefulness") is a trope for his brave effort to assume control of his history or tale (*and* of tale-telling) through artful acts of written composition. Thus, another aspect — perhaps *the* other aspect — of the Invisible Man's newfound freedom is that he may now pursue acts of written articulateness and literary form-making, filling the empty briefcase with what are in effect "protections" or "passes" from his *own* hand. To compose such "protections" is to assert a marvelous and heroic concept of self-willed mobility, an idea of mobility that is in keeping with the narrative's definition of hibernation:

"A hibernation is a covert preparation for a more overt action." The covert filling of the satchel with the self-authored "protection" that constitutes the completed narrative (tale *and* frame) is Ellison's most convincing expression of his hero's inevitable return, partly because it revoices a primary trope inaugurated in the tradition by Frederick Douglass.

All in all, the frame in *Invisible Man* is a familiar construction in Afro-American narrative literature, primarily because it is the mechanism for authentication and authorial control in the narrative. At the beginning of the frame, the competing or imposing fictions that surface in the tale as items in the hero's briefcase are generally defined — "When they approach me they see only my surroundings, themselves, or figments of their imagination — indeed, everything and anything except me." By the end of the frame those fictive "certainties" have been subsumed by the hero's own self-authored "plan of living" or, as he also calls it, his "pattern to the chaos." Perhaps even more impressive and resilient, however, is the manner in which this trumping of fictions with fictions is occasioned and sustained by Ellison's remarkably explicit expression of one authenticating strategy overtaking and making a joke out of another. In the tale, the Invisible Man's briefcase is much more than a repository of cultural signs and false "protections"; it is, most ironically and humorously, *the* trope for the strategy of self-authentication the Invisible Man values during most of the tale. He carries it everywhere, never realizing that it possesses him far more than he possesses it. At the beginning of the tale, in the battle-royal where he "earns" his briefcase and his first "protections" (the diploma and scholarship to Bledsoe's college), his speech full of echoes of Booker T. Washington's Atlanta Exposition Address is a signal not simply of initial rhetorical indebtedness to Washington, but (more profoundly) of an initial adherence to the Washingtonian strategy of narration and self-authentication as résumé. The briefcase substantiates this idea because it is, in effect, a résumé edited and amended by acts of sign gathering during the course of the tale. In vivid contrast to Washington, however, the Invisible Man learns not only that he lacks a grand public speech to be authenticated by a tale of his life, but also that his accumulated résumé isn't his tale.

MAKING LIGHT OF THE LIGHT

Like *The Autobiography of an Ex-Coloured Man* and *Black Boy*, *Invisible Man* presents, as part of its narrative machinery, a series of portraits — on the wall as well as in the flesh — that may be loosely termed the narrative's portrait gallery. While it can be argued that any mobile or immobile character in any narrative is in some sense a portrait, the portraits which I'm about to discuss are special. They comprise a narrative strategy by which various models of voice and action are

kept before the questing narrator, and by which the full range of human possibility in the differing social structures of the narrative may be defined and seen.
In the chapter on *The Autobiography* [in *From Behind the Veil*], I described at
some length the portrait gallery in the parlor of the Ex-Coloured Man's Club; it
is important to recall that gallery here, because it is our best example of a symbolic construction in which all of the models (from Frederick Douglass to the
minstrel who yearns to be a Shakespearean) are valorized as heroic examples that
the narrator would do well to emulate. The whole point to the construction is
that the Ex Coloured Man could have learned from these "portraits," but
didn't — because he could not really see them, let alone see through them. In
Black Boy, virtually the opposite is true. Few if any portraits are displaced on the
walls of the narrative's prison-like interiors; the major portraits are intentionally
"in the flesh" and, with the possible exceptions of Ella (the schoolteacher who
tells the story of Bluebeard), the editor of the Negro newspaper, and the
Irishman who surreptitiously lends his library card to young Richard, they are all
of men and women who are "warnings" rather than "examples." While the Ex-
Coloured Man cannot fully see the heroic examples before him, and thus not only remains a non-hero but effectively relinquishes the narrative's space for heroic
posturing to figures such as "Shiny," Wright's persona pursues a far different
and aggressive course. In *Black Boy* the potential or assumed examples, especially the elder kinfolk, are systematically de-valorized and portrayed as
"warnings" — partly so that a hellish landscape may be depicted and peopled,
but mostly so that Wright's persona, as an emerging articulate survivor, may not
only control but also fill the narrative's space for heroic posturing. In this way
Wright's persona, unlike Johnson's Ex-Coloured Man, sees and aggressively *sees
through* the major "portraits" in his tale. For this reason, to cite only one example, the persona meticulously buries his father alive in the red clay of Mississippi.

    Invisible Man retains certain aspects of the portrait galleries found in both
The Autobiography and *Black Boy*. The narrative offers portraits both on the
wall and in the flesh, and the portrait motif is indeed central to Ellison's strategy
of keeping both examples and warnings before the questing narrator. But more
significant is how *Invisible Man* bursts beyond the strategies of portraiture and
gallery construction that we find in Johnson's and Wright's prefiguring texts. At
first glance, the portrait gallery in *Invisible Man* is much like that in *Black Boy*,
in that it is not confined to a ritual space such as the Ex-Coloured Man's Club (or
the outdoor revival in which the preacher, John Brown, and the master singer,
Singing Johnson, are sketched) but is dispersed throughout the narrative.
Furthermore, as in *Black Boy*, the portraits in *Invisible Man* are usually dismantled or demystified — that is, the figures are usually less then heroic. But this
is also where the different treatment of this motif begins in each narrative. In

Black Boy, one senses that Wright's portraits of would-be examples, such as the father and the presona's Uncle Tom, are *always* demystified; the figures thereby plummet from their assigned (if not always earned) heights to the depths of life as it is lived by partially animate warnings. But to judge from *Invisible Man,* Ellison appears perennially suspicious of such simple dichotomies, and in pursuit, therefore, of more complex and differentiated expressions. Hence we discover in his narrative that while Bledsoe, Norton, and the one-eyed Jack are indeed warnings, not examples, Trueblood, Brother Tarp, and most especially the advice-giving grandfather are neither examples nor warnings, but enigmas of varying sorts. They occupy and enlarge a fresh narrative space.

While the demystification of these would-be examples is a prerequisite for the Invisible Man's blossoming as a truly literate figure, the thrust of the narrative is not to replace these portraits with that of the Invisible Man as a heroic example. Rather, it is to *identify* Bledsoe, Norton, and the rest as varying fictions of reality and history which must be deposed or, as we soon will see, defiled in order for the fiction that is the narrative to be imagined. The narrative and not the narrator, the "principle" and not the "men," and the frame far more than the tale collectively constitute the heroic example forwarded by Ellison's narrative and rhetorical strategies. To see this is to know a major way in which *Invisible Man* aggressively contradicts the abiding idea of the artist in *Black Boy,* and to know as well how it assumes its place in the Afro-American narrative tradition.

One final preliminary point is that the portrait motif in *Invisible Man* is joined by, and in some sense conjoined to, what I am going to call the narrative's museum motif. There are at least three great "museum collections" in the narrative, and these are important to the narrative's machinery as contexts or syntaxes, just as the portraits are important as relatively discrete expressions. What binds the portrait motif to the museum motif is not simply the fact that portraits frequently form an integral part of certain specific contexts or syntaxes, but that both motifs are reduced, in the narrative's frame, to being one and the same expression and sign — the collected and displayed light for which certain other people's measurements of reality cannot account. The narrator's warm hole is at once a portrait gallery of light and an exquisite museum collection of light; the light "confirms" his "reality" and "gives birth" to his "form," just as other, ostensibly more delineated, portraits and displayed objects confirm other realities and give birth to other forms — especially of a literary sort.

But perhaps, as the Invisible Man says of himself at the end of the beginning (which is the beginning of the end), I am moving too fast. The frame is not visible in its full splendor of invisibility unless we can see the proud visages and precious vestiges which it both visibly and invisibly frames. We must begin with *Invisible Man*'s tale — even though it is neither the narrative's beginning nor its end — and with the portrait of the grandfather who seems, as a highly visible invisibility, to begin and end it all.

The grandfather enters the tale at its beginning, in a speech — or, rather *as* speech: "'Live with your head in the lion's mouth. I want you to overcome 'em with yeses, undermine 'em with grins, agree 'em to death and destruction, let 'em swoller you till they vomit or bust wide open.'" This entrance is central to his place in the tale; he is a portrait-in-language that his grandson must learn to hear, read, and contextualize. But as the following passage from the end of the battle-royal episode instructs, the grandfather is as much a portrait on the wall (of the mind, as well as of the space called "family" or "home") as he is one in language:

> When I reached home everyone was excited. Next day the neighbors came to congratulate me. I even felt safe from grandfather, whose deathbed curse usually spoiled my triumphs. I stood beneath his photograph with my briefcase in hand and smiled triumphantly into his stolid black peasant's face. It was a face that fascinated me. The eyes seemed to follow everywhere I went.

Several things are afoot here, and one of them is certainly a radical revision of the "obituary" with which Wright's *Black Boy* persona buries his father alive by calling him a "stranger" and a "black peasant." In *Black Boy,* the implication is clearly that the father is a known quantity; that he is fixed or immobilized in a "culture's" time and space, and that his portrait has been completely and consummately read by his "civilized" questing kinsman. In *Invisible Man,* however, the grandfather is not quite so easily removed from the wall and (in that sense, among others) dismantled. As the phrase "the eyes seemed to follow everywhere I went" suggests, Ellison's narrator's grandfather is an unknown and mobile figure whose eyes are hardly "glazed" like those of the "dead" father in *Black Boy;* he will travel with and reappear before his youthful kinsman in word and image many times before the narrative's tale is finally complete. The grandfather, who provides the first portrait in the tale's portrait gallery, is neither a warning nor an example but a huge and looming question mark — an enigma. In this way his portrait prefigures those of other "peasants" in the narrative, such as Trueblood and Brother Tarp (Brother Veil? Brother Sail?), who are also enigmas, and the grandfather's portrait quite purposefully skews whatever preconceptions we might have regarding a simple system of dialectical or antipodal portraiture ("warning" / "example") in the narrative. The grandfather is, in short, a "Mr. In-Between," a Vergilian guide who occupies neither antipodal space, not because he is supposedly dead (or thought "mad" by the intervening generation, the Invisible Man's parents) but because of the implicit distinction which the narrative draws between the spoken and written word and, hence, between guides and artists.

Another method of dismantling and possibly debunking an antipodal system of portraiture is simply to inaugurate a presentation in which examples, warnings, and the world they define are eventually and comically turned inside out. Ellison does essentially this with the portraits in the campus episodes and with the initially Edenic campus as a world within the world of the narrative. His activity differs from Wright's in *Black Boy,* mainly because Wright never allows a model to become an example before he shows it to be warning, or a space to assume paradisaical proportions before he demonstrates that it is a circle of hell. In the campus episodes, the portraits begin with the bronze statue of the college Founder. Ellison has a lot of fun with both his narrator and the conventions of heroic portraiture while describing this work of art:

> It's so long ago and far away that here in my invisibility I wonder if it happened at all. Then in my mind's eye I see the bronze statue of the college Founder, the cold Father symbol, his hands outstretched in the breathtaking gesture of lifting a veil that flutters in hard, metallic folds above the face of a kneeling slave; and I am standing puzzled, unable to decide whether the veil is really being lifted, or lowered more firmly in place; whether I am witnessing a revelation or a more efficient blinding. And as I gaze, there is a rustle of wings and I see a flock of starlings fighting before me and, when I look again, the bronze face, whose empty eyes look upon a world I have never seen, runs with liquid chalk—creating another ambiguity to puzzle my groping mind: Why is a bird-soiled statue more commanding than one that is clean?

Of course, there is much serious activity here that advances the narrative's discussion of what is visible and invisible, seen and unseen. The second veil of a very organic tulle joins the first, of bronze, adding a necessary complexity to the abiding question of who is the prophet, who the sheep, and what indeed can that prophet see. Furthermore, it prefigures other tropes in the narrative, such as the Liberty Paint Factory's celebrated optic white paint. But basically this comic portrait of Founder and narrator achieves its humor not so much because a heroic example is draped in guano or because the youthful narrator attempts to make and unmake a philosophical puzzle out of that event. Rather, its humor arises from the more profound incongruities that displace the narrator as seer from the Founder who, according to one definition of history, is a Seer, but who, according to at least one other definition, is the seen.

This high comedy continues in the narrative when Homer A. Barbee, the noted blind minister, preaches on and adds further luster to the legend of the Founder's death. Indeed, the inanimate statue on the lawn and the highly animated tale or "lie" as sermon are parts of the same composite portrait of the Founder. Through a marvelous orchestration of images, reminding us of many other train rides in written and verbal art (recall, for example, Lincoln's cortege in Whitman's "When Lilacs Last in the Dooryard Bloom'd"), Homer Barbee transports us on another ride, a solemn ride of sorrowful rest and joyous resurrection: "'When the train reached the summit of the mountain, he [the Founder] was no longer with us. . . .'" But there is a new and finally quite funny twist to all of this: Barbee and Bledsoe, like two disciples become vaudevillians, are on board. Were you there when they crucified my Lord? Yessir, as a matter of fact I was! Me and Bledsoe! Right there!

Barbee's sermon is finally less a valorization of the Founder than of A. Herbert Bledsoe. To put it another way, the text of his sermon is less a strategy for authenticating the legend of the Founder than one for authenticating the equally supreme fiction with which Bledsoe wields power and proffers a particular construction of historical reality:

> "Oh, yes. Oh, yes," he [Barbee] said. "Oh, yes. That too is part of the glorious story. But think of it not as a death, but as a birth. A great seed has been planted. A seed which has continued to put forth its fruit in its season as surely as if the great creator had been resurrected. For in a sense he was, if not in the flesh, in the spirit. And in a sense in the flesh too. For has not your present leader become his living agent, his physical presence? Look about you if you doubt it. My young friends, my dear young friends! How can I tell you what manner of man this is who leads you! How can I convey to you how well he has kept his pledge to the Founder, how conscientious has been his stewardship?"

With words like these Homer Barbee demonstrates how he and Herbert Bledsoe — the Preacher and the Principal — are indeed quite a team, more than likely one of the most extraordinary comedy teams in Afro-American narrative literature. Evidently they have made a long black joke out of the long black song of the Founder's long black train. Who follows in his train? The shadows do.

After the portrait of the Founder, the next arresting portrait in the campus episodes is of Norton's daughter. Appropriately enough, her image is not a photograph on the wall or a totem on the lawn, but something of a cameo which her father reverently carries on his person, as close to his waist as to his heart:

Suddenly he fumbled in his vest pocket and thrust something over the back of the seat, surprising me.

"Here, young man, you owe much of your good fortune in attending such a school to her."

I looked upon the tinted miniature framed in engraved platinum. I almost dropped it. A young woman of delicate, dreamy features looked up at me. She was very beautiful, I thought at the time, so beautiful that I did not know whether I should express admiration to the extent I felt it or merely act polite. And yet I seemed to remember her, or someone like her, in the past. I know now that it was the flowing costume of soft, flimsy material that made for the effect; today, dressed in one of the smart, well-tailored, angular, sterile, streamlined, engine-turned, air-conditioned modern outfits you see in the women's magazines, she would appear as ordinary as an expensive piece of machine-tooled jewelry and just as lifeless. Then, however, I shared something of his enthusiasm.

Of course, the immediate business at hand here is a citing and sighting of Norton's erection of a pedestal for his "biblical maiden" of a daughter, which will soon crumple as he hears the sorrowful tale of Jim Trueblood. Perhaps, too, Ellison is up to some devilish tricks regarding what is unstated about Mr. Dalton and his virginal Mary in *Native Son*. Surely it is not stretching things to draw a parallel between Norton giving money for toys to the Truebloods and Dalton giving pingpong paddles to the "bloods" at the South Side Boys Club.

More to the point, however, regarding Ellison's demystification of this portrait, are the Invisible Man's remarks about Miss Norton's costume in the miniature, and what she would have looked like in contemporary "engine-turned" dress. In truth, at this point in the tale he hasn't met the likes of her; but he is about to meet her again and again — and phrases like "an expensive piece of machine-tooled jewelry" instruct us as to where and when. The portrait of Miss Norton in her father's vest pocket is but an abiding fiction of "modern" women like Emma and other women in the Brotherhood episodes — but especially of Emma, who, like a slick magician performing an ancient trick, will pull the narrator's new name out of her otherwise empty but interesting bosom. Miss Norton, or rather her portrait, may return to New York in her father's pocket; but it is clear that, as that portrait is dismantled, it (and she) will not remain there. Indeed, one of the most remarkable images offered by the New York episodes is that of Norton's "daughters" entertaining the Brotherhood at the chic Chthonian, while Norton himself is lost in the subway.

But we're not yet ready to go to New York; we must return to the campus and to Bledsoe's office—which is a kind of annex to the college's museum of slavery, although no one there would dare call it that. Several aspects of this museum will be discussed shortly, but what interests me here are the "frame portrait photographs and relief plaques of presidents and industrialists, men of power." Evidently these portraits are redoubtable examples of heroic portraiture in which the "men of power" appear as heroic examples, or gods. In the process of attempting to describe their extraordinary presence in Bledsoe's *sanctum sanctorum,* the Invisible Man unwittingly stumbles upon much of the symbolic space's hidden significance when he writes that these men are "fixed like trophies or heraldic emblems upon the walls." He's right: the "men of power" *are* Bledsoe's "trophies"—he has bagged them (or, got them by their bags) in many senses of the term. The phrase "heraldic emblems" is also apt, because these men are messengers of given sovereignties, as well as of given fictions of historical reality. As such, they are harbingers of war, morticians to the dead, and custodians of national and genealogical signs. This fits them and, indeed, destines them for positions of stewardship to constructions such as Bledsoe's college; this is much of what the Invisible Man may finally see about them, once he is released from the pattern of their certainties and deep into the task of creating a competing fiction. In Bledsoe's office, however, wherein our hero is summarily expelled from "nigger heaven," the "men of power" are but a mute angelic choir (to Bledsoe's St. Peter) whose collective voices and visages seem to condemn him all the more with their silence.

In the Brotherhood episodes, Ellison continues to give his portraits a comic texture, but he also seems intent on enlarging the space for enigmatic models in which the grandfather has already been situated. Quite fittingly, these portraits appear on the walls of the Invisible Man's office within the Brotherhood's Harlem headquarters, constituting a significant portion of the narrative strategy by which that space is positioned (and thereby read) within a spatial dynamic that also embraces Bledsoe's "trophy room" and the framing warm hole. Especially in their conversation with one another, the portraits expose the hidden seams in the elaborate fiction that the Invisible Man jokingly calls, in retrospect, his "days of certainty" with the Brotherhood. The controversial "rainbow poster," for example, is described matter-of-factly—but not without a dollop of Ellisonian humor:

> It was a symbolic poster of a group of heroic figures: An American
> Indian couple, representing the dispossessed past; a blond brother
> (in overalls) and a leading Irish sister, representing the dispossessed

present; and Brother Tod Clifton and a young white couple (it had been felt unwise simply to show Clifton and the girl) surrounded by a group of children of mixed races, representing the future, a color photograph of bright skin texture and smooth contrast . . . [its] legend:

"After the Struggle: The Rainbow of America's Future"

The rhetoric of heroic example offered here is at once antithetical to that put forth by Bledsoe's display of the "men of power," and yet much the same as that rhetoric in that it is another imposed fiction of reality. However, at this point in the narrative the Invisible Man cannot see or read this rhetoric, any more than he can comprehend what certain Brotherhood members found objectionable about the poster. (Here, it is reasonable to assume that some brothers viewed the poster as being too "racial" and / or "nationalistic" in its statement and, therefore, insufficient as an expression of the international class struggle.) One guesses that the Invisible Man probably overheard some Harlemite in a bar telling a "lie" about Josephine Baker and her "rainbow tribe," and "ran" with the idea in his own newly ideological way. All such guesses aside, however, it is clear that the rainbow poster portrays not just a rhetoric our hero thinks he can see, but also a compromise he has made which he *can't* see.

The other portrait on the wall helps Ellison make much the same point. The first of several gifts the Invisible Man receives from Brother Tarp, it is of Frederick Douglass, and it is the first portrait of a truly heroic example to be hung in the narrative's gallery. But, unlike Johnson with his Ex-Coloured Man, Ellison is neither about the task of providing redoubtable examples for his confused protagonist nor about that of lamenting the sad fact that his narrator cannot see or see through Douglass. In the scene where the Douglass portrait is discussed, we receive instead another example of the Invisible Man's partial comprehension of a heroic rhetoric:

> I liked my work during those days of certainty. I kept my eyes wide and my ears alert. The Brotherhood was a world within a world and I was determined to discover all its secrets and to advance as far as I could. I saw no limits, it was the one organization in the whole country in which I could reach the very top and I meant to get there. Even if it meant climbing a mountain of words. For now I had begun to believe, despite all the talk of science around me, that there was a magic in spoken words. Sometimes I sat watching the watery play of light upon Douglass's portrait, thinking how magical it was that he had talked his way from slavery to a government ministry, and so swiftly. Perhaps, I thought, something of the kind is happening to

me. Douglass came north to escape and find work in the shipyards; a big fellow in a sailor's suit who, like me, had taken another name. What had his true name been? Whatever it was, it was as *Douglass* that he became himself, defined himself. And not as a boatwright as he'd expected, but as an orator. Perhaps the sense of magic lay in the unexpected transformation. "You start Saul, and end up Paul," my grandfather had often said. "When you're a youngun, you Saul, but let life whup your head a bit and you starts to trying to be Paul — though you still Sauls around on the side."

Several things stand out in this remarkable piece of writing. One of them is the presumably naive way in which the Invisible Man convinces himself of the great truths subsumed within the fiction he is living by means of creating an authenticating fiction for his own life story. At the heart of this fiction is his questionable assertion that Douglass defined himself as an orator — as a private-become-public act of speech. Abetting this assertion are several revealing revisions of Douglass's language in the 1845 *Narrative:* "from slavery to a government ministry" is, for example, a remarkable revision or misreading of Douglass's famous "from slavery to freedom." Of course, he has the goal all wrong; but even more disastrously wrong than the goal is the misconception of literacy and its uses that lies behind it.

In the Douglas *Narrative,* the phrase "from slavery to freedom," or more fully "the pathway from slavery to freedom," is Douglass's most felicitous expression for acts of reading and writing. He writes in chapter 6 of what he learned when Mr. Auld forbade Mrs. Auld to instruct him any further in "The A B C": "From that moment, I understood the pathway from slavery to freedom. It was just what I wanted, and I got it at a time when I the least expected it. . . . Though conscious of the difficulty of learning without a teacher, I set out with high hope, and a fixed purpose, at whatever cost of trouble, *to learn how to read"* (italics added). This is the abiding idea of literacy and its uses in the *Narrative* (and in the Afro-American tradition). Given the events of the *Narrative,* it isn't stretching things to say that, for Douglass, acts of literacy include acts of reading the signs and events, or "patterns of certainties," that comprise oppressive and imposing fictions of reality. Douglass didn't "talk" his way to freedom; rather, he "read" his way and, as far as the *Narrative* is concerned (it being his personal history as and in a literary form), "wrote" his way.

In the Brotherhood episode wherein Douglass's portrait is hung, it is clear that the Invisible Man only partially comprehends the heroic example and rhetoric captured in that usually fierce visage, mainly because he is still wrapped up in the idea of composing a fiction in which he himself is a great speaker or act

or sound. Somehow he senses — perhaps because Douglass's portrait forces him
to hear unwelcome echoes of his grandfather's voice — that Douglass is as much
an enigma to him as the grandfather, that both images will remain looming
question marks in his mind. Surely he will later sense that Douglass poses some
very substantial questions about the fiction he is living, when he returns to
Harlem to discover that Tod Clifton and Brother Tarp are missing and that
Douglass's portrait has been torn down as well. In the meantime, however, during those days of certainty, the portraits on the walls of the narrator's bustling office only exhibit to him a full and sufficient expression of himself as a brother in
the struggle — and on the make.

As I have suggested before, there is a museum as well as a portrait gallery in
Invisible Man; that museum contains various collections that are contexts or syntaxes for certain portraits and, more to the point here, certain cultural artifacts or
material objects. While a given portrait and artifact may function (and possibly
resonate) in the narrative in much the same way, an essential distinction must be
drawn between how the portraits as a group (the gallery) and the artifacts as a
group (the museum) operate as narrative strategies, especially within the tale.
While the portraits present the full array of examples, warnings, and enigmas
before the questing narrator, the artifacts present the full array of prescribed or
pre-formed patterns of mobility. Of course, the collected portraits and artifacts
alike are, at base, systems of models; but in *Invisible Man* they are differing
systems, in so far as the portraits are prototypes for the self and the artifacts are
prototypes for the self-in-motion.

Returning to Bledsoe's office, which I have described before as an unofficial
annex to the college's museum of slavery, we are led to discover, amid the heavy
furniture, mementos of the Founder, and collective gaze of the "men of power,"
an artifact of which Bledsoe as both curator and custodian is very proud:

> He looked at me as though I had committed the worst crime imag-
> inable. "Don't you know we can't tolerate such a thing? I gave you
> an opportunity to serve one of our best white friends, a man who
> could make your fortune. But in return you dragged the entire race
> into the slime!"
>
> Suddenly he reached for something beneath a pile of papers, an
> old leg shackle from slavery which he proudly called a "symbol of our
> progress."
>
> "You've got to be disciplined, boy." he said. "There's no ifs and
> ands about it."

I have quoted from the text at some length because we must see the leg shackle
both as an object and as language. As Ellison makes so very clear, as an object it

is *not* a charmingly rustic paperweight gracing Bledsoe's many papers, but something far more sinister and weapon-like that must be concealed—perhaps, as in this instance, by a cloak of words. As language, the leg shackle is less a silence or pause than a transitional phrase—a veritable link—between the two cited parts of Bledsoe's speech. For Bledsoe, the shackle is a charged rhetorical object in the present ("a 'symbol of our progress'"), principally because it is also a rhetorical expression of the past (the "slime" which is invariably the nearly excremental quicksand of slavery; recall here, in contrast, Du Bois's swamp) and a paradigm for a fiction that may be imposed selectively on the future—in this case, the narrator's future. The half-dozen or so letters of introduction (the "protections")—which Bledsoe is able to produce so mysteriously in thirty minutes' time, and which allow the Invisible Man no mobility whatsoever except, ironically, a bus ride to New York (undoubtedly on the Bloodhound or North Star line)—are prefigured before, in all of their nefarious qualities, by the "pile of papers" in collusion, as it were, with the leg shackle.

Another telling aspect of Bledsoe's shackle is that it is smooth and unsullied, perhaps still gleaming as if brand new—or not yet put to its purpose. But we do not learn this until Brother Tarp presents the narrator with a very different leg iron, in the same Brotherhood episode when he hangs the portrait of Frederick Douglass:

> He was unwrapping the object now and I watched his old man's hands.
>
> "I'd like to pass it on to you, son. There," he said, handing it to me. "Funny thing to give somebody, but I think it's got a heap of signifying wrapped up in it and it might help you remember what we're really fighting against. I don't think of it in terms of but two words, *yes* and *no;* but it signifies a heap more. . . ."
>
> I saw him place his hand on the desk. "Brother," he said, calling me "Brother" for the first time, "I want you to take it. I guess it's a kind of luck piece. Anyway, it's the one I filed to get away."
>
> I took it in my hand, a thick dark, oily piece of filed steel that had been twisted open and forced partly back into place, on which I saw marks that might have been made by the blade of a hatchet. It was such a link as I had seen on Bledsoe's desk, only while that one had been smooth, Tarp's bore the marks of haste and violence, looking as though it had been attacked and conquered before it stubbornly yielded.

With these words the Invisible Man receives the first and only viable "protection" he is given in the tale. Shortly thereafter he fits the leg iron on his hand as if it were a pair of brass knuckles ("Finding no words to ask him more about it, I slipped the link over my knuckles and struck it sharply against the desk"), never dreaming that he will soon use it in this very manner in a pitched battle with Ras and his followers. Here we receive nothing less than a deft and momentous construction and ordering of the narrative as a whole. Tarp's shackle, in contrast to Bledsoe's, is worn, not just in the sense that it bears the marks of a violent attack and defeat, but also in that it has been literally worn — for nineteen years — by Brother Tarp. This suggests that Tarp is a very different kind of "curator" and, in some sense, *author* of the leg shackle and its accompanying fictions than is Bledsoe — recall here Tarp's earlier remark, " 'I'm tellin' it better'n I ever thought I could.' " As an author, Tarp has been both in and out of his tale, and has thereby gained the perspectives and techniques with which to *see* the tale and *tell* it well. He — like certain other "peasants" in the narrative, such as the grandfather, Trueblood, and Frederick Douglass — is something of an artist, while Bledsoe — like certain other "uplifted" types, including Brother Jack — is not so much an artist or tale-teller as a manipulator of them. In either case, Tarp's or Bledsoe's, the leg iron which each man possesses, displays, and in varying senses gives away is an abiding expression of a posture as a "man of power" in the narrative, especially as far as art-making is concerned.

Related is the substantial matter of how the two leg irons prompt another review of Bledsoe's and the Invisible Man's offices as contrasting symbolic spaces. I have already suggested how the portraits alone help to construct these spaces, but what is pertinent here is how they are further assembled by the beams of meaning that stretch between portrait and artifact. The heart of the matter, I believe, is that once the portraits and leg irons are bound before us, we see more clearly the profound distinction between a rhetoric of progress and one of liberation. In Bledsoe's office, the "men of power" are the smooth, closed shackle — and the shackle the men — not only because the men are, in various meanings of the term, a "closed circle," but also because the rhetoric of progress which they as trustees (or is it trusties?) oversee, and in that sense enclose far more than they author, is as fixed or static as their conception (and perception) of the present. Indeed, much as Bledsoe is characterized in another episode as a "headwaiter" and not a consummate chef (hence the continuity in his career, from his college days as the best "slop dispenser" up to the narrative present), the "men of power" must be seen as figures who "serve" power: they dispense its prevailing fictions, yet are shackled to those fictions. The unending circle of Bledsoe's leg iron is a remarkable manifestation of a particular and prevailing uplift myth in which "service" is not just equated with "progress," but is also its literary form.

In the Invisible Man's office, the portrait of Frederick Douglass is modally bound to the violently opened leg shackle partly because Douglass, like Tarp, set himself free, and partly because Douglass, like the filed-open shackle, is an expression of human possibility. The key, as it were, to this construction is the exquisitely rude aperture that "defiles" the otherwise completed (or closed) form of the leg iron. On one level, that space is an exit or entrance; on another, it is a void to be filled, not once and for all but continually. Douglass and the open shackle speak as one, not just of human possibility but also of artistic possibility. To fill the space is less to close the form than to shape the form; and, to be sure, there can never be only one form. After all, hadn't Douglass written at least three *tales* of his life? Hadn't he hung a mighty door in his shackle's space and shaped his form not once but three times? Douglass's breaking of the shackle, his artful movement out and back in and out of the shackle, and his forming and (in all senses of the term) *reforming* of the shackle is finally *the* trope before the questing narrator for a viable pattern of mobility and a viable system of authorial control. Once the Invisible Man takes Tarp's shackle with him down into the narrative's framing warm hole and learns to *read* it, as well as to *hear* his grandfather and to *return* Douglass's gaze, he is ready to hibernate and write. Once these portraits and artifacts are removed from what Ishmael Reed has called "Centers of Art Detention" and are displayed in that Center of Art Retention which Ellison calls the mind, he is ready to "birth his form."

It would appear, then, that Ellison is pursuing a narrative strategy in which aspects of the tale are turned inside-out in the frame, much as the narrator is transformed from an illiterate to a literate protagonist. But this is not the case. The means by which Ellison avoids such a closure — which would destroy his narrative — tell us much about the strategies by which he seeks to burst beyond the prototypical narratives of ascent and immersion provided by Frederick Douglass and W. E. B. Du Bois. Here I wish to suggest nothing less than that, on a level not altogether removed from the inner workings of *Invisible Man,* Bledsoe's smooth and closed shackle is a trope for inherited and, to a degree, imposed narrative forms in the tradition (of which Douglass's and Du Bois's forms are the dominant forms), and that Tarp's rudely opened shackle symbolizes both the release from these forms and the new form which is *Invisible Man.* Ellison appears only too aware that any step outside the shackles of what other men call reality necessitates an accompanying step outside what other men, including kinsmen, call literary form.

Douglass's 1845 *Narrative* is built upon a strategy and rhetoric of triumphant reversal: "how a man became a slave" becomes "how a slave became a man." Furthermore, the world of the narrative reverses somehow, in accord with the reversal of the persona's condition, even though the persona is still situated in an imposed social structure. *Invisible Man* breaks with this strategy most obviously by removing the transformed narrator from social structure, but also more subtly by not completing all aspects of the reversal in the first place. While the Invisible Man does indeed "reverse" from visible to invisible (or invisible to visible) as well as from illiterate to literate, and while the portraits and artifacts of the tale move from the surfaces of the tale's symbolic interiors to those of the narrator's mind, the darkness or dimness that once occupied his mind is *not* transposed to the surfaces of the new symbolic space (the hole). Instead, it quite simply and profoundly vanishes. What *are* on these surfaces are expressions, if you will, not of darkness but of light; there are 1,369 light bulbs, and apparently more to come. These lights "speak" not of a former somnolent dimness, but of a contemporary illuminated wakefulness. And in addition to not expressing the narrator's previous abiding "dim-wattedness," the many lights are not portraits and artifacts like those in the tale. They are not competing or guiding fictions, but expressions of something that is distinctly pre-fiction, pre-form, and pre-art. In the warm hole of hibernation (or so Ellison's new construction informs us), what is so "torturous" about writing is not that one must work in the presence of already formed artworks, but that this work must be accomplished under the scrutiny of a certain radiant and self-inflicted brilliance.

The "brilliance" interests me principally because it is a constructed brilliance and, as such, part of a strategy by which Ellison bursts beyond the narrative model provided by Du Bois. Of course, the model as a whole is *The Souls*, but the particular aspect of that model which Ellison must revoice and revise in order to achieve a new narrative expression is the obviously Romantic primary scene at the end of the narrative, where brilliance makes its visit to the self-conscious artist in the form of an enlightening "sunshine." By way of a reminder, let me mention further that in *The Souls* Du Bois's light must *enter* his persona's private space, and that it is above all a natural energy that binds him to whatever "Eternal Good" resides in this and other worlds. Furthermore, once these beams are entwined with those of the songs of his generations ("My children, my little children, are singing to the sunshine"), they bind him to his "tribe" as well, and, more specifically still, to his tribe's *genius loci*. Quite to the point, and in full accord with other Romantic aspects of the model, Du Bois remarks on how these magnificient energies are "free"; these remarks are as conspicuous as the absence of even a veiled suggestion that he, too, is free. This primary scene in *The Souls* indicates that a price must be paid for accomplishing immerson; it is the other side of the coin, as it were, to being self-consciously situated in an isolated space, where the windows are few and "high" and latticed with bars of light and song. The brilliance that enlightens Du Bois's persona as self and artist speaks as much of loss as of gain, and this brilliance and its accompanying idea of artistic compensation must be radically revoiced in order for the "shackle" of the immerson narrative form to be broken.

Ellison's deliberate positioning of the brilliance before his narrator *inside* the hole, all over the hole, and with many bulbs instead of a few high windows, is the beginning of such a revision and revoicing. Of course, there is more to his expression than this: the brilliance is a constructed brilliance in that it is man-made or "tinkermade," and it is an interior brilliance most particularly in that it is mind-made or "thinker-made." Indeed, as the Invisible Man informs us in the prologue, it is the self-work of a "'thinker-tinker,'" an "inventor" with a "theory and a concept" who is almost anything but an embodiment of an "Eternal Good." This brilliance is "free" in a sense of the term very different from the one which Du Bois advances. In *The Souls,* the entwining beams of light and voice are free *only* in the sense that they are as visible, audible, and mobile as those who reside within the shadows of the Veil are invisible, inaudible, and im-mobile. This is clearly the sense of Du Bois's language when he writes:

> If somewhere in this whirl and chaos of things there dwells Eternal Good, pitiful yet masterful, then anon in His good time America shall rend the Veil and the prisoned shall go free. Free, Free as the sunshine trickling down the morning into these high windows of mine, free as yonder fresh young voices welling up to me from the caverns of brick and mortar below.

However, as I've suggested, these energies are not free to the persona; he has paid for them in various ways, including the undertaking of a requisite pilgrim-mage into more oppressive systems of social structure. For these reasons I think it might be said that the immersion narrative, like the narrative of ascent, is less about strategies for avoiding payment than about strategies for making payment that yield, in turn, a fresh posture within social structure which is somehow *worth* that payment—or *more than worth it.* Viewed in this way, ascent and im-mersion narratives are very much of a piece, and so it would appear that a strategy for bursting beyond the one is also a scheme for release from the other.

Ellison achieves such a strategy when he makes it clear that his narrator has found a way not only to stop paying for his life within what other men call reali-ty, but also to avoid paying for his enlightenment once he has fallen outside those imposing fictions. The former discovery releases him as Du Bois and others are not released from various rhetorics of progress; the latter discovery allows him to gain as few others have gained a rhetoric of liberation. Above and beyond the hilarious joke of "socking it" to the power company with every socket in-stalled (or of "screwing" them with every screw of a bulb) lies the very serious point that the self-initiated and self-constructed brilliance before the hibernating narrator does not, and in fact cannot, reverse the charge: it comes free and freely without a service payment, without a loss that the narrator must balance against his gain. In the narrative of hibernation — for so we must call it, because it is a new form in the tradition — what defines the new resulting posture and space for the questing narrator has nothing to do with whether he is situated in the most or least oppressive social structure of the narrative, and little to do with how much space lies between his hole and the "ornery" world above (after all, the Invisible Man can smell the stench of Spring), but everything to do with whether it is a context in which the imagination is its own self-generating energy. The new resulting posture and space beyond those of the ascent and immersion narratives are ones in which the narrator eventually gains complete authorial control of the text of the narrative, and of the imagination as a trope subsumed within that text. (For those who have said through the years that Ellison has "grabbed all the marbles," but who don't know by what sleight of hand he did it — this is how he did it.)

I have not forgotten that Du Bois's enlightening brilliance is an exquisite commingling of light *and* song — nor apparently has Ellison. Indeed, just as the Invisible Man wants more and more light, he also desires more and more machines with which to play Louis Armstrong's "What Did I Do to Be so Black and Blue." This music, like the light it accompanies, does not have to waft in some high window, but emanates instead from *within* the space; it is a "thinker-tinker" music, music that has been improvised upon. The Invisible Man touches on this matter when he writes:

> Sometimes now I listen to Louis while I have my favorite dessert of vanilla ice cream and sloe gin. I pour the red liquid over the white mound, watching it glisten and the vapor rising as Louis bends that military instrument into a beam of lyrical sound. Perhaps I like Louis Armstrong because he's made poetry out of being invisible. . . . And my own grasp of invisibility aids me to understand his music. . . . Invisibility, let me explain, gives one a slightly different sense of time, you're never, quite on the beat. Sometimes you're ahead and sometimes behind. Instead of the swift and imperceptible flowing of time, you are aware of its nodes, those points where time stands still or from which it leaps behind. And you slip into the breaks and look around. That's what you hear vaguely in Louis' music.

With these words Ellison clarifies an essential distinction between immersion and hibernation that is at root, in the terms afforded here, a distinction between embracing the music you hear and making the music you hear your own. The counterpointing image that immediately appears before us is one in which the good doctor is ensconced in his study, awaiting those entwined beams from above, while dear Louis is fashioning beams of a certain brilliance all his own. But of course the grand trope before us is the one with which we (and, in a certain sense, Ellison) began: Tarp's open leg shackle. Louis Armstrong's bending of a "military instrument into a beam of lyrical sound" is a magnificent and heroic revoicing of Tarp's defiling of the shackle. As these brilliant images conjoin and speak as one, we see as perhaps never before the extent to which each figure is a poet of invisibility, not because they make art out of chaos or out of nothingness, but because they make art out of art. As master craftsmen to whom the Invisible Man is apprenticed, their master lesson for him (and us) is that, while the artist must be able to burst beyond the old forms, he also must be able to make light of the light that fills the resulting hole—"slip into the breaks and look around." In *Invisible Man*, "making light of the light" is a rhetoric of liberation, a theory of comedy, and a narrative strategy rolled into one. Once Ellison's questing narrator becomes a hibernating narrator and finally comprehends all of this, he may truly say, "Light confirms my reality, gives birth to my form."

SUSAN L. BLAKE

Ritual and Rationalization: Black Folklore in the Works of Ralph Ellison

The predominant theme in the works of Ralph Ellison is the quest for cultural identity. Although he does not realize this himself, the protagonist of *Invisible Man* seeks identity, not as an individual, but as a black man in a white society. He encounters and combats the problem Ellison identified in an interview with three young blacks writers in 1965: "Our lives, since slavery, have been described mainly in terms of our political, economic, and social conditions as measured by outside norms, seldom in terms of our *own* sense of life or our *own* sense of values gained from our *own* unique American experience." The Invisible Man searches for self-definition in terms of the sense of life and values gained from the unique black American experience. His quest, however — like that of almost every other Ellison protagonist — ends in the conviction that the black experience is not so unique: "Who knows but that, on the lower frequencies, I speak for you?" Cultural identity becomes indistinguishable from the human condition.

I

One way that Ellison bridges the gap between the uniqueness and the universality of black experience is by use of black folklore. *Invisible Man*, most of Ellison's short stories, and the pieces of his partially published second novel, "And Hickman Arrives," are packed full of folktales and tellers, trinkets, toasts, songs, sermons, jazz, jive, and jokes. In his essays and interviews, Ellison has repeatedly singled out black folklore as the source of genuine black self-definition:

From *PMLA* 94, no. 1 (January 1979). © 1979 by the Modern Language Association of America.

In the folklore we tell what Negro experience really is. We back away
from the chaos of experience and from ourselves and we depict the
humor as well as the horror of our living. We project Negro life in a
metaphysical perspective and we have seen it with a complexity of vision that seldom gets into our writing.

("Discipline")

Negro folklore, evolving within a larger culture which regarded it as
inferior, was an especially courageous expression. It announced the
Negro's willingness to trust his own experience, his own sensibilities
as to the definition of reality, rather than allow his masters to define
these crucial matters for him.

("The Art of Fiction: An Interview")

At the same time, however, Ellison insists that "on its profoundest level American experience"—and, it is implied throughout *Shadow and Act,* human experience—"is of a whole"; that behind John Henry is Hercules, behind specific
folk expression, "the long tradition of storytelling . . . of myth." So when
Ellison uses black folklore in his fiction, he consciously adapts it to the myths of
the "larger" American and Western cultures:

For example, there is the old saying amongst Negroes: if you're
black, stay back; if your're brown, stick around; if you're white,
you're right. And there is the joke Negroes tell on themselves about
their being so black they can't be seen in the dark. In my book this
sort of thing was merged with the meanings which blackness and
light have long had in Western mythology: evil and goodness, ignorance and knowledge, and so on. In my novel the narrator's development is one through blackness to light; that is, from ignorance to
enlightenment: invisibility. . . .

It took me a long time to learn how to adapt such examples of
myth into my work—also ritual. The use of ritual is equally a vital
part of the creative process. I learned a few things from Eliot, Joyce
and Hemingway, but not how to adapt them.

("The Art of Fiction")

Ellison's use of terms is confusing here: the saying "if you're black, stay
back" is not myth but folk wisdom; ritual is not completely independent of
myth, it is the form through which myth is often expressed. What Ellison
learned to do, in order to adapt black folk expression in literature, was to turn it
into ritual and to put it at the service of a myth "larger," or other, than itself.
Folklorists, myth theorists, and literary critics—as groups and as individuals—

differ widely on the definition of "myth" and its relationship to the rest of folk-lore. Whether they say, however, that myths involve divine characters and folk-tales human, that myths take place in prehistoric and folktales in historic time, or that myths are believed by teller and audience and folktales told as fiction, they are acknowledging a not necessarily sharp distinction between two levels of folk belief—one concrete, temporal, and specific to the folk group; the other abstract, "eternal," and "universal." "Eternal" and "universal" are here relative terms; they refer to times and worlds larger than those of the immediate social context—how much larger is unimportant. For the purposes of this paper, "myth" refers to the abstract level of folk belief; "folk expression," to the concrete.

Ritual is the repetition of action for symbolic purpose. It abstracts experience from history by extending it over time and emphasizing form over context. We need not get into the question of whether myth or ritual comes first in order to say that ritual, theoretically at least, turns social experience into the symbol of mythic experience. When Ellison puts elements of black American folk experience into series with similar elements of American or Western mythology, he is ritualizing them, making each experience a repetition of the other. He is removing the black experience from its historical time and place and replacing it in the long run of time, erasing its distinctiveness, heightening its similarity to other experience. He is translating an expression of the way things work in a particular, man-made, social world to an expression of the way they work in a larger, uncontrollable, cosmic world.

The specific implications of the difference between a social and a mythic view of folk experience can be illustrated by considering Ellison the critic's discussion of the Battle Royal scene in *Invisible Man:*

> Take the "battle royal" passage in my novel, where the boys are blindfolded and forced to fight each other for the amusement of the white observers. This is a vital part of [the] behavior pattern in the South, which both Negroes and whites thoughtlessly accept. It is a ritual in preservation of caste lines, a keeping of taboo to appease the gods and ward off bad luck. It is also the initiation ritual to which all greenhorns are subjected. This passage which states what Negroes will see I did not have to invent; the patterns were already there in society, so that all I had to do was present them in a broader context of meaning. In any society there are many rituals of situation which, for the most part, go unquestioned. They can be simple or elaborate, but they are the connective tissue between the work of art and the audience.
>
> ("The Art of Fiction")

The battle-royal is rooted in the slave experience. It goes back to the many-versioned folktale "The Fight," in which Old Marster and his neighbor pit their two strongest slaves against each other and stake their plantations on the outcome. It has been used by Wright in *Black Boy,* Faulkner in *Absalom, Absalom!,* and Killens in *Youngblood* to dramatize social relations between whites and blacks. It encapsulates the physical, economic, psychological, and sexual exploitation of slavery (and dramatizes the slaves' comprehension of it). By identifying this ritual of a slave society as a "keeping of taboo to appease the gods" and an "initiation ritual to which all greenhorns are subjected," Ellison turns it into an essentially religious ritual in commemoration of implicitly immutable laws and connects it with other such rituals across cultures. By emphasizing the symbolic rather than the social components, Ellison transforms a social experience into a mythic one.

The social and mythic interpretations of a ritual of situation might coexist peacefully if the situation were not a function of so abnormal a condition as slavery. But the mythic interpretation of the battle-royal contradicts and negates its social meaning. As a social ritual, the battle-royal reflects the limitation of blackness in the face of white power. As an initiation ritual, it reflects the limitation of youth in the face of maturity. The youth can expect to become mature; the black cannot expect to become white. The initiation ritual symbolizes the relationship of an individual to his own community; the social ritual symbolizes the relationship of an oppressed people to an oppressive people. The initiation ritual celebrates a natural process, maturation, that has been ritualized because it cannot be circumvented; the social ritual celebrates a man-made convention that has been ritualized to prevent its circumvention. Because the social ritual and the mythic ritual reflect different relationships between people and power, they do not have compatible meanings. To equate the battle-royal with an initiation or an appeasement of the gods is to assume that the relationship between blacks and whites that it dramatizes is divinely sanctioned and eternal. Although that relationship has often seemed permanent, black folklore is based on the premise that it is not; the folk connections between Old Marster and divinity are all ironic.

In his theoretical analysis, Ellison places this ritual of situation in a context that distorts its social meaning. In *Invisible Man,* he makes it one of a series of initiations that finally demonstrate not the politics of slavery but the chaos of the universe. In his fiction in general, he fits black American folk expression into the forms of American and Western myth. To do so, he must ignore, minimize, distort, or deny the peculiarities of the folk expression. Since the peculiarities of black folklore reflect those of the peculiar institution, the effort to transcend them results in the denial of the circumstances that distinguish black experience from all others. The end of the identity quest in Ellison's fiction betrays the beginning.

II

Some of Ellison's short stories illustrate the process of adapting black folk experience to the forms of ritual and the meanings of myth. The quest for identity is the quest for manhood (quite literally: Ellison's only significant female character, Mary Rambo, *knows* who she is). Ellison mounts the quest on rituals of situation like the battle-royal—characteristic social situations that are repeated over and over again in black life, folklore, and literature because they so accurately express the conflict between black manhood and white power in American society. In his earliest stories, Ellison exploits only the social dimensions of the rituals of situation and the social dimensions of the protagonists' struggles for manhood. In "Slick Gonna Learn," an excerpt from an unfinished first novel, Slick escapes the expected retribution for accidentally striking a policeman but gets picked up by a carful of off-duty cops for a verbal assault when he thinks he is free; he escapes again when the policemen, who are planning to "give this nigger the works," get a radio call and dump him out into the rainy night with only a few kicks and some pistol shots that miss. In "The Birthmark," Matt and Clara, who have gone to the woods with a policeman and the coroner to identify the body of their brother, are forced to accept the story that he has been hit by a car, when he has obviously been lynched with the cooperation of the police. The title refers not only to an identifying mark on the body but also to the castration wound and to blackness itself. Both stories probe the helplessness and frustration of black characters in the face of a capricious and all-powerful white law. Both use the ritual qualities of the situation to illuminate social experience.

The Buster-and-Riley stories—"Mister Toussan," "That I Had the Wings," and "A Coupla Scalped Indians"—use folklore more symbolically. Buster and Riley are two little boys looking for adventure and fulfillment in a world circumscribed by God, the white folks, and their elders, who interpret God and the white folks for them. In "Mister Toussan," they get carried away retelling the story of Toussaint L'Ouverture that Buster has heard from his teacher. In a call-and-response collective composition with the style of a toast and the rhythmic climax of a folk sermon, they create a heroic badman who makes "those peckerwoods" beg for mercy:

> "They said, Please, Please, *Please, Mister Toussan*. . . ."
> ". . . We'll be good," broke in Riley.

"Thass right, man," said Buster excitedly. He clapped his hands and kicked his heels against the earth, his black face flowing in a burst of rhythmic joy.

"Boy!"

"And what'd ole Toussan say then?"

"He said in his big deep voice: *You all peckerwoods better be good, 'cause this is sweet Papa Toussan talking and my nigguhs is crazy 'bout white meat!*"

Their story of Toussan both arises from and is applied to the social conflict between blacks and whites. Buster and Riley have just been chased out of their white neighbor's yard for asking whether they could pick up cherries from under his trees—as the birds are doing undisturbed. The irony of the birds' freedom and the sound of his mother inside singing the protest spiritual "I Got Wings" makes Riley ask Buster what he would do if he had wings. Buster replies that he would go to Chicago, Detroit, the moon, Africa, "or anyplace else colored is free." The mention of Africa brings up the school books' view that Africans are lazy, and this leads to the story of the black hero. Their story of Toussan is a flight of fancy that develops the theme of freedom introduced by Buster's answer to Riley's question; identification with Toussan gives them the courage to think about another attempt on Old Rogan's cherries.

"That I Had the Wings" continues the theme of freedom through flying, but freedom in this story means freedom from the limitations of childhood and humanity. Riley, frustrated in his own wish to learn to fly, tries and fails to teach some chicks. He is defeated by his Aunt Kate, Ole Bill the boss rooster (the identity Riley would choose if he were to die "and come back a bird like Aunt Kate says folks do" and gravity. The obstacles to manhood in this story are not social but universal—immaturity and earthboundedness.

In "A Coupla Scalped Indians," the quest for manhood is specifically sexual. Buster and Riley, who, still sore from circumcision, have been out in the woods performing Boy Scout tests (with a view to becoming, not Boy Scouts, but Indians), have to pass the house of Aunt Mackie, a reputed conjure woman, whose very name makes Riley shiver. In the course of trying to get by Aunt Mackie's dog, Riley somehow gets himself inside her yard and ever closer to her house, where he sees her dancing naked before the window and is surprised at the youthful body beneath her wrinkled face. She discovers him, brings him in, makes him kiss her ("You passed all the tests and you was peeping in my window"), demands to see his circumcision wound, and fills him with the confusing emotions of pain, need, shame, and relief. The only conflict in the story is sexual, and the elements of folklore, Aunt Mackie's "conjure" and Buster's eulogy to the dozens (a game of competitive insult usually focusing on the sexual behavior of the opponent's female relatives), are metaphors for the power of sex. The definition of manhood in the early stories becomes more and more general, and the elements of black folklore become less and less connected with specifically black social experience.

Both "Mister Toussan" and "That I Had the Wings" make central use of the ability to fly as a metaphor for freedom and manhood. "Flying Home" develops this metaphor further and, through it, shows the effect of framing black folk materials in Western myth. Flying is a predominant motif in black American folklore as well as in Western myth; its meanings vary from one tradition to another. In Greek mythology, flying represents the superhuman power of the gods; in Freudian psychology, it symbolizes male sexual potency; in black American folklore, it means freedom. In a folk context the aspiration to fly recalls Harriet Tubman's dream of flying over a great wall, the numerous references in the spirituals to flying to freedom in Jesus, the Sea Islands legend of the Africans who rose up from the field one day and flew back to Africa, and the humorous folktale of the Colored Man who went to heaven and flew around with such abandon that he had to be grounded but who boasted that he was "a flying black bastard" while he had his wings. Although the mythic and sexual meanings of the metaphor are of course implicit in the aspiration to freedom, the emphasis in the folk concept of manhood is on the freedom, and the obstacles to freedom are seen to be in the social structure, not in oneself or the laws of the physical universe.

"Flying Home" presents at least four folk variations on the flying motif and as many more mythic ones. The story is based on the former military practice of withholding from blacks the opportunity to fly airplanes, a historical situation that so largely bore out the folklore of flying that it immediately became part of it. The protagonist in the story is a student at the Negro air school in Tuskegee, established during World War II in response to complaints about discrimination against blacks in pilot training. The story about the school was that it trained black men to fly but never graduated them to combat. Todd, the flier in this story, who feels he acquires dignity from his airplane and the appreciation of his white officers and shame from his relationship with ignorant black men, has run into a buzzard and crashed in a white man's field. Jefferson, the "ignorant black man" who finds him, sends for help, and keeps him company while they wait, tells him two folktales—a brief anecdote about seeing two buzzards emerge from the insides of a dead horse and the comic story of the Colored Man who tore up heaven flying.

The buzzard is a common figure in black folklore, representing sometimes the black person scrounging for survival, sometimes his predators, and always the precariousness of life in a predatory society. In one story, told by Mrs. I. E. Richards, the buzzard is represented as a bird that flies higher than the average but has to come down to get food; this story is told to impress children that "regardless of what you might have . . . we all have to live on the same level." All these folk associations are active in the references to buzzards in "Flying Home." The birds are black; Jefferson says that his grandson Teddy calls them jimcrows. Representing not only the black man, Todd, but the Jim Crow society, they symbolize the destructiveness of both. Todd thinks of himself as a buzzard when he cries, "Can I help it if they won't let us actually fly? Maybe we are a bunch of buzzards feeding on a dead horse, but we can hope to be eagles, can't we?" But there is also a clear analogy between him and the horse's carcass ("Saw him just like I see you," says Jefferson of the horse: he is being devoured by both the Jim Crow society and his own shame at blackness. Todd (*Tod* 'death') is, in trying to destroy old Jefferson, also feeding on his own dead self. So the moral of Mrs. Richards' buzzard story also applies to Todd: he learns that he cannot set himself above other blacks because, as Jefferson reminds him, "You black son. . . . You have to come by the white folks, too."

The tale of the Colored Man in heaven also applies to Todd, who "had been flying too high and too fast" and "had climbed steeply away in exultation" before going into a spin and crashing. Todd recognizes this application in anguish: "Why do you laugh at me this way?" he screams while Jefferson is laughing at the punch line. The point of the folktale, which Jefferson emphasizes by adding the "new turn" that "us colored folks had to wear a special kin' a harness when we flew," is that the black man is a man despite the obstacles put in his way: even with the harness, he outflies the other angels; even grounded, he remains brash and confident. Together, the moral of this story and the implications of the buzzard associations compose the explicit message of "Flying Home": manhood is inherent, neither tendered nor rescinded by white society; to try to achieve manhood by escaping blackness is only self-destructive, because "we all have to live on the same level."

As Joseph F. Trimmer has pointed out, "Flying Home" also recalls the myth of Icarus and alludes to the myth of the phoenix, the Christian doctrine of the fortunate fall, and the parable of the prodigal son. The stories of Icarus, the fall, and the prodigal son all involve men trying to transcend their condition, as Todd is trying to transcend blackness. The story of Icarus parallels Mrs. Richards' comments on the high-flying buzzard. The idea of the fortunate fall and the story's final image of the buzzard flying into the sun and glowing gold like the phoenix both suggest, as the folk referents in the story do, that the flier's failure is in some way a victory. But there are important differences between the meanings of the myths alluded to in the story and those of the folk sources. First, the strivers in the stories of Icarus and the fall of man are trying to improve their position with respect not to other men but to God. Even the Prodigal Son is presented in that context in this story, through the opening lines of James Weldon Johnson's "Prodigal Son" in *God's Trombones*, which Todd remembers his grandmother reciting as a warning when he was a child:

> *Young man, young man,*
> *Yo' arms too short*
> *To box with God.*

But Todd's fault—and that of the high-flying buzzard—is to try to set himself above other men. Second, all these myths, including that of the phoenix, which cremates and resurrects itself, imply that the hero is the sole cause of his own fall. By thus obscuring the duality of the buzzard symbol and ignoring the social basis of the story, the mythic allusions dull the irony of the folk associations and shift the emphasis from manhood to mortality. In the end, Todd flies "home" to freedom in the sense of the Sea Islands legend, by flying "home" to his people and to himself like the Prodigal Son. But as the final image of the buzzard glowing gold like the phoenix seems to imply, he is also dying, flying "home" to acceptance of the universal human condition of mortality, which is not at all the same as the perpetual precariousness of life in a predatory society. Nor is it the same as the "home" or "heaven" of the black spiritual tradition, for there, in a reversal of the conventional relationship between the concrete and abstract terms of metaphor, both "home" and "heaven" often connote the geographical North and social freedom.

The mythic context subtly changes the meaning of the themes embodied in the folk foundation of "Flying Home." It transforms acceptance of blackness as identity into acceptance of blackness as limitation. It substitutes the white culture's definition of blackness for the self-definition of folklore.

III

The theme of *Invisible Man* is similar to that of "Flying Home." The novel presents itself as an epic statement of the need for black self-definition. The protagonist of the novel, characterized as a representative black man on an identity quest, finds himself only when he gives up his white masters' definition of reality and adopts that asserted by the black folk tradition. Ironically, however, the definition of reality that Ellison attributes to the folk tradition is the very one maintained by the whites.

What functions as black folklore in the novel is everything the protagonist initially rejects as manifesting a Sambo mentality and finally learns to accept as basic to his true identity. It includes almost anything rooted in or associated with slavery, the South, the established body of southern folklore, or its northern ghetto mutations. And it comes from the traditions of both the black slave and the white plantation. Nothing could be more apparently contradictory than the images of the black man offered by these traditions, which differ simply as the perspectives of slave and master. The archetypal black man of slave folklore is John, the hero of an extensive cycle of tales, who comically but constantly says "no" to Old Marster and the slave system he represents. The stereotypical black man of the plantation tradition is Sambo, who grins, sings, fawns, and otherwise says "yes" to Old Marster, old times, and the old Kentucky home. John may appear to acquiesce, but he manages to subvert Old Master's intentions; Sambo may appear mischievous, but he is fundamentally loyal. *Invisible Man* attempts to reconcile the two images through both the plot, in which the protagonist must learn to stop fleeing from Sambo in order to find himself, and the pattern of folklore allusion, which treats Sambo and John as though they were one and the same.

The novel chronicles three stages in the protagonist's life — education, employment, and political activity — framed by his entry into the life of society (or, in the novel's terms, history) through high school graduation and his exit from it through disillusionment with political organization. Each stage in the protagonist's personal history corresponds to an era in the social history of black Americans. His sojourn in a southern black college modeled on Tuskegee Institute corresponds to Reconstruction; he has entered it on a scholarship presented in a parody of Emancipation, and he leaves it under compulsion, in the company of a disillusioned World War I veteran, in a manner representative of the Great Migration. His first few weeks in New York — job hunting, working in the paint factory, encountering unionism, and undergoing electric shock treatment — contain the elements of the hopeful twenties, when industry was god, self-reliance its gospel, and unionism an exciting heresy; when timidly rebellious young heirs like Emerson, Jr., frolicked in Harlem and psychology was the newest toy. His experience in the Brotherhood reflects the Great Depression, when dispossession was the common complaint and communism the intellectual's cure; his disillusionment with the Brotherhood parallels the general post-Depression retreat from communism. And the riot in which he drops out — of sight, of history, of the novel — suggests the Harlem riot of 1943.

The protagonist enters each stage hopefully and is ejected forcibly. His hopefulness is based on faith in the word or belief or method that each historical age has offered as the solution to the difficulties blackness has always presented. In school and college, it is accommodation — the principles of Booker T. Washington, as quoted by the protagonist in his graduation speech, eulogized by the Rev. Homer Barbee in his chapel-service account of "the Founder's" life, and practiced by Dr. Bledsoe in the administration of the college. In the business world, it is capitalism, individualism, Emersonian self-reliance. In politics, it is "brotherhood" — whether of class, as maintained by the Brotherhood itself, or of race, as insisted by its chief competition, the Garvey-esque Ras the Exhorter. The distinction between Ras and the Brotherhood is ultimately unimportant, for all the recommended solutions to the problem of blackness — accommodation; capitalism; its briefly introduced corrective, union-ism; communism; nationalism — prove to be false. Reliance on these conventional principles leads the protagonist not to security but to the chaos that propels him from one stage to another — from the battle-royal, to the melee at the Golden Day, to the paint factory explosion, to the Harlem riot. And the proponents of these principles — Jack, Norton, Emerson — merge in the protagonist's mind by the end of the novel "into a single white figure," with which Bledsoe, too, is elsewhere associated.

Opposed to the conventional and apparently rational doctrines of the white world are the wisdom and experience of the black folk tradition, which exposes the falseness of the white view of reality and offers an alternative vision testified to by the protagonist's grandfather, the pushcart man, the vet, and, ironically, Bledsoe and Emerson, Jr. Each of these characters has some link with the folk past. The grandfather has been a slave; the pushcart man talks rhymes and fables and sings the blues; the vet, though educated and erudite, is connected in the protagonist's mind with the pushcart man; Bledsoe is modeled on Booker T. Washington, a legend in himself and a real-life reflection of the traditional trickster; even Emerson, Jr., is a primitivist, who frequents Harlem nightclubs, collects African art, and reads *Totem and Taboo*. These characters are also linked — as Bledsoe, Emerson, Norton, and Jack are on the other side — by the advice they give the protagonist for dealing with blackness.

The protagonist regards the businessmen's smoker at which he delivers his graduation speech and receives his scholarship to the state college for Negroes as his emancipation from the degradation created by slavery, but it is also here that he is compelled to participate in the battle-royal. Folk wisdom would show this "emancipation" and each successive one to be just variations on the fundamental condition of slavery. The protagonist's grandfather warns him in a dream that the scholarship certificate in his briefcase advises "Whomever It May Concern" to "Keep This Nigger-Boy Running." The prediction recalls the trick some masters played on their illiterate slaves, writing them passes that invited the reader to administer a flogging. It is fulfilled by both Bledsoe, whose treacherous letters of introduction request the reader to help the bearer "continue in the direction of that promise which, like the horizon, recedes ever brightly and distantly beyond the hopeful traveler," and Jack, who the protagonist realizes, when he sees that the handwriting on a threatening note is the same as that which has informed him of his Brotherhood name, "named me and set me running with one and the same stroke of the pen."

The principle of emancipation through accommodation is refuted by the folk storyteller Trueblood: "I done the worse thing a man could ever do in his family and instead of chasin' me out of the country, they gimme more help than they ever give any other colored man, no matter how good a nigguh he was." The principle of emancipation through capitalism is punctured by the folk rhyme the protagonist remembers when he hears of Bledsoe's treachery: "They Picked Poor Robin Clean" explains not only what Bledsoe has done to him but what Liberty Paints has done to Lucius Brockway and will do to him and what capitalistic industry generally strives to do to all its workers. The irony of Brother Jack's betrayal is sharpened by the background of the John-and-Old-Marster tales: "Brother Jack," whose name is a variant of "Brother John," reminds the protagonist of "old Master," a bulldog he "liked but didn't trust" as a child, and becomes in the end "Marse Jack." Even Brotherhood—which, as both abstract philosophy and political movement, promises the ultimate liberation—offers only the same old oppression.

What the folk perspective substitutes for the "rational" programs to order chaos is acceptance of chaos as reality. Under the stream of conventional advice on how to deal with blackness runs a current of counteradvice introduced and distilled in the protagonist's grandfather's deathbed dictum: "overcome 'em with yeses, undermine 'em with grins, agree 'em to death and destruction"—the "beginning" to which the narrator returns on the first page of chapter 1. The grandfather, the vet, the pushcart man, Bledsoe, and Emerson offer a vision of reality based on contradiction: yes is no, freedom is slavery, things are not what they seem. The pushchart man sings the characteristic contradiction of the blues,

> "She's got feet like a monkey
> Legs like a frog—Lawd, Lawd!
> But when she starts to loving me
> I holler Whoooo, God-dog!
> Cause I loves my baabay,
> Better than I do myself . . ."

leaving the protagonist to wonder whether the song expresses love or hate and whether he himself is hearing it with pride or disgust. "Play the game, but don't believe in it," counsels the vet. "You're black and living in the South," exclaims Bledsoe, "did you forget how to lie?" "For God's sake, learn to look beneath the surface," exhorts the vet. "Aren't you curious about what lies behind the face of things?" asks Emerson, Jr. What lies behind the face of things is, like the black dope in the white paint, contradiction.

The inclusion of Emerson, Jr., and Bledsoe as spokesmen for the "folk," as well as for the white, point of view is not self-contradictory but illustrative of the simultaneous sway of opposites that Ellison sees as the heart of the folk vision. A yam may be good and sweet and call up memories of all that is good in the past and in the South; or it may be bitter. A leg shackle may be a "symbol of our progress," as Bledsoe calls the memento on his desk; or it may be a symbol of continued slavery, as Bledsoe's seems to be in comparison with Brother Tarp's filed-open shackle. The meaning is not in the thing itself but in the way it is used.

The function of folklore in chapter 11, in which the protagonist undergoes electric shock treatment in the paint factory hospital, applies this point to the protagonist's identity and the Sambo image. When the doctors and nurses refer to Brer Rabbit in their efforts to draw the protagonist a new personality after erasing the old one electrically, they clearly have the Sambo image in mind. They have just played with the shock treatment as the traditional cracker plays with pistol shots:

> "Look, he's dancing," someone called
> "No, really?"
> An oily face looked in. "They really do have rhythm, don't they?
> Get hot, boy! Get hot!" it said with a laugh.

When they ask in sequence "What is your name?" "Who was your mother?" "Who was Buckeye the Rabbit?" and "Who was Brer Rabbit?" they are regarding folklore as the expression of a childish personality, safe and hence "normal" in a black subject. The protagonist identifies with the folklore — "Somehow I was Buckeye the Rabbit" — but while the doctors mention the Rabbit with the expectations of the nursery, the protagonist replies in the idiom of the dozens:

> BOY, WHO WAS BRER RABBIT?
> He was your mother's back-door man, I thought. Anyone knew they were one and the same: "Buckeye" when you were very young and hid yourself behind wide innocent eyes; "Brer" when you were older.

Even Sambo, the image of subjugation, has simultaneous, opposite meanings. He is not only the embodiment of degradation but also, as Dr. Bledsoe, Trueblood, Lucius Brockway, and Tod Clifton all demonstrate in one way or another, a source of power. "I's big and black and I say 'yes, suh' as loudly as any burrhead when it's convenient," Dr. Bledsoe concedes, "but I'm still the king down here." Sambo represents not only powerlessness but the knowledge of

powerlessness, not only the absence of identity but knowledge of the absence —
and knowledge is a kind of power in itself. Tod Clifton, selling Sambo dolls,
even being shot by the police, is in greater control of his own destiny than the
protagonist, who is still being manipulated, like one of Clifton's dolls, by the
Brotherhood. Clifton has acknowledged and rejected the Brotherhood's manipulation; the protagonist is still dancing on a string unawares.

Sambo is, in effect, the lesson the protagonist has rejected all along: that,
in the terms of the white world he has been relying on for guidance and identity,
he is nobody, invisible, Sambo — something his advisers have been telling him
from the beginning. Whether invisibility is identity or nonidentity depends on
your point of view: "You're nobody, son," barks Bledsoe, speaking for the white
point of view. "You're hidden right out in the open," says the vet, from the
black. "Identity! My God! Who has any identity any more anyway?" laments
Emerson, Jr., from the nihilistic. The protagonist's challenge is to look at things
from the black point of view, the underside, from which the contradiction, the
chaos, is apparent.

The folk influences in *Invisible Man* define not an action but an attitude of
ironic withdrawal from the white world, an attitude represented metaphorically
by the lives of all those characters — Bledsoe, Trueblood, Brockway, and Rinehart — who deal with it successfully and finally by the protagonist's withdrawal
into his well-lighted cellar. All the characters who function well in the white
world inhabit some sort of underworld: Bledsoe's is calculated humility; Trueblood's, the subconscious; Brockway's, the cellar of Liberty Paints; Rinehart's,
organized crime. And they all accept the chaos apparent from down below.
"You have looked upon chaos and are not destroyed?" Mr. Norton asks Trueblood. "No suh, I feels all right." "This here's the uproar department and I'm in
charge," boasts Lucius Brockway (Lucifer Breakaway) from his cellar. Rinehart
does not simply live with chaos; as Rine the runner, Rine the gambler, Rine the
briber, Rine the lover, and Rine the Reverend, he *is* chaos:

> Could he be all of them? . . . Could he himself be both rind and
> heart? . . . It was true as I was true. . . . The world in which we
> lived was without boundaries. A vast seething, hot world of fluidity,
> and Rine the rascal was at home. Perhaps only Rine the rascal was at
> home in it. It was unbelievable, but perhaps only the truth was
> always a lie.

When the protagonist comes to this insight, realizes that he has "no longer to
run for or from the Jacks and the Emersons and the Bledsoes and Nortons, but
only from their confusion, impatience, and refusal to recognize the beautiful
absurdity of their American identity and mine," and goes underground, he is

following the model of these folk characters and the wisdom of his folk advisers and is acting out the lesson that folk allusions have helped to develop: that meaning is all in your mind.

This ironic withdrawal is presented as negation of the white world and its absurdity. The protagonist looks on his retreat as a relief from the "ill[ness] of affirmation, of saying 'yes' against the nay-saying of my stomach — not to mention my brain." The characters he is imitating are all, from the conventional point of view, a bit diabolical, and those whose advice he is following — the crazy grandfather, the insane vet, the neurotic young Emerson — are all a bit mad. It is against this perceived negation that Ellison sets the contrived reinterpretation of the grandfather's advice ("Could he have meant — hell, he *must* have meant that we were to affirm the principle on which the country was built and not the men . . .") and the unsupported retraction of the book's dramatic statement: "Perhaps that's my greatest social crime, I've overstayed my hibernation, since there's a possibility that even an invisible man has a socially responsible role to play."

But withdrawal into a hole is not negation. To say that the world is absurd, that the only reality is in the mind, is a way of saying that the world and the falsehoods that make it absurd are unimportant. And that is, if not affirmation, at least acquiescence. The goal in *Invisible Man* is to know, not to change; knowledge is presented as the equivalent of change. But knowledge does not necessarily produce change. Whether or not Sambo knows is something Old Marster never knows, it is only when Sambo shows he knows that the relationship changes — and then Sambo is not Sambo at all, but John, Old Marster's natural equal and moral and intellectual superior. When John says "yes" to Old Marster, he is either covering up his crimes against slavery or setting up new ones. The result is, at least, a couple of chickens in his pot; at most, some erosion of the power of slavery that Old Marster is forced to acknowledge: Old Marster gets whipped, Old Miss gets slapped, or Old John gets freedom. The affirmation of *Invisible Man* is neither the survival technique of John the chicken thief nor the political weapon of John the social saboteur, for the negation behind it is all in the mind. The ultimate effect of *Invisible Man*'s reinterpretation of the black folk image is not to elevate Sambo, the cellar rebel, to the status of John but to reduce the archetypal black folk hero to Sambo. Thus the result of the protagonist's identity quest is not self-definition at all but reaffirmation of the identity provided by the white culture.

There are two folk characters in the novel who have the potential for representing a positive interpretation of the black folk perspective: Mary Rambo and Brother Tarp. Both are explicitly characterized as anchors against chaos. The protagonist thinks of Mary as "a force, a stable familiar force like something out of my past which kept me from whirling off into some unknown which I dared not face." He regards Brother Tarp's gift of the sawed-open chain link as a "paternal gesture which at once joined him with his ancestors, marked a high point of his present, and promised a concreteness to his nebulous and chaotic future." Both offer the protagonist advice in direct opposition to the counsel to go underground:

> "It's you young folks what's going to make the changes," [Mary says]. "Y'all's the ones. You got to lead and you got to fight and move us all on up a little higher. And I tell you something else, it's the ones from the South that's got to do it, them what knows the fire and ain't forgot how it burns. Up here too many forgits."

Brother Tarp echoes her with the gift of the legchain link:

> "Even when times were best for me I remembered. Because I didn't want to forgit those nineteen years I just kind of held on to this as a keepsake and a reminder. . . . I'd like to pass it on to you, son. . . . Funny thing to give somebody, but I think it's got a heap of signifying wrapped up in it and it might help you remember what we're really fighting against. I don't think of it in terms of but two words, *yes* and *no;* but it signifies a heap more."

These passages root both the activist perspective and the stabilizing effect of Mary and Tarp in slavery, the South, the past — the black folk experience. The anchor against chaos that each provides is a clear perception of the source of the chaos, not as general absurdity, but as the specific legacy of slavery, something to be confronted in the world, not just the mind. But the perspective of Mary and Brother Tarp is not the perspective of the novel. Ellison does not follow up the implications of their characterization. Their advice is never confirmed, never refuted, never even dramatized. Though they are introduced as admirable and illuminating characters, they are soon dropped and forgotten. Mary Rambo is further developed in an unused chapter entitled "Out of the Hospital and under the Bar," but even if it were included, she would still have no sustained effect on the novel. The final perspective remains that of the grandfather, who has said "no" so secretly that even his family is shocked to hear him call himself a traitor.

IV

The long-projected novel "And Hickman Arrives" follows up on the final, universalizing sentence of *Invisible Man:* "Who knows but that on the lower frequencies, I speak for you?"

Judging by the published fragments, "Hickman" explores the relationship between a representative white American and a group of blacks who are, in two ways, his. Senator Sunraider is a representative American in that he is a legislative representative, and he is a representative white man in that his views, though racist in the extreme, represent the quintessence of white consciousness of whiteness. The black characters are "his" not only in the sense that he acts as though he owns them but also, paradoxically, in the sense that he belongs to them. Senator Sunraider, like Faulkner's Joe Christmas, is a man of ambiguous ancestry. We see him in "Juneteenth," "The Roof, the Steeple, and the People," and the flashback in the title story as a light-skinned foundling in a black community in the South, a child-prodigy preacher named Bliss, foster son and pupil of Rev. A. Z. Hickman, "God's Trombone." He has grown up to be, inexplicably, a white racist senator from a New England state. As Hickman and his congregation watch the Senator from the Senate visitors' gallery, they recognize in the very rhetoric with which he humiliates black people the gestures and cadences of the southern black preacher: "'why, Reveren', that's *you!* He's still doing you! O, my Lord . . . still doing you after all these years and yet he can say all those mean things he says. . . .'" The Senator is *of* what he is *against;* his roots are in what he so strenuously denies; and he denies it so strenuously *because* he is rooted in it. The implication is that the Senator's apparently bizarre relationship with Hickman is actually the archetypal relationship of white America to black: something more than brotherhood — identity, perhaps — denied.

The relationship is developed by stitching together elements of the black experience and elements of American popular culture into a patchwork myth of American identity. Like a quilter making two-color patterns, Ellison matches black folk characters to white racist stereotypes, the folklore of race relations to the conventions of southwest humor, and ultimately the emancipation of black folks from slavery to the emancipation of whites from racism. The patterns are set against a background of allusions to stories — historical and literary — that have already become myths of American identity.

Daddy Hickman, the folk preacher, and Senator Sunraider, the southern politician (though northern: North and South are one and the same) relate to each other as Uncle Remus and the Little Boy. Hickman treats the child Bliss, the grown-up Senator, and all whites with the patronizing patience characteristic of the stereotypical plantation storyteller. Bliss and Sunraider portray the two sides of the white child, who is both the child and the master, both the "son" and the "son-raider," kidnapper, castrater. The relationship between Senator Sunraider and his living past culminates when he is shot from the Senate visitors' gallery in a gesture that, ironically, recalls the assassination of Lincoln the Emancipator (and seems to divine, in 1960, an element of the American experience revealed in the ensuing decade with the assassinations of John and Robert Kennedy, Malcolm X, and Martin Luther King).

In a further twist to the irony, the assassination does emancipate Senator
Sunraider by making him acknowledge his sonship and hence himself. In his
delirium he calls for Daddy Hickman and reenacts sermons he has helped Hickman preach. The role of Bliss in these sermons has been to dramatize the theme
of life-out-of-death. In the sermon in "And Hickman Arrives," he rises on cue
from a little white satin coffin clutching his teddy bear and an Easter bunny. As
the Senator relives the experience of the sermon, falling again under the influence of Hickman's rhetoric as he remembers it, he undergoes the rebirth that the
sermon is about. The "Juneteenth" sermon, preached on the annual celebration
of Emancipation among blacks in the Southwest, applies the resurrection theme
to the history of a people and the awakening of Senator Sunraider to the
redemption of American society. In this sermon, Hickman calls the enslavement
and emancipation of his people "a cruel calamity laced up with a blessing—or
maybe a blessing laced up with a calamity. . . . because out of all the pain and
the suffering, out of the night of storm, we found the Word of God." As Hickman develops this theme, Bliss acts it out. "WE WERE LIKE THE VALLEY OF DRY
BONES!" he shouts. When the bones begin to stir, Bliss begins to strut. When
Bliss, the child of his memory, is moved, the dry bones of the Senator begin to
stir. When Senator Sunraider comes to himself, he emancipates both the blacks
he has assumed power over and the blackness, the humanity, in himself.

The relationship between black and white outlined in the main plot is repeated with variations in a comic subplot in which the assassination of Senator
Sunraider is parodied by the sacrifice of a gleaming white Cadillac. This episode,
contained in "Cadillac Flambé" and "It Always Breaks Out," is a chain of reactions
to the Senator's half-facetious but characteristic public statement that the Cadillac
has become so popular with blacks that it ought to be renamed the "Coon Cage
Eight." Each of the characters in this subplot is both a racial and a literary
stereotype, characterized by both the content and the form of a speech on race
relations.

LeeWillie Minifees, who immolates his Cadillac on the Senator's front lawn,
is the Black Militant and literary Badman. He acts in the tradition of a decade of
ghetto rioters, draft-card burners, and self-immolating Buddhist monks; he
speaks with the style and defiance of a Shine or a Stackolee:

> "YOU HAVE TAKEN THE BEST," he boomed, "SO, DAMMIT, TAKE ALL
> THE REST! Take ALL the rest!"
> "In fact, now I don't want anything you think is too good for me
> and my people. Because, just as the old man and the mule said, if a
> man in your position is against our having them, then there must be
> something WRONG in our wanting them. So to keep you happy, I me,

LeeWillie Minifees, am prepared to WALK. I'm ordering me some clubfooted, pigeon-toed SPACE SHOES. I'd rather crawl or fly. I'd rather save my money and wait until the A-RABS make a car. The Zulus even. Even the ESKIMOS! Oh, I'll walk and wait. I'll grab me a GREYHOUND or a FREIGHT! So you can have my coon cage, fare thee well!

. . . And thank you KINDLY for freeing me from the Coon Cage. Because before I'd be in a CAGE, I'll be buried in my GRAVE — Oh! Oh!"

McGowan, a journalist who comments on the conflagration from the leather-upholstered luxury of his club, while the "inscrutable but familiar Negro waiter" Sam unobtrusively serves drinks, is both the Unreconstructed Rebel and the Big Braggart of southwestern humor. The main body of "It Always Breaks Out" is McGowan's long, hyperbolic dissertation on the thesis "everything the Nigra does is political." If he buys a washing machine or more than one TV, wears a dashiki or a homburg, joins the Book-of-the-Month Club or likes Bill Faulkner, drives a Volkswagen or a Cadillac or an Imperial when he can afford a Cadillac (and so on for nine pages), he is being political. "But gentlemen," McGowan concludes, with the inconsistency of wishful thinking, "to my considerable knowledge no Nigra has ever even *thought* about assassinating anybody."

The journalist who narrates both LeeWillie's action and McGowan's reaction is, in his own words, "a liberal, ex-radical, northerner" — in folk-literary tradition, the Gullible Greenhorn. He reports the conflagration on the Senator's front lawn with meticulous attention to detail, and with all the insight of the narrator of "The Big Bear of Arkansas" or "The Celebrated Jumping Frog of Calaveras County."

For now, having finished unpacking, the driver . . . picked up one of the cases — now suddenly transformed into the type of can which during the war was sometimes used to transport high-octane gasoline in Liberty ships (a highly dangerous cargo for those round bottoms and the men who shipped in them) — and leaning carefully forward, began emptying its contents upon the shining chariot.

And thus, I thought, is gilded an eight-valved, three-hundred and fifty-horsepowered air-conditioned lily!

For so accustomed have we Americans become to the tricks, the shenanigans, and frauds of advertising, so adjusted to the contrived fantasies of commerce — indeed, to pseudo-events of all kinds — that I thought that the car was being drenched with a special liquid which would make it more alluring for a series of commercial photographs.

The reporter's careful, conscientious, and convoluted report is his "speech"; he comments by his very attempt to report without commenting.

For all their difference in style, the narrator and McGowan speak from equal ignorance, obtuseness, and presumption. Neither can see the implications of his own speech; neither can conceive of a black person's destroying a symbol or representative of American society. The narrator does not see LeeWillie any more than McGowan notices Sam. The northern and southern journalists are both like the northern-southern Senator, and he is like both of them. All three deny black humanity. All three, in doing so, make themselves ridiculous. The narrator has a glimpse of this connection when he observes Sam, the one character of the four who comments by silence:

> Was he, Sam, prevented by some piety from confronting me in a humorous manner, as my habit of mind, formed during the radical Thirties, prevented me from confronting him; or did he, as some of my friends suspected, regard all whites through the streaming eyes and aching muscles of one continuous, though imperceptible and inaudible, belly laugh? *What the hell,* I thought, *is Sam's last name?*

In among the jibes at journalists, liberals, and advertising stunts, the episode of the burning Cadillac makes the point that the humanity of such paper-doll characters as McGowan and the narrator is tied up in that of the Sams and the LeeWillies, that it is their refusal to acknowledge the humanity of the Sams and the LeeWillies that stereotypes them and robs them of their own humanity. If the message of *Invisible Man* and Ellison's early short stories is that blackness is humanity, the message of "And Hickman Arrives" is that humanity—and particularly American humanity—is blackness.

Given Ellison's acute consciousness of literary tradition and national myth, it is probably more than coincidence that Hickman bears the same name as the focal character in Eugene O'Neill's *Iceman Cometh,* another mythic rendition of the American experience. Each of them, Theodore Hickman ("Hickey") the salesman and A. Z. Hickman the preacher, is both preacher and salesman. Each comes to his potential converts—Hickey, as Iceman, "cometh" to Harry Hope's saloon, Hickman "arrives" in Washington—with a gospel of self-recognition. Each preaches birth into a new life through death to a false one. Each establishes a sense of identity between himself and his subject. Though Hickey's gospel is ultimately ironic and Daddy Hickman's straight, Ellison uses the mythic character of the consummate salesman to touch the themes of illusion and identity and to tie his conception of the American experience to what American society already accepts as an American myth. The distinction between black and white, Daddy

Hickman is saying, is one of those illusions we think we need in order to live, but we do not really live until we see it as an illusion and give it up. "And Hickman Arrives" is a mythic and metaphorical amplification of the theme of an essay Ellison wrote for *Time* entitled "What America Would Be without Blacks" (6 April 1970). In this essay Ellison identifies two fundamental contributions of blacks to American culture: a cultural style and a moral center — "for not only is the black man a co-creator of the language that Mark Twain raised to the level of literary eloquence, but Jim's condition as American and Huck's commitment to freedom are the moral center of the novel." A patchwork of American archetypes and stereotypes, "Hickman" attempts to give a moral center to the myth of American democracy. In the *Time* essay Ellison says that the presence of an incompletely free group of people represents both the performance and the possibilities of American democracy, and in the novel he suggests that the function of black suffering is to emancipate white humanity. As Hickman, looking back on the night in which he now realizes his foster son "began to wander," confesses to Sunraider, "all that time I should have been praying for you." Ellison's manipulation of folklore in "Hickman" subordinates black experience to American redemption.

V

Ellison's ability to adapt, rather than simply to include, black folklore in his fiction is regarded as his special contribution to the literary interpretation of both folklore and black culture. A few commentators have criticized this adaptation of black folklore for its dependence on Western mythology. Larry Neal, who singles Ellison out for his broad and profound understanding of Afro-American culture, considers the fact that Ellison "overlays his knowledge of Black culture with concepts that exist outside of it" a sign of confusion. George K. Kent regards Ellison's use of the folk and cultural tradition in *Invisible Man* with "a certain unease," "inspired by the elaborate system of interconnection with Western symbols and mythology, and our awareness that Blackness is more in need of definition than Western traditon, which has had the attention of innumerable literary masters." Both these comments treat the elements of blackness and Western tradition in Ellison's fiction as separable. But Ellison's adaptation of black folklore produces an alloy rather than a plate. The process of ritualization itself changes the meaning of the folklore.

Although rituals do undergo change, they do so much more slowly than other aspects of life, and fixity remains the principle of ritual as a form. People use ritual to deal with "those sectors of experience which do not seem amenable to rational control," or as Ellison himself puts it,

> People rationalize what they shun or are incapable of dealing with; these superstitions and their rationalizations become ritual as they govern behavior. The rituals become social forms, and it is one of the functions of the artist to recognize them and raise them to the level of art.
>
> ("The Art of Fiction")

Thus ritual, by its very nature, formalizes the relationship of individuals to an order they do not understand and think they cannot change. By formalizing, it perpetuates; by perpetuating, it celebrates. As a form, ritual tends to affirm the powerlessness of human beings and the permanence of a fixed order.

Emulation of ritual in literature applies the implications of the form to the conflict between characters and the social, natural, or metaphysical forces controlling their lives. It diminishes the role and responsibility of individuals for shaping their own world, personifies impersonal forces and dehumanizes social institutions, homogenizes human experience by emphasizing continuity rather than development, and reduces any particular human action to an insignificant gesture among many in the long run of time. Ultimately, it reduces the significance of the very conflict it expresses by setting it in the context of innumerable others, past and future, by foreordaining the outcome, and by approving the outcome as a contribution to maintaining the order.

Ritualization of black folklore applies the implications of ritual to the specific social conflict between black people and the institution of slavery or Jim Crow. It implies that this conflict is part of a general, eternal, and inescapable conflict between human beings and their limitations. It transforms the social conflict at the heart of the folk expression into the metaphysical conflict of the framing myth, thus denying the social conflict any importance of its own. But the relationship between an oppressed people and an oppressive society *is* social; it is the result of human action and can be changed by human agency. To imply otherwise is, in Ellison's own words, to rationalize.

Rationalization is in fact just what Ellison's ritualization of black folklore accomplishes. It implicitly justifies the relationship between black people and American society by effectually denying it. Putting the experience of the flier in "Flying Home" into a context that includes the stories of Icarus, the Prodigal Son, and the fall of man changes it from an experience with racism to an example of hubris. It changes the image of the buzzard, a folk symbol of the destructiveness of racism, to that of the phoenix, a mythic symbol of the redemptiveness of destruction. The folk advisers in *Invisible Man* offer the protagonist a way of looking at society that allows him to live with it as it is. They teach him to consider invisibility a personal asset, rather than a social liability, to embrace chaos as the natural order, to regard Sambo as John, yes as no. But invisibility in the novel *is* a social liability; chaos is racism; Sambo is an attitude of acquiescence; and yes means no only in the mind of the speaker. In both *Invisible Man* and "Flying Home," Ellison offers folk expression as a definition of blackness, then uses folk characters and allusions to deny the social reality that has created the folk identity.

In "Hickman," Ellison uses the materials of black folklore and American popular and literary culture to broaden the context of black experience and reduce the significance of its social dimension. "Oh God hasn't been easy with us because He always plans for the loooong haul," Hickman preaches. "He's looking far ahead and this time He wants a well-tested people to work his will" ("Juneteenth"). As Hickman, in folk-preacher tradition, puts the experience of slavery into the context of Christian myth, Ellison puts it into the context of American myth. "And Hickman Arrives" characterizes the black experience as a test of American humanity and takes the same patient and paternal attitude toward its failure that Hickman takes toward the prodigal Senator Sunraider.

By enlarging the context of the relationship between black people and American society, all these works come to a positive conclusion. They suggest that the nature of the relationship can be changed by changing the perspective from which it is viewed and thus, implicitly, that the relationship exists only in the minds of the victims, as the Invisible Man's exists in his mind. This shift in perspective shifts the burden of change from the racist society to the oppressed race. Even in "Hickman," where Senator Sunraider, who represents American society, does apparently change, it is Hickman's uniquely paternal and pastoral attitude that effects the change. By denying the need for real change, broadening the context of black folklore perpetuates the oppressive relationship on which it is based. Thus the definition of black experience achieved by Ellison's ritualization of black folklore is ultimately not black but white — white not only because the "larger" contexts into which ritual fits the folklore are those of predominantly white American and Western societies but also because the very idea that a change in mental context can change social reality supports the interests of white society by implicitly denying those of the black. Ellison's adaptation of black folklore, however involuntarily, exchanges the self-definition of the folk for the definition of the masters — an effect it would not have if it did not undertake to define black identity.

CHARLES T. DAVIS

The Mixed Heritage
of the Modern Black Novel

Friendship is where we begin. Once upon a time there were three friends, Wright, Ellison, and Baldwin, and Wright, it was, who served as the central person in the relationship, extending the arm of affection to his two younger colleagues, Ellison and Baldwin. They were not friendly at the same time. Ellison was close to Wright until his departure for France and permanent exile in 1947, just at the time that he was beginning to write *Invisible Man,* and Baldwin sought out Wright in Paris during the early years of his residence there. Friendship is not always a pact made in heaven; it resembles at times an insurance policy. That is to say, there are terms, and if the terms are ignored, the friendship is strained, frequently to the breaking point.

Now the accepted element in the Wright-Ellison-Baldwin alliance was that Wright was the dominant father figure, offering advice to his younger associates, directing their reading. As everyone knows, fathers, in the course of things, are destined to be rejected—indeed, in suffering such rejection, some attain unexpected heights. The young associate, seeking distance from an all-embracing arm that has become too confining, can manage his rejection with discretion or with rudeness.

Ellison was discreet. We might expect that he would be, since he was well brought up in Oklahoma and has paid in his autobiographical pieces respect for his elders, especially to a Mr. Randolph, his adopted grandfather, who served as the learned caretaker of the library of the Oklahoma legislature. Ellison, in an

From *Black is the Color of the Cosmos: Essays on Afro-American Literature and Culture, 1942–1981.* © 1982 by The Estate of Charles T. Davis. Garland Publishing Inc., 1982. Originally entitled "The Mixed Heritage of the Modern Black Novel: Ralph Ellison and Friends."

interview published in *The Massachusetts Review* in the Autumn 1977 issue, voiced his rejection in a measured way:

> Most friendships have their vague areas of mystery and the older member of a relationship between writers might himself project the younger in a role which obscures the extent of his intellectual maturity or the extent and variety of his experience. One of my early experiences with Dick Wright involved such an underestimation, with him assuming that I hadn't read many books with which I was, in fact, quite familiar. . . . Well, among others, he assumed that I hadn't read any of Marx . . . Conrad . . . Dostoevsky . . . Hemingway—and so on. I was somewhat chagrined by his apparent condescension, but instead of casting him in the role of misunderstanding "father," I swallowed my pride and told myself, "Forget it, you know what you know, so now learn what he thinks of in terms of his Marxism and the insights he's gained as a developed writer of fiction." And that was the way it went.

On the other hand, Baldwin was a good deal less discreet. After all, he came from a background charged by evangelical religion, and his long suit, if you forgive the mixed metaphor, was conversion, not cultivation. Baldwin attacked Wright in a famous essay written in the mid-fifties entitled "Everybody's Protest Novel," in which he lumped together *Native Son* and *Uncle Tom's Cabin* and asserted, with some pretension, that both failed to qualify as high art. Baldwin said then that the novel should have to do not with society but rather with "the power of revelation," the "journey toward a more vast reality which must take precedence over all other claims." It matters little now that Baldwin was wrong, fuzzily wrong. He was mistaken about the relationship between the novel and society, about the worth of *Native Son,* even about the artistic value of that extraordinary fusion of sentiment and propaganda that is *Uncle Tom's Cabin.* What does matter in our context is that the Wrights (Richard and Ellen) never forgave him, even though they realized that he was reflecting, simply, the pressures of a singularly smug and complacent decade. I say Wrights, by the way, because Ellen, Richard's socond wife, still remembers the assault upon her husband and the objectionable piety that accompanied it. I should add that the last word on this controversy has yet to be printed. There exists now in the Beinecke Library, where the whole Richard Wright Archive now rests, a completed novel, *The Island of Hallucinations,* the second work in a projected trilogy begun by *The Long Dream,* which presents a particularly unpleasant character named "Mr. Mechanical." Some of us, including Michel Fabre, see a striking resemblance between that character and a former intimate associate of Wright's.

Ellen Wright, at the moment, will not permit the publication of the novel because it contains matter damaging to the reputations of people still living.

We are not essentially interested really in the flow and ebb in friendship, but in a moment in the history of Afro-American literature when these interests of Wright, Ellison, and Baldwin converged. This would be in the years 1952 and 1953, when *Invisible Man, The Outsider* by Wright, and *Go Tell It on the Mountain* by Baldwin appeared. The dominant force in the literary ferment created by this convergence was exercised by Ellison, not Wright, the distant master.

Ellison is the writer who comes to mind when we retrace the beginnings of a truly modern tradition in black fiction. Indeed, Ellison's is the achievement that black critic Addison Gayle must reject when he wishes to replace a complex and perhaps perverse heritage with a simple art of straightforward expression and black pieties. Happily, such a replacement is impossible as well as unthinkable, and the dream of it is destined to go the way of the philistine complaint against Henry James, that James's fiction would somehow be stronger, healthier, and more American if he had tended the flame of his genius at Washington Square. The fact is that Ellison for all of his readers, his admirers as well as his detractors, created a new thing in the black novel, shaped a new climate, and forced upon his audience a new pattern of expectations for the art of black fiction, and he did so not by denying the Western tradition in a foolish gesture that would cost him half of the resources of his imagination and his language, but by using it and combining an essentially "white" heritage with the matter and the manner of a rich black oral culture.

Though everyone admits that a break of some kind in the continuity of black fiction occurs with Ellison, few critics, especially those so passionately opposed to his malign influence, can say exactly what it is. Certainly, there is nothing unique about stirring into the same pot white art forms and black folklore, soup stock and exotic herbs. Chesnutt had done this with some commercial success in the 1890s, notably in *The Conjure Woman;* but there is a great difference here in both ingredients and cuisine. Chesnutt used the fictional forms from the conservative genteel tradition, the short narrative carefully tailored for the reading audience of *Scribner's, Century, Harper's, The Critic,* and *The Dial,* which respected a cultivated middle-class sensibility that welcomed titillation but not trauma. Nothing ever really changes in the psychic life of the retired couple who listen to the yarns of Uncle Julius in *The Conjure Woman.* It costs the husband a few dollars now and then and rather more time, but the exposure to black folklore is managed at a proper distance and with a display of civilized tolerance that survives quite easily the odd happenings among lesser black folk. True, Chesnutt's style at its best approaches an irony that might unsettle the most sensitive. The folklore center within the genteel envelope of a typical Chesnutt tale has vitality, but this matter is tempered, too. All of the attention to goophering and transformation tended to sustain conventional moral standards and values, if not in blacks directly, indirectly in the whites, punishing excess in human appetites, and rewarding, at times in odd ways, fidelity and endurance. The precedent for handling folk matter in this way was established, no doubt, by George Washington Cable in the decade preceding the emergence of Chesnutt as a writer, when the quaint ways of the Creoles in Louisiana charmed Eastern audiences, not entirely to the satisfaction of the residents of New Orleans, Plaquemines, and Natchitoches.

The comparison of Chesnutt and Ellison is a device for measuring Ellison's achievement, providing the terms for a proper evaluation. Ellison does not rely upon the more conservative models provided by the mainstream of the American narrative, which would be in the late 1940s a still vigorous Naturalism. Now, "conservative" in this context has nothing to do with politics. The reality is that the American political Left applied the formulas of Naturalism with a new rigor and a new intensity, giving to the achievement of James Farrell and Richard Wright an authority not to be lightly dismissed. A writer of this school practiced exact, detailed representation and looked to the social sciences, at times to Marxist notions of history, for ways of structuring human behavior. The emphasis was always upon the society, not upon the rare individual who dropped out of a well-defined place or a well-clocked time; the challenge for the Naturalistic hero was inevitably adjustment, not psychic trauma that might be magnified in proportion to the character or sensitivity of an individual consciousness. The Naturalist was always about the business of Man, with a capital M, and it helped little to make him Common and to claim that his low state came from a pathological environment. The consequence is an art of constraints: more, indeed, for Wright than there were for Dreiser, since Wright bore consciously and deliberately, but with much turmoil, a commitment to the Communist Party.

I suppose that Wright's inner doubts and his frequent questions were as much responsible as his continuing faith in the Party for the fact that he wrote the finest proletarian novel ever written in America, *Native Son*. But a complete break with his Naturalistic models was unthinkable for Wright while he was a Party member and while he remained in America. Not so for Ellison, who stood at the periphery of the New York political scene in which Wright was a central actor, and who came from a background dominated by an interest in several of the arts rather than a single one. He was also southern in a way that Wright was not. Ellison was prepared, in short, to turn his back on both American Naturalism and the American Left and to welcome aspects of a southern exposure not recognized by Wright, or Chesnutt either, for that matter.

Ellison tells us that *Invisible Man* had its beginnings on a farm in Vermont in the summer of 1945 when he read *The Hero* by Lord Ragland and speculated on the nature of black leadership in the United States. Ellison never intended to construct an odyssey of a representative man, a standard exercise in Naturalism, given its direction by an inflexible social milieu. From the start, he was concerned with a hero with especially endowed characteristics and possibilities, perhaps even with talents not unlike his own. Ellison had read Conrad, Henry James, and Dostoevsky, even before Wright in New York guided the younger writer to James's "Prefaces," the letters of Dostoevsky, and the critical commentary of Joseph Warren Beach. He admits now to "playing possum" with Wright, simulating an innocence of knowledge that he did not possess when they talked in the early forties. After all, T. S. Eliot, whose imprint upon *Invisible Man* is to be seen everywhere, especially on the early pages and in the conclusion, was a Tuskegee discovery like the fine black woman pianist Hazel Harrison. Ellison had a talent for sculpture too, as well as for music, and he was able to recognize a certain naiveté and unsophistication in the sculptor Richmond Barthé, with whom he studied briefly. As a consequence, he adopted a style that was always eclectic, changing to reflect the psychological shifts within his unnamed narrator. He has associated in "The Art of Fiction," an interview published in *The Paris Review* in 1955, a particular and distinctive style with each of the three sections of the novel: Naturalism with the adventures in the South, though it is Naturalism of a highly symbolic kind, when we move away from the well-manicured lawns of the black college; impressionism for the early efforts of the hero to establish himself in the North; and surrealism with the documentation of the hero's fall from grace in the Brotherhood. We may quibble, as I do, with the accuracy of these labels, but not with the presence of a staggering virtuosity in technique that brought into being *Invisible Man*. The point is that Ellison casts off the shackles of Naturalism, both in matter and in manner.

Nowhere is the departure from Naturalism more evident than in the way that environment is rendered, the always richly documented background demanded by that form of the novel extended by Norris and Dreiser, one which devoted attention to the central forces that shape life. Even in the more Naturalistic pages of *Invisible Man*, we find a Melvillian duality, a delight in playing with two equally valid but opposed physical realities — the gleaming and orderly campus of the college, with its suggestions of New England and the triumphs of Christian faith and hard work, and the unsightly cabins of Trueblood and his brothers, sisters, and children, reminding us and Mr. Norton, the trustee from the North, of unattended back alleys of the spirit, unmistakably black and recalling an instinctive life that cannot be forgotten.

This duality is to be found wherever background is sketched in *Invisible*

Man; in the Liberty Paint factory, in the domains of Kimbro and Brockway; in upper Manhattan itself, with a topside of apartments and stores, and a bottom equipped with the most elaborately illuminated basement ever rendered in literature or in life. It is clear that the essentially fictional problem is not adjustment, since no one knows to what he might adjust; rather, the more desperate question is ordering one's tradition, history, and psyche, best put by one of Ellison's favorite authors at the time, Eliot, at the conclusion of *The Waste Land:* "These fragments I have shored against my ruins." No more. And the unnamed narrator confesses that he is only half prepared to emerge from his hole. A little like Louis Armstrong, who would "Open the Window and let the foul air out," knowing all the time that the "Old Bad Air" was responsible for the good music.

Perhaps the plainest indication of Ellison's reliance upon the rich tradition in experimental Western art is the title itself. "Invisibility" is not simply a characteristic first given visual expression by the fine British actor Claude Rains in a horror movie, nor even first used as a metaphor for blackness in 1948 by George Orwell. It is a concept that owes something to European Expressionism, in which the dominant idea in a complex whole of a community of values or of a social system or a culture or a human relationship is extracted, magnified, distorted, and allowed to stand for the whole. For precedents of this kind, we do not need to look to the dramatists Kaiser or Capek with their experiments in Europe, but closer at hand to O'Neill in *The Hairy Ape,* or, indeed, to Eliot, in "The Hollow Men." What is exaggerated, of course, is what some of us still remember from the bad days before the black revolution, the tendency of whites to ignore or to make easy generalizations about blacks; this is not so prevalent since the publication of *Invisible Man* and the parade of liberated, individualized black psyches that followed in print.

We are dealing in halves here, since the break with Naturalism constitutes only one half of the meaning of Ellison's achievement. The flip side of the coin that represents his contribution to the modern black novel is all black and connected directly with a black oral tradition. Chesnutt, we must recall, used only that folk matter that could be absorbed with comparative ease by a genteel reading audience. He wrote about conjurers, mostly women, who restricted their practice of the black arts to blacks, in general, and blacks in a reasonably remote community in North Carolina at that. Zora Hurston knew much more than Chesnutt did about the black folk tradition, especially the animal tales, the boasts and jokes, and the rituals in folk medicine, but in her fiction she tended to separate the white world and the black, following Chesnutt's pattern, but often rendering black life with more dignity, fullness, and wonder. It was Ellison who suggested a subversive dimension for the black arts.

Ellison uses the matter and the style of a black folk culture with a new broadness and with an incredible range, from music through the spoken word to the icon. His blackness is much more accessible and much more threatening. Trueblood demonstrates this early on when Norton, the college trustee, has the temerity to stray away from the neatly landscaped grounds of the narrator's institution. But there is much more. Louis's trumpet blues complain eloquently about the unchanging condition of blackness in white America, played off the beat, of course, and making marvelous art from "bad air." The characters from beast fables, Buckeye Rabbit and Jack the Bear, appear as symbols representing the narrator's psychological states, documenting the measure of his submission to or evasion of inhuman white authority. Cryptic folk rhymes stir racial memories that would moderate somewhat the narrator's headlong pursuit of conventional goals within the context of commercial New York. The extraordinary "Prologue" contains, along with snatches of blues and other bits of folk matter, an irreverent folk sermon on the text "Blackness of Backness," and it offers a summary description of the action which is hard to improve upon:

> "Black will make you . . ."
>
> . . . .
>
> ". . . or black will un-make you"

And the response of the assembled congregation in this dream sequence seems wholly appropriate: "Ain't it the truth, Lawd?" An object, not simply a musical line or a phrase, has the power in *Invisible Man* to link past and present. We think of Brother Tarp's leg chain, a device associating two kinds of bondage: chattel slavery in the South and absolute allegiance demanded by the Brotherhood. The chain, though not folk art in any true sense, has the effect of an iron in that it arouses memories of almost unbreakable intensity of the cruelty of black servitude in the South. Illustrations accompanying the slave narratives when they appeared in the North during three decades of appeal to the American conscience just before the Civil War frequently presented a black and his leg chain.

To give a proper estimate for what Ellison has accomplished we must record it in black and white, that is to say, within the framework of a vital and comprehensive black folk culture and within the emerging tradition of the experimental modern novel. He breaks decisively, on both counts, from the practice of his immediate predecessors, and such is the power of his genius that he leaves the impression that by his efforts alone he has prepared the way for the bold achievements in black fiction that are to come.

To believe so would be to attribute too much to Ellison, great as his work is,

and to ignore the time. The crucial period of gestation and formation of the
modern black novel is the late forties and early fifties. Indeed, the culminating
years for these pioneer efforts are 1952 and 1953, a two-year period during which
not only *Invisible Man* appeared, leading the way in 1952, but *Go Tell It on the
Mountain,* and also *The Outsider* by Richard Wright, which appeared a year
later in 1953.

We tend to ignore *The Outsider* in this context, probably because of the
false assumption that his self-imposed and widely advertised exile in France had
deprived Wright of the nourishment of American society. It is the old provin-
cialism again, underestimating, as it always did, the power of a really strong imagination. In fact, *The Outsider* is a new departure for the old master of
Naturalistic fiction, demonstrating that Wright in his own way had shared the
same road with Ellison, not too unexpected given that they were firm friends in
the early forties.

The Outsider has a protagonist who is also extraordinary and who very early
in the action seeks to shape his own life by assuming a new identity: Cross
Damon becomes Lionel Lane; the black postal worker in Chicago becomes an
important, though unofficial, member of a local cell of the Communist Party in
New York. We sense in both Ellison's hero and Wright's that they have the
potential for leadership, though circumstances of life are not favorable. What is
important, finally, for both is not success but coming to terms with themselves.
The Invisible Man must develop, first, an awareness of his needs as a person;
Cross makes what he considers, at last, to be the wrong decision about his need,
and faces, in his dying moments, the human consequences of a freedom gained
by violating accepted moral standards and living outside of society. Both protagonists drop out of time; for Ellison, such an escape is short-term therapy that
works, for Wright it is ultimately disastrous, destroying the connection, the
"bridge from man to man," which is, Cross maintains, all we have: "starting
from scratch every time is . . . is no good."

Despite a certain identity in theme and in fictional strategies, the two works
are remarkably different. Ellison's is a personal odyssey that leads to the discovery of a rich black folk heritage, which accompanies the acquisition of a psychological equilibrium at the end, almost sufficient to face a chaotic and often
senseless world. There are few such positive assurances in *The Outsider,* singularly devoid of allusions to a racial heritage or to psychic traumas that oppress the
Invisible Man. Wright's novel is, instead, a form of fable in which personal relationships and their exploration count for little. What matters is a philosophical
point: the power and the cost of the condition of conscious alienation debated
with brilliance by Cross and Ely Houston, the District Attorney of New York City,
two outsiders, one a black criminal evading capture and the other a hunchback

lawman with the capacity to reconstruct the motivation of the man whom he hunts and about whom he can speak, at his death, with the voice of a brother. Raskolnikoff and Porfiry, we think, in *Crime and Punishment,* and we are not far off. Wright's fable, relying on reason and philosophical discussion rather than upon psychological development, makes a powerful statement about the human condition, which is clear and unqualified: "Alone a man is nothing." The narrative, despite its lean, even ascetic technique, manages to view the future in a hopeful light, assuming, indeed, the presence of an audience that might learn from a well told lesson. Beyond the horror, Cross's four murders, rests a promising prospect: "Man is returning to the earth finding himself in a waking nightmare. . . . The real men, the last men are coming." Nothing so hopeful as this emerges from *Invisible Man,* though Ellison's hero, despite temptation, is never moved to resort to such violent means to achieve his ends.

One critic has called Wright a birthright existentialist, which is an affirmation that criticism will use any science or pseudo-science to make its point, even dialectics. I prefer to think of Wright as a home-grown existentialist, made so by his traumatic childhood in Mississippi, his reading of the more libertarian Naturalists like Dreiser, who scorned moral conventions and inhibitions supported by religion, and his trials in the Communist Party.

What is inescapable, with both Ellison and Wright, is that the discovery of blackness and its meaning represents a starting point for the artists; Wright's experience, as we have seen, leads to an existential view of reality. Ellison states his notion of what constitutes a beginning best in a remarkable article on the art of his friend Romare Bearden.

> I refer to that imbalance in American society which leads to a distorted perception of social reality, to a stubborn blindness to the creative possibilities of cultural diversity, to the prevalence of negative myths, racial stereotypes and dangerous illusions about art, humanity and society. Arising from an initial failure of social justice, this anachronism divides social groups along lines that are no longer tenable while fostering hostility, anxiety and fear; and in the area to which we now address ourselves it has had the damaging effect of alienating many Negro artists from the traditions, techniques and theories indigenous to the arts through which they aspire to achieve themselves.

Ellison practices what he counsels: he addresses "social imbalance," using the full range of the techniques available to him from contemporary fiction, music and the plastic arts, and the folk tradition.

James Baldwin, like Ellison and Wright, explored in *Go Tell It on the*

Mountain the problems of a potential leader, though of a special kind. The intellectual context for the coming of John, to echo Du Bois for a moment, is religious and psychological, not political or philosophical. John, Baldwin's protagonist, has the talent and the temperament to become a preacher, a wise and compassionate shepherd for a black congregation; but he lacks the spirit, the sense of mission that comes from the experience of conversion. John's difficulty rests not with the attraction to sin, which he resists without real conflict, but in the hatred of his stepfather, Gabriel, once a powerful preacher in the South, now brought low because he has yielded to lust and pride. John must moderate his antipathy for Gabriel before he can join the community of the saints of the Temple of the Fire Baptized in Harlem. He does so by absorbing the testimonies, "prayers" Baldwin calls them, of his aunt, his stepfather, and his mother. We know that John in this way has acquired an understanding of, if not a complete sympathy for, the adults of his family, because snatches from their statements, their responses to the call of the preacher to come to God, appear in the remarkable record of his conversion. The family's collective guilt, as well as its collective memory, weighs him down as he approaches the agony and the light on the threshing-floor. This necessity to reckon with a black past, to learn it and to accept it, follows the pattern of Ellison's nameless hero who eats a yam in public as a step toward establishing his racial identity.

Though the essential fictional problem owes little to Naturalism, the description of the background in Harlem, with its dirt, smells, rats, and harlot cries, displays an indebtedness that is quite clear. It is firm until John slips off into Central Park and we discover ourselves suddenly upon a hill in Judea with a view of a sinful city below. Baldwin's South has even less the shape of a readily identifiable land; the terrain is rather the mountains and the valleys of the Old Testament prophets. By the time we reach the threshing floor, the landscape is wholly surrealistic.

Certainly one of the great triumphs of *Go Tell It on the Mountain* is the imaginative use of a folk art form, specifically the folk sermon. Ellison was ingenious, too, in the way that he absorbed folk materials within the structure of *Invisible Man,* but he did not take Baldwin's longer step in this respect. The entire novel is a response to a folk sermon, culminating indeed in a conversion scene. The black preacher's call to "Come" results first in "Telling," the testimonies of members of the Grimes family and then the descent of God's grace upon John. At the end of the narrative John is saved, but he has yet to be tried. His faith will be tested when he himself goes forth to spread the Word, risking the hazards to the psyche that will afflict him when he struggles to ascend the steep side of the mountain, as Gabriel had attempted to do. I can think of no other example in modern fiction in which a form derived from folk art exercises such commanding authority.

It is time now to take stock, to sum up the most visible consequences of this artistic revolution in the early fifties. We know now that it is not simply Ellison that we must thank or damn, but Wright and Baldwin too, whose more modest participation must be counted. This new literature is a record of an exceptional sensibility as it copes not so much with a hostile world but with the terrors of its own creation. What is prized more than anything else is an understanding of one's black self, and this requires a reconciliation of some sort with the black heritage, family and folk, in America. Almost in his dying words, Cross Damon warns: "Starting from scratch every time is . . . is no good." No good it is for any of these writers.

Ellison, Wright, and Baldwin depart from Naturalistic techniques to render the turmoil of the psyche. Ellison uses dream sequences and violent distortions of reality, both clocked to a remarkable sense of place and of pace. Wright constructs a morality tale, a modern fable permitting a naked and a full discussion of such issues as freedom, power, and human connection. Baldwin fashions what might be called a counter-sermon, fleshing out what rests behind the audience's "Amen" and ending in a description of a convulsive transcendence that is one of the extraordinary achievements in modern literature. For all three, the old verities no longer work. Theirs are now the realities beyond success, freedom, and salvation, and we inherit a house of black fiction that has yet to settle securely on a foundation so recently reclaimed from the marshes of the psyche.

If we look more closely at *Native Son*, we can observe that the signs of change are already in the air in 1940. I refer to the third book of the novel, still often criticized for being inconsistent with the brilliant Naturalism of the first two books. We recall that Bigger, after his conviction for murder, throws the crucifix out of his cell when he is visited by a black preacher bringing the chance to repent and to acquire, at the last moment, divine grace, and we listen with astonishment to the rejection of the Marxist vision of his lawyer, Max, when Bigger insists that his murders were not the consequence of society's pathology but the result of his own will. And to Max's dismay, Bigger asserts that the murders were good since they gave him a human dimension that he never possessed before. Bigger, after his resurrection in the final act, may be a phenomenon that is premature; but with the perspective of literary history, we can say that he has brothers in the heroes of novels published more than a decade later, in the fifties.

HOUSTON A. BAKER, JR.

Creativity and Commerce
in the Trueblood Episode

Them boss quails is like a good man, what he got to do he do.
—Trueblood

In such close alliance with his predecessor of blue-black, inversive rites of the black underground—indeed, a protégé—yet so anxious to scandalize the name of Wright, Ralph Ellison suggests the agonizing dues extracted from the author who writes the blues book most excellent—who fitly and brilliantly achieves a form that fulfills the American Dream. Dunbar's dilemma and Wright's magnificent expressive strategies in creating authoritative rites that mark a modern Afro-American narrative tradition combine in the career of the author of *Invisible Man.* The combination provides extraordinarily rich and subtle texture for that career. Appearing to mediate between a consuming desire for "literary" form and an overwhelming attraction to the expressive desires of a black blues life, Ellison sometimes seems suspended just above a bedrock ground whose touch would renew him, make him whole. Yet this suspension, like all acts of levitation, is merely an appearance—part of the magic of the crafty blues artist who knows which way the bad wind is blowing. Under blues analysis, Ellison's career emerges as a productive reconciliation of Dunbar's dilemma and Wright's achievement. *Invisible Man* reflexively and nimbly negotiates not only the economics of slavery, but also the *break* held to obtain between "the forms of things unknown" and the "evolved" forms of English and American literatures. The novel not only discovers *AMERICA* in a stunningly

From *Blues, Ideology, and Afro-American Literature.* © 1984 by The University of Chicago. The University of Chicago Press, 1984. Excerpted from a chapter entitled "A Dream of American Form."

113

energetic blues manner, but also sets that idea singing in ways unheard before its production and unequaled since its first appearance in 1952. To study the fulfillment of a dream of American form is to read *Invisible Man* as a brilliant expressive moment that achieves both the limitless freedom of myth and the remarkably efficacious passage through rites of the blue-black, underground (w)hole.

In his essay "Richard Wright's Blues," Ralph Ellison states one of his cherished distinctions: "The function, the psychology, of artistic selectivity is to eliminate from art form all those elements of experience which contain no compelling significance. Life is as the sea, art a ship in which man conquers life's crushing formlessness, reducing it to a course, a series of swells, tides and wind currents inscribed on a chart." The distinction between nonsignificant life experiences and their inscribed, artistic significance (i.e., the meaning induced by form) leads Ellison to concur with André Malraux that artistic significance alone "enables man to conquer chaos and to master destiny."

Artistic "technique," according to Ellison, is the agency through which artistic meaning and form are achieved. In "Hidden Name and Complex Fate" he writes:

> It is a matter of outrageous irony, perhaps, but in literature the great social clashes of history no less than the painful experience of the individual are secondary to the meaning which they take on through the skill, the talent, the imagination and personal vision of the writer who transforms them into art. Here they are reduced to more manageable proportions; here they are imbued with humane value; here, injustice and catastrophe become less important in themselves than what the writer makes of them.

Even the thing-in-itself of lived, historical experience is thus seen as devoid of "humane value" before its sea change under the artist's transforming technique.

Since Ellison focuses his interest on the literary, the inscribed, work of art, he regards even folklore as part of that realm of life "elements . . . which contain no compelling significance" in themselves. In "Change the Joke and Slip the Yoke," he asserts:

> the Negro American writer is also an heir to the human experience which is literature, and this might well be more important to him than his living folk tradition. For me, at least, in the discontinuous, swiftly changing and diverse American culture, the stability of the Negro folk tradition became precious as a result of an act of literary

discovery . . . For those who are able to translate [the folk tradition's] meanings into wider, more precise vocabularies it has much to offer indeed.

During a BBC program recorded in May 1982 and entitled "Garrulous Ghosts: The Literature of the American South," Ellison stated that the fiction writer, to achieve proper resonance, must go beyond the blues—a primary and tragically eloquent form of American expression:

> The blues are very important to me. I think of them as the closest approach to tragedy that we have in American art forms. And I'm not talking about black or white, I mean just American. Because they do combine the tragic and the comic in a very subtle way and, yes, they are very important to me. But they are also limited. And if you are going to write fiction there is a level of consciousness which you move toward which I would think transcends the blues.

Thus Ellison seems to regard Afro-American folklore, before its translation into "more precise vocabularies," as part of lived experience. Art and chaos appear to be homologous with literature and folklore.

To infer such a homology from one or two critical remarks, however, is to risk the abyss of "false distinction," especially when one is faced with a canon as rich as Ralph Ellison's. It is certainly true that the disparagement of folk expression suggested by these remarks can be qualified by the praise of folklore implicit in Ellison's assertion that Afro-American expressive folk projections are a group's symbolically "profound" attempts to "humanize" the world. Such projections, even in their crudest forms, constitute the "humble base" on which "great literature" is erected.

It does seem accurate, however, to say that Ellison's criticism repeatedly implies an extant, identifiable tradition of literary art—a tradition consisting of masters of form and technique who must be read, studied, emulated, and (if one is lucky and eloquent) equaled. This tradition stands as the signal, vital repository of "humane value." And for Ellison the sphere that it describes is equivalent to the primum mobile, lending force and significance to all actions of the descending heavens and earth.

Hence, while the division between folk and artistic may be only discursive, having no more factual reality than any other such division, it seems to matter to Ellison, who never, as far as I know, refers to himself as a folk artist. Moreover, in our era of sophisticated "folkloristics," it seems mere evasion to shy from the assertion that Ellison's criticism ranks folklore below literary art on a total scale of value. What I argue is that the distinction between folklore and literary art evident in Ellison's critical practice collapses in his creative practice in *Invisible Man's* Trueblood episode. Further, I suggest that an exacting analysis of this episode illuminates the relation not only between Ellison's critical and creative practices but also between what might be called the public and private commerce of black art in America.

The main character in the Trueblood episode, which occupies chapter 2 of *Invisible Man,* is a country blues singer (a tenor of "crude, high, plaintively animal sounds") who is also a virtuoso prose narrator. To understand the disjunctiveness between Ellison's somewhat disparaging critical pronouncements on "raw" folklore and his striking fictional representation of folk character in chapter 2, one must first comprehend, I think, the sharecropper Trueblood's dual manifestation as trickster and merchant, as creative and commercial man. Blues and narration, as modes of expression, conjoin and divide in harmony with these dichotomies. And the episode in its entirety is—as I demonstrate—a metaexpressive commentary on the incumbencies of Afro-American artists and the effects of their distinctive modes of expression.

In an essay that gives a brilliant ethnographic reading of the Balinese cockfight, Clifford Geertz asserts:

> Like any art form—for that, finally, is what we are dealing with—
> the cockfight renders ordinary, everyday experience comprehensible
> by presenting it in terms of acts and objects which have had their
> practical consequences removed and been reduced (or, if you prefer,
> raised) to the level of sheer appearances, where their meaning can be
> more powerfully articulated and more exactly perceived.

Catching up the themes of Balinese society in symbolic form, the cockfight thus represents, in Geertz's words, "a metasocial commentary . . . a Balinese reading of Balinese experience, a story they tell themselves about themselves." This implies that the various symbolic (or "semiotic") systems of a culture— religion, politics, economics—can themselves be "raised" to a metasymbolic level by the orderings and processes of "ritual interactions" like the Balinese cockfight.

The coming together of semiotic systems in ways that enlarge and enhance the world of human meanings is the subject of Barbara Babcock-Abraham's insightful essay "The Novel and the Carnival World." Following the lead of Julia Kristeva, Babcock-Abrahams asserts that a "metalanguage" is a symbolic system that treats of symbolic systems; for example, *Don Quixote* "openly discusses other works of literature and takes the writing and reading of literature as its subject." Both social rituals and novels, since they "embed" other semiotic systems within their "texture," are "multivocal," "polyvalent," or "polysemous" — that is, capable of speaking in a variety of mutually reflexive voices at once.

The multiple narrative frames and voices in Ellison's Trueblood episode include the novel *Invisible Man,* the protagonist's fictive autobiographical account, Norton's story recalled as part of the fictive autobiography, Trueblood's story as framed by the fictive autobiography, the sharecropper's own autobiographical recall, and the dream narrative within that autobiographical recall. All these stories reflect, or "objectify," one another in ways that complicate their individual and composite meanings. Further, the symbolic systems suggested by the stories are not confined to (though they may implicitly comment on) such familiar social configurations as education, economics, politics, and religion. Subsuming these manifestations is the outer symbolic enterprise constituted by the novel itself. Moreover, the Trueblood episode heightens the multivocal character of the novel from within, acting as a metacommentary on the literary and artistic system out of which the work is generated. Further enriching the burden of meanings in the episode are the Christian myth of the Fall and Sigmund Freud's mythic incest "narrative," which are both connoted (summoned as signifiers, in Babcock-Abraham's terms) and parodied, or inverted. I analyze the text's play on these myths later in my discussion.

For the moment, I am primarily interested in suggesting that the Trueblood episode, like other systematic, symbolic phenomena, gains and generates its meanings in a dialogic relation with various systems of signs. As a text this chapter derives its logic from its intertextual relation with surrounding and encompassing texts and in turn complicates their meanings. The Balinese cockfight, according to Geertz, can only tell a "metastory" because it is intertextually implicated in a world that is itself constituted by a repertoire of "stories" (e.g., those of economics and politics) that the Balinese tell themselves.

As a story that the author of Invisible Man tells himself about his own practice, the Trueblood episode clarifies distinctions that must be made between Ellison as critic and Ellison as artist. To elucidate its metaexpressive function, one must summon analytical instruments from areas that Ellison sharply debunks in his own criticism.

For example, at the outset of "The World and the Jug," a masterfully instructive essay on the criticism of Afro-American creativity, Ellison asks:

Why is it so often true that when critics confront the American as *Negro* they suddenly drop their advanced critical armament and revert with an air of confident superiority to quite primitive modes of analysis? Why is it that sociology-oriented critics seem to rate

literature so far below politics and ideology that they would rather
kill a novel than modify their presumptions concerning a given reality
which it seeks in its own terms to project?

What I take these questions to imply is that a given artistic reality designed to
represent "Negro-American" experience should not be analyzed by "primitive"
methods, which Ellison leaves unspecified but seems to associate with sociological, ideological, and political modes of analysis. In the following discussion I
hope to demonstrate that sociology, anthropology, economics, politics, and
ideology all provide models essential for the explication of the Trueblood episode. The first step, however, is to evoke the theater of Trueblood's performance.

II

Trueblood's narration has an unusual audience, but to the farmer and his
Afro-American cohorts the physical setting is as familiar as train whistles in the
Alabama night. The sharecropper, a white millionaire, and a naive undergrad-
uate from a nearby black college have arranged themselves in a semicircle of
camp chairs in the sharecropper's yard. They occupy a swath of shade cast by the
porch of a log cabin that has survived the ravages of climate since the hard times
of slavery. The millionaire asks, "How are you faring now? . . . Perhaps I could
help." The sharecropper responds, "We ain't doing so bad, suh. 'Fore they heard
'bout what happen to us out here I couldn't get no help from nobody. Now lotta
folks is curious and go outta their way to help." What has occurred "out here" —
in what the millionaire Mr. Norton refers to as "new territory for me" and what
the narrator describes as "a desert" that "almost took [his] breath away" — is Jim
Trueblood's impregnation of both his wife and his daughter. The event has
brought disgrace on the sharecropper and has mightily embarrassed officials at
the nearby black college.

The whites in the neighboring town and countryside, however, are scarcely
outraged or perturbed by Trueblood's situation. Rather, they want to keep the
sharecropper among them; they warn the college officials not to harass him or
his family; and they provide money, provisions, and abundant work. "White
folks," says Trueblood, even "took to coming out here to see us and talk with us.
Some of 'em was big white folks, too, from the big school way cross the State.
Asked me lots 'bout what I thought 'bout things, and 'bout my folks and the
kids, and wrote it all down in a book." Hence, when the farmer begins to re-
count the story of his incestuous act with his daughter Matty Lou, he does so as a
man who has thoroughly rehearsed his tale and who has carefully refined his
knowledge of his audience: "He cleared his throat, his eyes gleaming and his

voice taking on a deep, incantatory quality, as though he had told the story many, many times."

The art of storytelling is not a gift that Trueblood has acquired recently. He is introduced in *Invisible Man* as one who "told the old stories with a sense of humor and a magic that made them come alive." A master storyteller, then, he recounts his provocative exploits to an audience that is by turns shamed, indignant, envious, humiliated, and enthralled.

The tale begins on a cold winter evening in the sharecropper's cabin. The smell of fat meat hangs in the air, and the last kindling crackles in the dying flames of the stove. Trueblood's daughter, in bed between her father and mother, sleepily whispers, "Daddy." At the story's close, the sharecropper reports his resolution to prevent Aunt Cloe the midwife from aborting his incestuous issue. At the conclusion of his tale, he reiterates his judgment that he and his family "ain't doing so bad" in the wake of their ordeal.

Certainly the content and mode of narration the sharecropper chooses reflect his knowledge of what a white audience expects of the Afro-American. Mr. Norton is not only a "teller of polite Negro stories" but also a man who sees nothing unusual about the pregnant Matty Lou's not having a husband. "But that shouldn't be so strange," he remarks. The white man's belief in the promiscuity of blacks is further suggested by Mr. Broadnax, the figure in Trueblood's dream who looks at the sharecropper and his daughter engaged in incest and says, "They just nigguhs, leave 'em do it." In conformity with audience expectations, the sharecropper's narrative is aggressively sexual in its representations.

Beginning with an account of the feel of his daughter's naked arm pressed against him in bed, the farmer proceeds to reminisce about bygone days in Mobile when he would lie in bed in the evenings with a woman named Margaret and listen to the music from steamboats passing on the river. Next, he introduces the metaphor of the woman in a red dress "goin' past you down a lane . . . and kinda switchin' her tail 'cause she knows you watchin'." From this evocative picture, he turns to a detailed account of his dream on the night of his incestuous act.

The dream is a parodic allegory in which Trueblood goes in quest of "fat meat." In this episode the name "Mr. Broadnax" (Mr. Broad-in-acts) captures the general concepts that mark any narrative as allegory. The man whose house is on the hill is a philanthropist who gives poor blacks (true bloods) sustaining gifts as "fat meat." The model implied by this conceptualization certainly fits one turn-of-the-century American typology, recalling the structural arrangement by which black, southern colleges were able to sustain themselves. In one sense, the entire Trueblood episode can be read as a pejorative commentary on the castrating effects of white philanthropy. Trueblood's dream narrative is parodic because it reveals the crippling assumptions (the castrating import) of the philanthropic model suggested in "Broadnax." The man who is broad-in-acts in the dream is the one who refers to the sharecropper and his daughter as "just nigguhs." Further, his philanthropy — like Mr. Norton's — has a carnal undercurrent: it is dangerously and confusingly connected with the sexuality of Mrs. Broadnax. What he dispenses as sustaining "fat meat" may only be the temporarily satisfying thrill of sexual gratification. The "pilgrim," or quester, in Trueblood's dream allegory flees from the dangers and limitations of such deceptive philanthropy. And the general exposé effected by the narrative offers a devastating critique of that typography which saw white men on the hill (northern industrialists) as genuinely and philanthropically responsive to the needs of those in the valley (southern blacks).

Instructed to inquire at Mr. Broadnax's house, Trueblood finds himself violating a series of southern taboos and fleeing for his life. He enters the front door of the home, wanders into a woman's bedroom, and winds up trapped in the embraces of a scantily clad white woman. The gastronomic and sexual appetites surely converge at this juncture, and the phrase "fat meat" takes on a dangerous burden of significance. The dreamer breaks free, however, and escapes into the darkness and machinery of a grandfather clock. He runs until a bright electric light bursts over him, and he awakens to find himself engaged in sexual intercourse with his daughter.

In *Totem and Taboo,* Freud advances the hypothesis that the two taboos of totemism — the interdictions against slaying the totem animal and against incest — result from events in human prehistory. Following Darwin's speculations, Freud claims that human beings first lived in small hordes in which one strong, jealous man took all women to himself, exiling the sons to protect his own exclusive sexual privileges. On one occasion, however, Freud suggests, the exiled sons arose, slew and ate the father, and then, in remorse, established the taboo against such slaughter. To prevent discord among themselves and to ensure the survival of their new form of social organization, they also established a taboo against sexual intercourse with the women of their own clan. Exogamy, Freud concludes, is based on a prehistorical advance from a lower to a higher stage of social organization.

From Freud's point of view, Trueblood's dream and subsequent incest seem to represent a historical regression. The sharecropper's dreamed violations of southern social and sexual taboos are equivalent to a slaughter of the white patriarch represented by Mr. Broadnax, who does, indeed, control the "fat" and "fat meat" of the land. To eat fat meat is to partake of the totemic animal. And having run backward in time through the grandfather clock, Trueblood becomes the primal father, assuming all sexual prerogatives unto himself. He has warned away "the boy" (representing the tumultuous mob of exiled sons) who wanted to take away his daughter, and as the sexual partner of both Matty Lou and Kate, he reveals his own firm possession of all his "womenfolks"—his status, that is to say, as a sexual producer secure against the wrath of his displaced "sons." Insofar as Freud's notions of totemism represent a myth of progressive social evolution, the farmer's story acts as a countermyth of inversive social dissolution. It breaks society down into components and reveals man in what might be called his pre-social and unaccommodated state.

One reason for the sharecropper's singular sexual prerogatives is that the other Afro-Americans in his area are either so constrained or so battered by their encounters with society that they are incapable of a legitimate and productive sexuality. The sharecropper's territory is bounded on one side by the black college where the "sons" are indoctrinated in a course of instruction that leaves them impotent. On the other side lie the insane asylum and the veterans' home, residences of black men driven mad—or at least rendered psychologically and physically crippled—by their encounters with America. These "disabled veterans" are scarcely "family men" like Trueblood. Rather, they are listless souls who visit the whores in "the sun-shrunk shacks at the railroad crossing . . . hobbling down the tracks on crutches and canes; sometimes pushing the legless, thighless one in a red wheelchair." In such male company Trueblood seems the only person capable of ensuring an authentic Afro-American lineage. When he finds himself atop Matty Lou, therefore, both the survival of the clan and the sharecropper's aversion to pain require him to reject the fate that has been physically or psychologically imposed on his male cohorts. He says, "There was only one way I can figger that I could git out: that was with a knife. But I didn't have no knife, and if you'all ever seen them geld them young boar pigs in the fall, you know I knowed that was too much to pay to keep from sinnin'." In this reflection, he brings forward one of the dominant themes of *Invisible Man.* This theme—one frequently slighted, or omitted, in discussions of the novel—is black male sexuality.

Perhaps critical prudery prevents commentators from acknowledging the black male phallus as a dominant symbol in much of the ritual interaction of *Invisible Man.* In *The Forest of Symbols: Aspects of Ndembu Ritual,* Victor Turner provides suggestive definitions for both "ritual" and "dominant symbols." He describes ritual as "prescribed formal behavior for occasions not given over to technological routine, having reference to beliefs in mystical beings or powers. The symbol is the smallest unit of ritual which still retains the specific properties of ritual behavior; it is the ultimate unit of specific structure in a ritual context." For Turner, the most prominent—the "senior," as it were—symbols in any ritual are dominant symbols; they fall into a class of their own. The important characteristic of such symbols is that they bring together disparate meanings, serving as a kind of semiotic shorthand. Further, they can have both ideological and sensuous associations; the mudyi tree of Ndembu ritual, for example, refers both to the breast milk of the mother and to the axiomatic values of the matrilineal Ndembu society.

Ellison's *Invisible Man* is certainly an instance of "prescribed formal behavior" insofar as the novel is governed by the conventions of the artistic system in which it is situated, a system that resides ludically outside "technological routine" and promotes the cognitive exploration of all systems of "being" and "power," whether mystical or not. The black phallus is a dominant symbol in the novel's formal patterns of behavior, as its manifold recurrence attests. In "The Art of Fiction: An Interview," Ellison writes, "People rationalize what they shun or are incapable of dealing with; these superstitions and their rationalizations become rituals as they govern behavior. The rituals become social forms, and it is one of the functions of the artist to recognize them and raise them to the level of art." Stated in slighted different terms, Ellison's comment suggests an intertextual (indeed, a connoted) relation between the prescribed formal social behaviors or American racial interaction and the text of the novel. Insofar as Jim Crow social laws and the desperate mob exorcism of lynchings (with their attendant castrations) describe a formal pattern of Anglo-American behavior toward black men, this pattern offers an instance of ritual in which the black phallus gathers an extraordinary burden of disparate connotations, both sensuous and ideological. It should come as no surprise that an artist as perceptive as Ellison recognizes the black phallus as a dominant symbol of the sometimes bizarre social rituals of America and incorporates it into the text of a novel. In "The Art of Fiction," in fact, Ellison calls the battle-royal episode of *Invisible Man* "a ritual in preservation of caste lines, a keeping of taboo to appease the gods and ward off bad luck." He did not have to invent the ritual, he says; all he had to do was to provide "a broader context of meaning" for the patterns the episode represents.

The black phallus, then, does seem an implicit major symbol in Ellison's text, and there are venerable precedents for the discussion of male sexual symbols in ritual. For example, in "Deep Play" Geertz writes:

> To anyone who has been in Bali any length of time, the deep psychological identification of Balinese men with their cocks is unmistakable. The double entendre here is deliberate. It works in exactly the same way in Balinese as it does in English, even to producing the same tired jokes, strained puns, and uninventive obscenities. [Gregory] Bateson and [Margaret] Mead have even suggested that, in line with

the Balinese conception of the body as a set of separately animated parts, cocks are viewed as detachable, self-operating penises, ambulent genitals with a life of their own.

Certainly, the notion of "ambulent genitals" figures in the tales of the roguish trickster as recorded in Paul Radin's classic work *The Trickster*. In tale sixteen of the Winnebago trickster cycle, Wakdjunkaga the trickster sends his penis across the waters of a lake to have intercourse with a chief's daughter.

The black phallus as a symbol of unconstrained force that white men contradictorily envy and seek to destroy appears first in the opening chapter of *Invisible Man*. The influential white men of a small southern town force the protagonist and his fellow black boxers in the battle-royal to gaze on "a magnificent blonde — stark naked." The boys are threatened both for looking and for not looking, and the white men smile at their obvious fear and discomfiture. The boys know the bizarre consequences that accompany the white men's ascription of an animal-like and voracious sexuality to black males. Hence, they respond in biologically normal but socially fearful (and justifiably embarrassed) ways. One boy strives to hide his erection with his boxing gloves, pleading desperately to go home. In this opening scene, the white woman as a parodic version of American ideals ("a small American flag tattooed upon her belly"), is forced into tantalizing interaction with the mythically potent force of the black phallus. But because the town's white males exercise total control of the situation, the scene is akin to a castration, excision, or lynching.

Castration is one function of the elaborate electrically wired glass box that incarcerates the protagonist in the factory-hospital episode: " 'Why not castration, doctor?' a voice asked waggishly." In the Brotherhood, the class struggle is rather devastatingly transformed into the "ass struggle" when the protagonist's penis displaces his oratory as ideological agent. A white woman who hears him deliver a speech and invites him home seizes his biceps passionately and says, "Teach me, talk to me. Teach me the beautiful ideology of Brotherhood." And the protagonist admits that suddenly he "was lost" as "the conflict between the ideological and the biological, duty and desire," became too subtly confused. Finally, in the nightmare that concludes the novel, the Invisible Man sees his own bloody testes, like those of the castrated Uranus of Greek myth, floating above the waters underneath a bridge's high arc. In the dream, he tells his inquisitors that his testes dripping blood on the black waters are not only his "generations wasting upon the water" but also the "sun" and the "moon" — and, indeed, the very "world" — of their own human existence. The black phallus — in its creative, ambulent, generative power, even when castrated — is like the cosmos itself, a self-sustaining and self-renewing source of life, provoking both envy and fear in Anglo-American society.

While a number of episodes in *Invisible Man* (including Trueblood's dream) suggest the illusory freedoms and taboo-induced fears accompanying interaction between the black phallus and white women, only the Trueblood encounter reveals the phallus as producing Afro-American generations rather than wasting its seed upon the water. The cosmic force of the phallus thus becomes, in the ritual action of the Trueblood episode, symbolic of a type of royal paternity, an aristocratic procreativity turned inward to ensure the royalty (the "truth," "legitimacy," or "authenticity") of an enduring black line of descent. In his outgoing phallic energy, therefore, the sharecropper is (as we learn on his first appearance in *Invisible Man*) a "hard worker" who takes care of "his family's needs." His family may, in a very real sense, be construed as the entire clan, or tribe, of Afro-America.

As cosmic creator, Trueblood is not bound by ordinary codes of restraint. He ventures chaos in an outrageously sexual manner—and survives. Like the Winnebago trickster Wakdjunkaga, he offers an inversive play on social norms. He is the violator of boundaries who—unlike the scapegoat—eludes banishment. Indeed, he is so essential to whites in his sexual role that, after demonstrating his enviable ability to survive chaos, he and his family acquire new clothes and shoes, abundant food and work, long-needed eyeglasses, and even the means to reshingle their cabin. "I looks up at the mornin' sun," says the farmer, describing the aftermath of his incestuous act, "and expects somehow for it to thunder. But it's already bright and clear. . . . I yells, 'Have mercy lawd!' and waits. And there's nothin' but the clear bright mornin' sun."

Noting that most tricksters "have an uncertain sexual status," Victor Turner points out that on some occasions

> tricksters appear with exaggerated phallic characteristics: Hermes is symbolized by the herm of pillar, the club, and the ithyphallic statue; Wakdjunkaga has a very long penis which has to be wrapped around him and put over his shoulder in a box; Eshu is represented in sculpture as having a long curved hairdress carved as a phallus.

Such phallic figures are, for Turner, representatives of "liminality"—that "betwixt and between" phase of rites of passage when an individual has left one fixed social status but has not yet been incorporated into another. When African boys are secluded in the forest during circumcision rites, for example, they are in a liminal phase between childhood and adulthood. During this seclusion they receive mythic instruction in the origin and structures of their society. This instruction serves not only to "deconstruct" the components of the ordered social world they have left behind but also to reveal these elements recombined into new and powerful composites. The phallic trickster aptly represents the duality of this process. In his radically antinomian activities — incest, murder, and the destruction of sacred property — he symbolically captures what Turner describes as the "amoral and nonlogical" rhythms and outcomes of human biology and of meteorological climate, that is, the uncontrollable rhythms of nature. But the trickster is also a cultural gift bearer. Turner emphasizes that "the Winnebago trickster transforms the pieces of his broken phallus into plants and flowers for men." Hermes enriches human culture with dreams and music. In a sense, therefore, the phallic trickster is a force that is, paradoxically, both anticonventional and culturally benevolent. The paradox is dissolved in the definition of the trickster as the "*prima materia* — as undifferentiated raw material" from which all things derive. Trueblood's sexual energies, antinomian acts, productive issue, and resonant expressivity make him — in his incestuous, liminal moments and their immediate aftermath — the quintessential trickster.

In his sexual manifestation, Ellison's sharecropper challenges not only the mundane restraints of his environment but also the fundamental Judeo-Christian categories on which they are founded. As I have already noted, he quickly abandons the notion of the knife — of casting out, in Mr. Norton's indignant (and wonderfully ironic) phrase, "the offending eye." His virtual parodies of the notions of sin and sacrifice lend comic point to his latitudinarian challenge to Christian orthodoxy. When his wife brings the sharpened ax down on his head, Trueblood recalls, "I see it, Lawd, yes! I sees it and seein' it I twists my head aside. Couldn't help it . . . I moves. Though I meant to keep still, I moves! Anybody but Jesus Christ hisself woulda moved." So much for repentance and salvation through the bloody sacrifice of one's life. But Trueblood goes on to indicate why such sacrifice may not have been required of him: with the skill of a revisionist theologian, he distinguishes between "blood-sin" and "dream-sin" and claims, with unshakable certainty, that only the dream of his encounter at the Broadnax household led to his sexual arousal and subsequent incest.

But while this casuistic claim suffices in the farmer's interaction with the social world, his earlier appraisal of the event suggests his role as a cosmically rebellious trickster. He says that when he awoke to discover himself atop Matty Lou, he felt that the act might not be sinful, because it happened in his sleep. But then he adds "although maybe sometimes a man can look at a little old pigtail gal and see him a whore." The naturalness, and the natural unpredictability, of sexual arousal implied by "although" seem more in keeping with the sharecropper's manifestation as black phallic energy.

Trueblood's sexual energies are not without complement in the arid regions where the sharecropper and his family eke out their existence. His wife, Kate, is an awesome force of both new life and outgoing socioreligious fury. His yard is filled with the children she has borne, and his oldest child, Matty Lou, is Kate's double—a woman fully grown and sexually mature who looks just like her mother. Kate and Matty Lou—both moving with the "full-fronted motions of far-gone pregnancy"—are the first human figures Mr. Norton sees as he approaches the Trueblood property. The two bearers of new black life are engaged in a rite of purification, a workaday ritual of washing clothes in a huge boiling cauldron; which takes on significance as the men situate themselves in a semi-circle near the porch where the "earth . . . was hard and white from where wash water had long been thrown." In a sense the women (who flee behind the house at Norton's approach) are present, by ironic implication, as the share-cropper once more confessionally purges himself—as he, in vernacular terms, again "washes his dirty linen" before a white audience. Further, Matty Lou, as the object of Trueblood's incestuous desire, and Kate, as the irate agent of his punishment for fulfilling his desire, assume significant roles in his narrative.

The reversal of a traditional Freudian typology represented by Trueblood's dream encounter at the Broadnax Big House is reinforced by an implied parody of the Christian myth of the Fall. For if the white Mrs. Broadnax serves as the temptress Eve in the dream, then Matty Lou becomes an ersatz Eve, the paradoxical recipient of the farmer's lust. Similarly, if Mr. Broadnax—an inhabitant of the sanctuary-like precincts of a house of "lighted candles and shiny furniture, and pictures on the walls, and soft stuff on the floor"—is the avenging father, or patriarch, of the dream, then the matriarchal Kate replaces him in exacting vengeance. The "fall" of Trueblood is thus enacted on two planes—on a dream level of Christian myth and on a quotidian level of southern black actuality. In its most intensely conscious and secular interpretation, the incestuous act is a rank violation that drives Kate to blind and murderous rage: "I heard Kate scream. It was a scream to make your blood run cold. It sounds like a woman who was watching a team of wild horses run down her baby chile and she caint move. . . . She screams and starts to pickin' up the first thing that comes to her hand and throwin' it."

The "doubleness" of Kate and Matty Lou is felt in the older woman's destructive and avenging energies, which elevate her to almost legendary proportions. Her woman's wrath at the sharecropper's illicit violation of "my chile!" spirals, inflating Kate to the metaphorical stature of an implacable executioner: "Then I sees her right up on me, big. She's swingin' her arms like a man swingin' a ten-pound sledge and I sees the knuckles of her hand is bruised and bleedin . . . and I sees her swing and I smells her sweat and . . . I sees that ax." Trueblood tries to forestall Kate's punishing blow but, he says, he "might as well been pleadin' with a switch engine." The ax falls, and the farmer receives the wound whose blood spills on Matty Lou. The wound becomes the "raw and moist" scar the protagonist notices when he first moves "up close" on the sharecropper.

Kate becomes not only an awesome agent of vengeance in the sharecropper's account but also the prime mover of the parodic ritual drama enacted in the chilly southern cabin. It is Kate's secular rage that results in the substitute castration-crucifixion represented by Trueblood's wound. She is the priestess who bestows the scarifying lines of passage, of initiation—the marks that forever brand the farmer as a "dirty lowdown wicked dog." At her most severe, she is the moral, or socioreligious, agent of both Trueblood's "marking" and his exile. She banishes him from the community that rallies to support her in her sorrow. In keeping with her role as purifier—as supervisor of the wash—she cleans up the pollution, the dirt and danger, represented by Trueblood's taboo act.

It is important to bear in mind, however, that while Kate is a figure of moral outrage, she is also a fertile woman who, like her husband, provides "cultural gifts" in the form of new life. In her family manifestation, she is less a secular agent of moral justice than a sensitive, practical parent who turns away in sick disgust at the wound she inflicts on Trueblood. And though she first banishes the farmer, she also accepts his return, obeys his interdiction against abortions for herself and Matty Lou, and welcomes the material gains that ironically accrue after Trueblood's fall from grace. The sharecropper says, "Except that my wife an' daughter won't speak to me, I'm better off than I ever been before. And even if Kate won't speak to me she took the new clothes I brought her from up in town and now she's gettin' some eyeglasses made what she been needin' for so long."

As a woman possessed of a practical (one might say a "blues") sensibility, Kate knows that men are, indeed, sometimes "dirty lowdown wicked" dogs who can perceive a whore in a pigtailed girl. She is scarcely resigned to such a state of affairs where her own daughter is concerned, but like the black mother so aptly described in Carolyn Rodgers's poem "It Is Deep," Kate knows that being "religiously girdled in her god" will not pay the bills. She thus brings together the sacred and the secular, the moral and the practical, in a manner that makes her both a complement for Trueblood and (again in the words of Rodgers) a woman who "having waded through a storm, is very obviously, a sturdy Black bridge."

To freight Trueblood's sexual manifestation and its complement in Kate with more significance than they can legitimately bear would be as much a critical disservice as were previous failures, or refusals, even to acknowledge these aspects. For while it is true that sexuality burdens the content of his narrative, it is also true that Trueblood himself metaphorically transforms his incestuous act into a single, symbolic instance of his total life situation:

> There I was [atop Matty Lou] trying to git away with all my might, yet
> having to move *without* movin'. I flew in but I had to walk out. I had
> to move without movin'. I done thought 'bout it since a heap, and

when you think right hard you see that that's the way things is always
been with me. That's just about been my life.

Like the formidable task of the Invisible Man's grandfather, who gave up
his gun during the Reconstruction but still had to fight a war, Trueblood's problem is that of getting out of a tight spot without undue motion—without per-
ceptibly moving. The grandfather adopted a strategy of extrication by indirec-
tion, pretending to affirm the designs of the dominant white society around
him. Having relinquished his gun, he became "a spy in the enemy's country," a
man overcoming his adversaries with yeses. He represents the trickster as subtle
deceiver. Trueblood, in contrast, claims that to "move without movin'" means
to take a refractory situation uncompromisingly in hand: "You got holt to it,"
he says, "and yo caint let go even though you want to." He conceives of himself
in the throes of his incestuous ecstasies as "like that fellow . . . down in Bir-
mingham. That one what locked hisself in his house and shot [with a gun that he
had *refused to give up*] at them police until they set fire to the house and
burned him up. I was lost." An energetic, compulsive, even ecstatically expressive response is required:

> Like that fellow [in Birmingham], I stayed. . . . He mighta died,
> but I suspects now that he got a heapa satisfaction before he went. I
> *know* there ain't nothin' like what I went through, I caint tell how it
> was. It's like when a real drinkin' man gets drunk, or like a real sanc-
> tified religious woman gits so worked up she jumps outta her
> clothes, or when a real gamblin' man keeps on gamblin' when he's
> losing.

In his energetic response, Trueblood says a resounding no to all the castratingly
tight spots of his existence as a poor black farmer in the undemocratic south.

The most discursively developed *expressive* form of this no is, of course, the
narrative that Trueblood relates. But he has come to this narrative by way of
music. He has fasted and reflected on his guilt or innocence until he thinks his
"brain go'n bust," and then he recalls, "one night, way early in the mornin', I
looks up and sees the stars and I starts singin'. I don't know what it was, some
kinda church song, I guess. All I know is I *ends up* singin' the blues. I sings me
some blues that night ain't never been sang before." The first unpremeditated
expression that Trueblood summons is a religious song. But the religious system
that gives birth to the song is, presumably, one in which the term "incest" carries
pejorative force. Hence, the sharecropper moves on, spontaneously, to the
blues.

MICHAEL G. COOKE

Solitude

The mobile and urgent reaffirmation of the phrase "I am" in the opening paragraphs of the prologue to Ellison's *Invisible Man* bears scrutiny. It occurs eight times in sixteen lines (plus once in the preterit "I have been"). It occurs without clamor, without strain. What Bigger Thomas [in *Native Son*] gets by agony the Invisible Man seems to possess by instinct, or at least by virtue of irony. He plays at once with the fact of his being and with the social conception of his being black. With his unrolling of complements to complete the predication "I am"—"an invisible man," "not a spook," "nor . . . Hollywood-movie ectoplasm," "a man of substance, . . . even . . . [possessing] a mind," "invisible," "not complaining, nor . . . protesting"—he shows that he is marked by urbanity, forbearance, amusement, a wry touch of cultural history and mild debunking, and a gracious eschewing of rightful resentment. All in all, a prepossessing performance, and surely such as to reassure the likes of Boris Max in *Native Son*. The foursquare challenge and demand for recognition posed by Bigger is mollified here, and an easy if not simple mode of intercourse set up; no one need be alarmed about invisibility (caused by the society, suffered by the speaker), or about the social repercussions of invisibility (caused by the speaker, suffered by the society).

But abruptly the narrator shifts from the deft and authoritative "I am" into an impersonal, neutralized "you're," though still talking about himself. A kind of grammatical schizophrenia is taking place. And the evidence builds up that the difference between the unlettered Bigger and the literate, nearly elegant Invisible Man is more apparent than real. Jack-the-Bear also has eruptions of

From *Afro-American Literature in the Twentieth Century.* © 1984 by Michael G. Cooke. Yale University Press, 1984. Originally entitled "Solitude: The Beginnings of Self-Realization in Zora Neale Hurston, Richard Wright, and Ralph Ellison."

defensive violence, which he transposes on to the audience: "You ache with the need to convince yourself that you do exist in the real world . . . and you strike out . . . , you curse and you swear to make them recognize you." He too experiences self-cancelling dislocations, but into nightmares rather than magical movies and images: "You wonder whether you aren't simply a phantom in other people's minds. Say, a figure in a nightmare which the sleeper tries with all his strength to destroy." There is something of Bishop Berkeley in the idea of an entity existing only as a phantom in the mind, but the basic thrust of the language goes less toward epistemology than toward pathology; and the nightmare (which is the nightmare of reality for the black man) smacks of Goya or Fuseli.

The Prologue sets the amplitude of *Invisible Man,* from urbane humor to violence and phantasmagoria. The protagonist goes overnight from being a favored (if also carefully governed) student in a black college in the South to being an unwitting outcast who is "kept running" through a kaleidoscopic world of authoritarian business organizations and authoritarian political groups, on the one hand, and disorganized but rebellious and explosive individuals, on the other. He has the curious attribute of being a misfit everywhere, being too much of an organization man for the rebels and too much of a rebel for the authoritarians. But he is searching for a way to fit in, and keeps credulously thinking that a cryptic deathbed message from his grandfather or a supposed recommendation from his college president or a well-calculated political speech will do the trick. The emphatic repetition of the words "I am" in the Prologue is a confession of desperate need rather than a proof of self-knowledge. We will have to come to terms with the fact that, for all his elaborate experience, he ends in a state of confusedly expectant solitude. Ellison himself pointedly comments on the ironic freight of Jack-the-Bear's "infinite possibilities" (*Shadow and Act*).

Leaving the Prologue for the story proper, one finds the attributes of the "I am" all the more problematical. Jack-the-Bear says he took unusually long to "achieve a realization . . . [that] I am nobody but myself." This seems at first blush a sober and honorable piece of personal metaphysics, but it is shadowed by two pieces of problematical data. First, Jack-the-Bear's grandfather, a cryptic guru of the text, professes to "have been a traitor all my born days," and it is clear that he has been so not only to the white "enemy" but also to his unrealized self. His "yeses" and his "grins" are meant to keep the white man at bay, and perhaps to get the best of him. Presumably they constitute a form of signifying, but both significance and efficacy perish in the perfection of his gestures. Nothing is seen or known save yeses and grins. They are his legacy, but no one is sure how to interpret it, let alone use it. If a yes and a grin do not mean acquiescence, but defiance, this fact is virtually unrecognizable; the old man who advises his heirs to "yes them to death" has brought only himself to death, unfulfilled. His signifying signifies defeat. Ultimately the Invisible Man, though capable of believing that to ring changes on yes will enable him to "walk around in their guts with hobnailed boots," recognizes this for himself, recognizes that he has been outmanipulated, veritably "out-yessed": "by pretending to agree I *had* indeed agreed, had made myself responsible for that huddled form lighted by flame and gunfire in the street, and all the others whom now the night was making ripe for death."

Tod Clifton would stand as a better case of signifying, which Ellison himself defines as "rhetorical understatement" (*Shadow and Act*). Taken on the surface level of his behavior, Tod Clifton, of course, presents little evidence of understatement; even his friend the Invisible Man looks upon Tod's obscene sidewalk dolls as a shocking sign of degradation. But when Tod stands up for his honor against the policeman, it is clear that he has not simply come apart and sunk into cheap lewdness and greed. The dolls are telling us something besides what they say. In effect they are a prophecy of the revolt he soon makes explicit by defying the policeman; they reveal his opinion of society's taste and his knowledge of society's character. With Tod Clifton, Ellison condenses the slow social movement from signifying to rebellion. But when Tod in his use of his fists acts forthrightly, instead of signifying, the police take advantage of their position to signify by acting forthrightly: law enforcement is the vehicle for expressing an unstated will to destroy a Tod Clifton. The issue of the form of an act versus what that act signifies is of course a major bone of contention between the Invisible Man and the leaders of the Brotherhood; they see Tod in terms of what his act says socially, not what it signifies culturally and metaphysically.

Second, as George Kent has observed, Jack-the-Bear's "I am nobody but myself" is echoed exactly by Jim Trueblood, the incestuous father who tells of his act with an unsettled blend of shame and humor, and who profits from it with gratification and bafflement: "sings me some blues that night ain't never been sang before, and while I'm singin' them blues I makes up my mind that *I ain't nobody but myself*" (italics added). What is entailed in this sameness, at once linguistic and metaphysical, between the radically unreflective, shallowly sensual, blabbing protodegenerate Trueblood and the ambitious, fastidious, analytical, political, cautious, cryptoidealistic Jack-the-Bear? Like the Invisible Man the highly visible Trueblood has gone through unintended, though not finally unchosen, violations of taboos that *prove revelatory,* and both envision a definitive coming back to society that somehow does not amount to anything more than a suspended state of living off the white power structure. They further share a tendency to materialism, to blink basic human issues for the sake of what the ex-colored man calls "comfort and luxury" (it is not clear whether Jack-the-Bear abandons or is driven away from his materialism). It is notable too that

Trueblood's tale shows the same stylistic play of horror and comedy as the Invisible Man's narration, and that Trueblood, like the Invisible Man, is a renowned storyteller-speaker. Does Trueblood serve as a shamefully, and shamelessly, visible alter ego for the "invisible" Jack-the-Bear? Does he represent the *action* that identifies and isolates, to Jack-the-Bear's *conception* that identifies and isolates?

The subtlest but also perhaps the strongest link between Trueblood and the Invisible Man is their solitude. The relation between them is not parallel but complementary. Trueblood's is the solitude of an *unthinking* Oedipus. The ax-slash on his face corresponds to the Theban king's lost eyes, and marks him as one to be seen and shunned by the world; his experience has been social and external, and so is his penalty, without the psychomoral complexities of atonement. (Mythology offers us, in Philoctetes and Tiresias for example, the idea of injury as a sign of election. I do not see Trueblood as a figure in this scheme of understanding.) Jack-the-Bear knows the solitude of the *enlightened* Oedipus, whose blindness tells of his need not to see, or rather not to have seen a certain world.

In this connection let us recall that *Invisible Man* is framed by oblique violations of sex taboos, with Oedipal overtones. "Had the price of looking," Jack-the-Bear says of the naked blonde at the opening smoker scene, "been blindness, I would have looked," this despite his "irrational guilt and fear." In terms of strength of taboo, we may see here an analogy between incest and sexual activity with a white woman. This analogy is confirmed in Trueblood's dream, in which approaching a white woman is as full of dread as waking to recognize his daughter. The text gives indications that interracial sex may exceed incest in the strictness of its taboo, since Trueblood's transgression is indulged by the surrounding white community and proved dangerously attractive to Norton, whereas the final riot is set off by a black kid making a cop mad "by grabbing a candy named after a white woman." Even so indirect and trivial a "grabbing" as this triggers a possessive and punitive reaction. The taboo is not for the protection of society, but for the persecution and oppression of its black members.

Jack-the-Bear, or "Boogie Bear," is personally involved in this recrudescence of the taboo theme at the novel's end. He deliberately sets out to seduce a white woman, "one of the [Brotherhood's] big shots' wives," in a compound violation of sexual and political taboos. Nothing happens, in fact, but the posture, the *will* of violation is assumed and despite his final reneging the canonical consequence ensues: Jack-the-Bear loses connection with others, and indeed by calculation *chooses* disconnection from others. He has been much manipulated, it is true; when he finally stumbles upon this fact and, almost simultaneously, catches sight of the effectiveness of the protean Rinehart personality, he naturally is inclined to turn the tables and become the manipulator. But it remains true that manipulation equals violation. He inadvertently manipulates himself not only out of the artificial Brotherhood, but also out of the Harlem community, and ultimately out of the human community in his manhole existence.

It will be useful to distinguish between the way the novel associates Jack-the-Bear and Trueblood, on the one hand, and Jack-the-Bear and Rinehart on the other. Jack-the-Bear falls into the role of Rinehart, much as he falls into the manhole, by accident; and he makes use of the role of Rinehart, much as he does his sojourn in the manhole, to explore both the practical and the philosophical aspects of his experience. But he recognizes that the manhole is a stage, a convenient instrument for him, just as his assumption of the role of Rinehart has been. The Invisible Man is obliged to leave both this role and his manhole, or at least chooses to do so.

With Trueblood, he has no such choice. The association between them is not social and accidental, but primary and intrinsic. We may note that after each encounter with Trueblood and with Rinehart, the Invisible Man is thrown out of his established world, but in the Rinehart situation the sequence is merely adventitious. In fact, the plunging off the surface of life only extends the sense of instability and incoherence that the Rinehart episode induces. To the contrary, there is a genuine causal connection between the Trueblood episode and the Invisible Man's expulsion from college. (It is the Golden Day that, in the exposition of the novel, corresponds to the Rinehart episode with its confusion of identities and of values.) The identification between Jack-the-Bear and Trueblood, in short, tells us something basic about Jack-the-Bear, whereas the exchange of identity with Rinehart only tells us something about his world.

In the end Jack-the-Bear lives in indefinite solitude, in a world peopled by lights that offer number without substance or variety. It is as abstract as the first day of creation, and as pathetic as the impossibility of the second. The lights represent an obsessive literalization of his symbolic intent to bring light on his own situation and to bring its light to the world. He has a *fiat lux* at his disposal, but it is furtive and defiant. He is as improbable a "God" as Bledsoe, who dares to say to the sophomoric Jack-the-Bear: "your arms are too short to box with me." He is his own final mentor, and no more adept than a Bledsoe or a Jack or the ill-chosen Sybil who, far from making an illuminating and liberating pattern of the fragments of his sociopolitical experience, ties him to the cliché of overpowering sensuality ("you big black bruiser") that his being a black man triggers in her mind.

The fall into the manhole is a happy one, in that it saves his life. It is symbolically important too, not so much because it suggests the plunge "out of history" that he so dreads, but because it consummates the pattern of lurkings, twistings, and accidentality that informs the Invisible Man's experience. It follows the scene where he is most with others, with Dupre, Scofield, and the rest in the riot, but he joins them as superficially and as meaninglessly as possible, though ironically getting great credit for being there: "Brother . . . , you said you would lead us." It is more as if he were losing himself, "merging" in Bigger Thomas's escapist sense, than as if he were finding an identity. He says as much: "I was one with the mass, . . . my personality blasted."

Nor can he sustain even this limited condition; something impels him to detach himself, to opt for observation where he should take action: "Shouldering my way to the side I stood in a doorway and watched them move." The little he does on his own in tightening the tourniquet on the arm of an injured man only proves that he is essentially a bystander, without any reliable function or position in the scheme of things. He is astonished to be taken for a doctor. As he says, in a symbolic declaration of terrible simplicity: "I couldn't cure a headache." This moment, with its confusion of identity, reminds us of the Rinehart episode, but conveys a sense of beneficial action and healing, whereas Rinehart embodies only protean emptiness and escapism. The sense of possibility is not accepted, let alone sustained, by Jack-the-Bear. In the manhole he pronounces on his "infinite possibilities," but they are infinite mainly by virtue of having neither specificity nor focus.

Soon, too, pressed by Scofield, he is denying the name of "brother" that he had so proudly and enthusiastically adopted before. (It is ironic that the novel's theory of brotherhood should be confined to the cold political order.) The vocabulary of withdrawal and solitude gathers momentum rapidly: "I ran, going away, leaving Scofield"; "I went on, plunged in a sense of painful isolation"; "I am no longer their brother" (this in the midst of standing solitary against Ras and his henchmen); "If only I could . . . say, 'Look, . . . let's stop running and respect and love one another.' . . . If only . . ."; "as though I sat remote in a padded room"; and finally, in yet another point of identification with Trueblood, "I was caught like Trueblood's jaybird that yellow jackets had paralyzed in every part but his eyes." Trueblood, by analogy, gives us a singular insight into Jack-the-Bear's solitude, in its social and moral or spiritual dimensions. Actually, Jack-the-Bear articulates this:

> You stand naked and shivering before the millions of eyes who look through you unseeingly. *That* is the real soul-sickness, the spear in the side, the drag by the neck through the mob-angry town; the Grand Inquisition, the embrace of the Maiden, the rip in the belly with the guts spilling out, the trip to the chamber with the deadly gas that ends in the oven so hygienically clean—only it's worse because you continue stupidly to live.

But the fact that the Invisible Man articulates his position, and does not only embody it like Trueblood, implies at least a potential possession in the Du Boisian mode, and implies a potential freedom. He communicates from solitude. His knowledge that something is amiss with him becomes the instrument for social scrutiny ("Who knows but that, on the lower frequencies, I speak for you?") and the basis for a hope, even a program: "I'm shaking off the old skin and I'll leave it here in the hole. . . . And I suppose it's damn well time. . . . There's a possibility that even an invisible man has a socially responsible role to play." Solitude, or hibernation, takes on an idealistic color or, as Verlaine said of symbolism, *nuance*. Jack-the-Bear's is the voice of solitude, but the voice has a freedom and a mission that the Ex-Colored Man only briefly aspired to, and that Bigger Thomas never even brought to the pitch of aspiration. Cleansed of catchwords like "brother," the Invisible Man turns out to have more than a paralytic's eyes; he has a voice that speaks from solitude to, and sympathetically for, any man: ". . . I speak for you."

The significance of this projection bears spelling out, for the voice is what the Ex-Colored Man denied himself, what Janie [Crawford of *Their Eyes Were Watching God*] and Bigger Thomas were denied, and what Jack-the-Bear himself had dreaded to use save as a ventriloquist's dummy for a Bledsoe or a Jack. His voice means not only that he has a sense of having found himself, but also that he has found a basis of relationship with others. Someone else is there — the solitude is not perfect — and that someone is likely to be somehow genuinely accessible, akin to him. One goes back to the opening section of the novel with its subtle and complex cadences sustaining the bald avowal: "I am." We may say that the Invisible Man chooses himself in his hole, whereas the Ex-Colored Man chooses a hole for himself. What Ellison in "Richard Wright's Blues" calls "the American Negro impulse toward self-annihilation and going underground" (*Shadow and Act*) is inseparable from the impulse toward self-renovation, self-discovery, and self-assertion or, perhaps better, self-justification. That is to say, the self against all adversity and without glossing over its own weakness and waywardness reaches a point of readiness, a beginning that allows for purpose and tolerance, emphasis and irony, individuality and identification. As Ellison says, "being a Negro American involves a *willed* . . . affirmation of self against all outside pressures" (*Shadow and Act*).

This is a hard-won position. It must be remembered that the life condition of the black people the Invisible Man meets, from rural college days to city life and on to political life and even well into the climactic riot, shames and repels him. That is what he wishes, strives, to get away from. He identifies himself as a black man, rather than with the black man. When he eats the sweet yam on the street — already a departure from the upswing standards he has set for himself —

and pronounces with punning decisiveness, "I yam what I yam," it is a matter of a moment, a mood, rather than a turning point in his philosophy. Tod Clifton's death comes closer to constituting a change, but while it makes the Invisible Man, down in the subway, speak of "us transitory ones" in relation to the "three boys . . . distorted in the interest of design," it does not cause him to lose his "feverish isolation" or to intervene on behalf of the candy-filching boys near the five and ten (an old woman does that instead).

Only in the ultimate isolation of the manhole ("there is nothing like isolating a man to make him think") does he find a philosophy or a life posture that offers reconciliation with himself, his whole history, and his humanity. He can now "denounce and defend . . . , say no and say yes, say yes and say no." Nor does he speak only for himself. While at the outset of the novel he shifts from "I" to "you," striving for communion, here he shifts from "I" to "we," incorporating himself into humanity and humanity into himself: "Our fate is to become one, and yet many"; "sometimes I feel the need to reaffirm all of it, the whole unhappy territory and all the things loved and unlovable in it, for all of it is part of me."

And yet it is clear that the Invisible Man, like Bigger Thomas and Janie Crawford, has seen things intimately without achieving intimacy through them, just as he has recognized more than he has accepted kinship with other people.

Invisible Man is distinctly Janus-faced, looking back on accomplished events and looking forward to new accomplishment in personal action and being. This latter remains deeply problematical. The novel exhibits a conflict between (1) verification, or the reproduction of experience as having taken place, and (2) validation, or objective possession and articulation of his experience as belonging in a scheme of understanding and value. In fact, the speaker displaces validation unto the reader, unto *us* ("who knows but that . . . I speak for you?"). It might be urged that he has no choice, being uncertain of the reader's position. But that is to presuppose a white reader, indeed a hostile and unjust white reader, whereas the text holds out value and revelation to both black and white, both sympathetic and hostile readers. His tentativeness with us is a projection of inner doubt and irresolution. He says himself that he has accepted "the lesson," but he does not identify it and he is not sure what it amounts to, whether it puts him "in the rear or the *avant-garde*," reminding us of Ishmael Reed's mischievous declaration that "I called it pin the tail on the devil / they called it avant garde" ("if my enemy is a clown, a natural born clown," in *Conjure*). The Invisible Man's grandfather describes life as a situation in which one may "start Saul and end up Paul," and here again proves a cryptic if not devious guide. No conversion, no positive new commitment or conviction, actually emerges from the hole any more than the Invisible Man himself emerges. Indeed, he makes a point of suggesting that if he speaks for us we don't really know what he says: "So there you have all of it that's important. Or at least you *almost* have it." That *almost* does not refer to the few pages that remain to be written but to the reader's essential grasp, or more accurately, the writer's essential intention and conviction. If "all of it" is part of him, but he can't give us "all of it," the reverse becomes critical. We do not doubt him; he has achieved verification. But we cannot follow him, because he is not positively going anywhere; he remains suspended in hibernation, and short of validation.

In effect, Jack-the-Bear seems able to make only set speeches face to face. As he has been a hit-and-run orator in the eviction scene, so he becomes a hit-and-hide orator in the hole; in Addison Gayle's view, he is "faceless, formless, and rootless." If we go back to Trueblood for a moment, we can see that he displaces his will to violate taboo *and* his wish to seem to do so by accident or force of circumstances, unto the dream state, or unto his daughter's supposed sexual knowingness. That trick of displacement gives one sense of the Invisible Man's message about speaking for *us*. He will not speak forthrightly, in his own right; even his falling back on the Constitution is a poignant example of speaking by rote. Though he does invoke the Constitution, his solitude remains not only social and spiritual, but also political. He is cut off from any structure or mode of relationship that would bear on the organization and exercise of power in society. In this connection the Invisible Man differs from Janie and from Bigger Thomas by virtue of his half-hortatory, half-minatory desire to reach out, whereas Janie has no such desire and Bigger no opportunity.

The three texts of solitude, *Their Eyes Were Watching God, Native Son* and *Invisible Man,* represent frustrations of kinship and circumstantial violations of intimacy. If not the central then certainly the culminating action of each text is murder or widespread mayhem; each is marked by human dissociation or abuse. The protagonist in each case gains knowledge of a positive world, but remains unable to act on that knowledge, short of command or possession over anything but his or her own solitude. The failure of fulfillment is both psychic and social for Janie Crawford and Bigger Thomas; the act of homicide keeps one from one's kind.

The Invisible Man's failure has subtler causes. It is tied on one level to the obscure or displaced taboo violation of his experience, and on another to the fact that he simply does not know how to act on his own. He simply is accustomed to reacting and adjusting, taking his motive force from outside. Left to himself, he comes to a total halt. Still, he is the one who can look to something more than expiation of a specific crime, like Bigger, or devotion to a specific shrine, like Janie. He is the one with a catholic prospect: "all of it is part of me." That prospect is pivotal for the further development of Afro-American literature.

DOUGLAS ROBINSON

Call Me Jonah

In *Invisible Man* the Jonah motif is central. Not only is the novel plotted around a series of symbolic descents and returns, deaths and rebirths, but its macrostructure itself reflects the three phases of Jonah's ethical growth: (1) ironic phase—main narrative; (2) synecdochic phase—Prologue; (3) metonymical phase—Epilogue. This may seem a simplistic reduction of the novel to the terms of my Jonah motif, but if one reads the novel as an *elaboration* of this bare outline, I think it makes sense.

Consider, first of all, the parallels between Ellison's main narrative and the first chapter of the Book of Jonah. Like Jonah, Ellison's narrator moves through the novel in *flight,* an external and unconscious (though increasingly conscious) flight from a series of paternalistic manipulators (Bledsoe, Lucius Brockway, Brother Jack) who use him ostensibly in his own best interests, but in fact entirely for their own gain. This flight repeatedly leads him into apocalyptic situations that, as in Poe's *Pym,* develop by a sequential dynamic of intensification, each cataclysm more explosive than its predecessors: the battle-royal in chapter 1, the pandemonium at the Golden Day in chapter 3, the boiler-room explosion at the Liberty Paint factory in chapter 10, and the Harlem riot in chapter 25. As the apocalypses intensify, the reader's sense that the end of the world is in the offing grows, until in the Harlem riot it seems the end does finally impend, as interpreted by R. W. B. Lewis:

> The chaos is total and ubiquitous. It represents the considered program, as it were, of the agents of Antichrist for drawing the world

From *American Apocalypses: The Image of the End of the World in American Literature.*
© 1985 by The Johns Hopkins University Press.

onward to the great catastrophe—with the manifest intention of seizing power in the post-catastrophic wreckage. For Ellison has elevated his political theme, the familiar authoritarian strategy of making disaster serve the ends of conquest, into universal apocalyptic significance.

Even within the main narrative, however, this reading is questionable. Note how Lewis hedges on agents, for example. If they are of the biblical Antichrist, there is no need to seize power *after* the apocalypse, since Antichrist holds power now. And Lewis's "as it were" indicates that he really wants to use Antichrist metaphorically, to describe the displaced apocalyptic characteristics of political power-holders like Bledsoe and the Brotherhood—which is in fact the only Antichrist for which there is textual warrant. The problem is, if "Antichrist" is no more than an aggregate of powerful human beings, then the "great catastrophe" is only partial, and can have no "universal apocalyptic significance." Chaos may be ubiquitous, but it is by no means total. If men survive the great catastrophe to seize power in the "post-catastrophic wreckage," then it *wasn't* the great catastrophe.

Lewis's apocalyptic reading of *Invisible Man* becomes even more dubious when Ellison's narrator takes us out of the main narrative, out of history, into the mental landscape, the underground haunt—the whale's belly—of the Prologue and Epilogue. For the invisible narrator follows Jonah out of the external world of ships/riot and geographical travel into the internal world of dark imprisonment; as Jonah is swallowed by the whale, the Invisible Man is swallowed by the manhole in which he hides from his white pursuers:

> "You goddam black nigger sonofabitch," someone called, "see how you like this," and I heard the cover settle over the manhole with a dull clang. . . . [Ellipsis mine] Then I thought, This is the way it's always been, only now I know it—and rested back, calm now, placing the brief case beneath my head. I could open it in the morning, push off the lid. Now I was tired, too tired; my mind retreating, the image of the two glass eyes running together like blobs of melting lead. Here it was as though the riot was gone and I felt the tug of sleep, seemed to move out upon black water.
>
> It's a kind of death without hanging, I thought, a death alive. In the morning I'll remove the lid . . . Mary, I should have gone to Mary's. I would go now to Mary's in the only way that I could . . . I moved off over the black water, floating, sighing . . . sleeping invisibly [ellipses Ellison's].

But I was never to reach Mary's, and I was over-optimistic about removing the steel cap in the morning. Great invisible waves of time flowed over me, but that morning never came.

Here, at the close of the ironic phase in his Jonah-progress, the Invisible Man finds himself locked underground in total darkness, which he describes as at once "a kind of death" and a descent into invisible sleep. "This is the way it's always been," he now realizes, "only now I know it"—it's always been dark, he's always been invisible. The reality he thought was substantial is revealed as illusion—apparent presence is revealed as absence, and the absence of total dark is revealed as the only presence he has ever known.

Once the absence of his invisible has been revealed as *internality,* as the inwardness of his underground prison, the Invisible Man begins the labor of converting inwardness into outwardness, dark into light—the synecdochic phase of his progress described in the Prologue. Another way of describing this second phase might be to see in it an inversion of Plato's allegory of the cave: outside the cave, under the sun, the Invisible Man learns negatively, he *unlearns,* a process figured by the encroaching chaos of apocalypse; in the cave, he begins in the darkness of shadowy ignorance and gradually generates *truth* (figured both by the artificial light of 1,369 lightbulbs and the sound of the blues on the phonograph) out of his own imagination. By synecdochic substitution, the apocalyptic dynamic of intensification here becomes a dynamic of *internalization.* Reality is turned inside out; the external historical reality that physically encloses his haunt becomes itself enclosed by the internal reality of the mind, lit by electric light, filled with the vibrations of the blues, wound up in the string of words that produces the novel.

Like Jonah's three days and three nights in the belly of the whale, of course, this is a solipsistic retreat; but it is a solipsism that is both necessary and fruitful, for it marks the narrator's realization of his invisibility and therefore of the imperative of transforming it. His task in this second phase is to reverse the part-whole, inside-outside alignments imposed on him by the outside world, discovering in his invisibility the true reality and in the white blindness that fails to see him the illusion that till now has passed for reality. As he says in the opening words of the Prologue:

> I am an invisible man. No, I am not a spook like those who haunted Edgar Allan Poe; nor am I one of your Hollywood-movie ectoplasms. I am a man of substance, of flesh and blood, fiber and liquids—and I might even be said to possess a mind. I am invisible, understand, simply because people refuse to see me. Like the bodiless heads you

see sometimes in circus sideshows, it is as though I have been surrounded by mirrors of hard, distorting glass. When they approach
me they see only my surroundings, themselves, or figments of their
imagination — indeed, everything and anything except me.

"You wonder," the narrator goes on, "whether you aren't simply a phantom in other people's minds. Say, a figure in a nightmare which the sleeper tries
with all his strength to destroy." The synecdochic reversal recorded in the Prologue, one might say, is an iconological reversal, in which the shadowy nightmare image perceived as a mental phantom by whites is revealed as physical
body, the *soma phusikos* or *sarx*, "flesh and blood, fiber and liquids," and the
bodily reality above ground is conceived as illusory shadow. Mirrors, then, as the
Invisible Man points out, create not images of the true substance, but *desub-
stantiate* by reflecting a distorted image, an illusion projected onto the night.
When a white man insults the narrator on a dark street, he beats the man and
nearly kills him — but suddenly "it occurred to me that the man had not *seen*
me, actually; that he, as far as he knew, was in the midst of a walking nightmare!
. . . Then I was amused. Something in this man's thick head had sprung out
and beaten him within an inch of his life." The confrontation is the product of
competing iconologies: whereas the narrator conceives both self and other as
substantial, as embodied minds, the white man, in a secularized inversion of
medieval demonology, images the narrator as a black spirit in the illusory guise
of a body — an illusion that would later, no doubt, mystify him by leaving visible
bruises.

What the apocalyptic events throughout the ironic main narrative destroy,
therefore, is not the world but the Invisible Man's vision of the world as projected through the lenses of the white man's iconology. The realization that he is
invisible marks the nadir of his ironic flight and necessitates the synecdochic
reimaginings of the Prologue; there, trapped in his underground hole, the narrator turns his world upside down — or, like Dante climbing down Satan's
chained body, finally comes to see the world right-side up. The difficulty with
this synecdochic understanding, however, is that while it reconciles the Invisible
Man to *himself*, it does not go far toward reconciling him to the *world*. The explosion of the white man's iconology in the narrator's mind does nothing to erase
it in the world, in the minds of others; and without such erasure, obviously, the
narrator's *social* circumstances can never change. "Hence again I have stayed in
my hole," he tells us in the Epilogue, "because up above there's an increasing
passion to make men conform to a pattern." The narrator now understands and
knows what he doesn't want; but what is there left for him to want? Why should
he come out of his hole? What can he *do* in the world above ground? What is

needed is some route to compromise that will not destroy the Invisible Man's new-found inward integrity—and the last few pages of the Epilogue record just this search, the search for a passage into Jonah's last phase of metonymical compromise. The narrator offers two alternatives: "Until some gang succeeds in putting the world in a strait jacket, its definition is possibility. Step outside the narrow borders of what men call reality and you step into chaos—ask Rinehart, he's a master of it—or imagination."

Chaos—or imagination. Chaos is what remains when one rejects the prevailing ideological fiction and has nothing to offer in its place—an ironic formlessness that Rinehart, the great swindler, represents and exploits. Rinehart is *free*—but for Ellison, freedom in a surrealistic world of shifting images is meaningless, and the narrator rejects it. What is needed is *imagination,* the recreation of reality in a more human form. Although the narrator never quite tells us what he plans to do with his life above ground—what the form of his metonymical compromise will be—my guess is that he intends to publish his novel, the novel that he has been writing in his underground haunt: the novel that has guided *him* to insight by the very act of writing and that may guide others as well. The clue to this reading appears in the last two paragraphs of the novel, in the narrator's two-fold reversal of his Prologue positon. Whereas earlier, before the narrator had written the novel, he denied any claim to social responsibility and insisted on his own substantiality, here, guided by artistic creation to deeper truths, he offers a new manifesto:

> I'm shaking off the old skin and I'll leave it here in the hole. I'm coming out, no less invisible without it, but coming out nevertheless. And I suppose it's damn well time. Even hibernations can be overdone, come to think of it. Perhaps that's my greatest social crime, I've overstayed my hibernation, since there's a posibility that even an invisible man has a socially responsibile role to play.
>
> "Ah," I can hear you say, "so it was all a build-up to bore us with his buggy jiving. He only wanted us to listen to him rave!" But only partially true: Being invisible and without substance, a disembodied voice, as it were, what else could I do? What else but try to tell you what was happening when your eyes were looking through? And it is this which frightens me:
>
> Who knows but that, on the lower frequencies, I speak for you?

Just when did he become "without substance, a disembodied voice"? He did so, I suggest, when he came to conceive himself not as a political activist nor as a solipsistic hermit, but as a *fictional speaker.* Invisibility, that is, is here reified as the imaginative power of voice, the narrator's inward vision metonymically reduced to black words on a white page that both move and illuminate as no political action can, because they allow readers to reify *their* invisibility as well. The novel is Ellison's verson of Jonah's plant — a visible reduction of inward vision that transcends compromise by *teaching*, by implanting itself, as it were, in the reader's imagination. Thus, far from predicting the imminent end of the world, Ellison's novel takes us through the symbolic landscapes of Jonah's descent and return, embodying for us not apocalypse but ethical growth — growth toward *ethos*, a fully developed and integrated self.

BERNDT OSTENDORF

Anthropology, Modernism, and Jazz

Ralph Waldo Ellison, though conscious of what he does and eloquent about the meaning of his art, is in his own words not a systematic thinker, certainly not one with a blueprint or program. Least of all does he believe in radical utopias or fundamental certainties. In all his work there is a healthy distrust of simple answers. Hence, any attempt to chart a map of his thinking about American literature and culture is doomed to a certain measure of failure. For he belongs, like his protagonist in *Invisible Man* to the tradition of American tinkerers, and he is, like his namesake Ralph Waldo Emerson, a manipulator of words—the French would call him a *bricoleur* of language.

And yet, the cumulative evidence of his stories, his essays, his novel and his carefully choreographed interviews, all of which will be treated as one universe of discourse, allows us to identity certain recurrent strategies of thinking, typical scenarios and interactions, arguments and scripts. I should watch my words, in keeping with the care Ellison brings to naming, and ought not to use terms which are conceptual straight jackets. The very caution against narrow pigeon-holing or against static certainties, however, brings us to a first and duly large discrimination. If we were to divide aesthetic paradigms and their attendant world views into those based on "being" and those based on "becoming" Ellison would favor the latter, and therefore opt for ritual, open-endedness, latency, ambivalence, and anti-structure. In all his work there is a negative bias against paradigms of being and hence against dogma, closure, blueprints, and structures. His temperament is antinomian, anti-ontological, pragmatic, and dramatistic. His meanings are therefore temporary and transient, or, in his own words,

© 1986 by Berndt Ostendorf. Published for the first time in this volume.

145

"experimental." His answers are of the yes—but sort, shot through with disclaimers and contradictions which mirror, condense, and clarify (but rarely resolve) the political and social ambiguities of black American existence in the New World.

Though Ellison favors dynamic paradigms, in his artistic practice he is said to have written himself into a Modernist deadlock. His work, in particular his novel, has become an awesome prisonhouse circumscribed by expectations of more and better things to come. This contradiction between open, fluid, improvisational social ideals and intimidating writerly practice needs to be elaborated. His fluid anthropology and stern Modernism are at odds or, perhaps, in constant negotiation. They could be seen as thesis and antithesis; and jazz might be the synthesis.

The three encompassing frames and their antagonistic relationship give meaning and direction both to his work and to his opinions. None of these frames takes on the hard contours of a program, to which Ellison would at all times be loyal. Rather he plays with them or improvises on them, as a jazz musician would use a head arrangement or chord progressions. To modify Kenneth Burke's metaphor, he "dances" in and around these frames. And both jazz and dance are of course key traditions of black expressive culture with deep meaning for Ellison's art.

Briefly defined, these three frames are (1) a ritual theory of culture and society which derives its vocabulary from symbolic action and anthropology. This frame includes and structures his ideas on black folklore. (2) Modernism, which shapes his ideas of a personal and collective literary tradition. This includes and structures his views on the place of the novel and on the antinomian function of black art in white society. Modernism in this sense is a loose periodization marking the rise of a special consciousness in Western art. Its theory of knowledge grows out of the ruling episteme of the late nineteenth century, put on the agenda by Marx, Nietzsche, and Freud. Their larger interest focused on the latency of the world, and their appropriate critical strategy was to bring the hitherto invisible into visibility. Marx attacked ideology as false consciousness; Freud, chief poet of the age, charted a deep and hidden cultural map of the mind; and Nietzsche destabilized tacit assumptions and taught us to take nothing for granted. While for many European Modernist artists this was an episteme of crisis and decline, Ellison, as American latecomer and black outsider, would read it as one of possibility. One of his root metaphors after all combines latency and possibility: "hibernation." (3) The third frame is the *world* of jazz. Again my choice of words is deliberate, for jazz is understood not only as one of several discrete genres of music, but as a pervasive cultural style. Louis Armstrong, first in Ellison's hall of fame, allegedly once said "what we play is life." Jazz represents a working out of an American vernacular, a national style. In fact, for Ellison all American culture including baseball, is "jazz-shaped." Jazz is an example and chief exhibit for Ellison's conception of a pluralist culture which, as opposed to bounded social and political systems of power, knows no fixed frontiers, whether marked by color or genes. The process of cultural give and take has its own logic, and it is basically assimilative. Jazz then is a new American mix; a creole representative of the complex history of white and black interaction under conditions of racial hegemony. It serves also as a shorthand metaphor for the relationship between subculture and mainstream, between high Modernist and vernacular black traditions. Of these three frames jazz is the most inclusive, for it incorporates and synthesizes the contradictions of the previous two. Not only is jazz a symbolic action, it is the true musical idiom of Modernism.

For the sake of completeness one more frame ought to be mentioned, which calls out from Ellison's name, that of the moral and aesthetic universe of nineteenth-century American literature and philosophy. This heritage has found much attention and may, on balance, receive short shrift in this essay.

I. RITUAL: THE DANCING OF AN ATTITUDE

Ellison's many references to Lord Raglan and the Cambridge School of ritual and his many quotes from Kenneth Burke indicate a pervasive interest in dramaturgical metaphors to describe cultural and social processes. The social sphere is conceived as an arena or a stage where the individual may use his or her cultural resources and personal talent not only to master the game of life, but even to transcend personal or social limitations. Though Ellison makes a great deal of the term "consciousness," his characters and individuals are rarely mere *Kopfmenschen,* cerebral constructs or mental abstractions. Long before any theories of body language were current, Ellison played with the embodiment of language on the one hand, and with the body and its signals on the other. Ellison's understanding of the meaning of style is anthropological rather than narrowly technical. Style refers to the handling of language as well as to the handling of the body: "It has been said that Escudero could recapitulate the history and spirit of the Spanish dance with a simple arabesque of his fingers" (*Shadow and Act*). The same could be said of Louis Armstrong's authoritative statement in "Potato-Head Blues"; and the complicated history of black American dance and of American minstrelsy is present in Bojangles Robinson doing the Buzzard Lope. Vernacular dance, vernacular language, and vernacular music represent, for this high-cultural Modernist, a total body of culture. And Ellison wants to translate that energy into the organized discipline of his art.

Discrete items of black culture, say a blues piece by Jimmy Rushing, are for him synecdoche, metonymy, and metaphor of the cumulative historical experience of black people in the United States. Jazz, dance, and language all partake of a total world view and of a total way of life. Hence, one of the most critical asides which Ellison ever said about Richard Wright was that "he knew very little about jazz and didn't even know how to dance" (*Remembering Richard Wright*).

Transformations

Ellison's interest in becoming as opposed to being and in open-ended possibility rather than in closed systems explains his preoccupation with transformations, metamorphosis, and hibernation. These processes involve transition, waiting, and hope. Afro-Americans, he writes, have been kept in a state of alert, biding their time; they are in a situation of watchful waiting and suspension of final judgment. Not being part of the finite and closed world of white power, circumscribed by racist paranoia, may have its advantages, says Ellison. As Diderot has it, the lord may have the title, but the bondsman is in possession of the things of life. Or as Hegel suggests, the former is constrained by the finite limitations of power, whereas the latter has before him infinite possibilities and may live in a world of hope. His advantage is described by Kenneth Burke in a most Ellisonian manner: "We win by capitalizing on our debts, by turning our liabilities into assets, by using our burden as a basis of insights," thus fooling or subverting power structures, a strategy which the Invisible Man advocates shrewdly.

The interest in states of becoming and in crisis points of the life cycle lets Ellison choose as heroes youngsters and adolescents who are on the verge of breaking into responsibility. His interest in heroes generally concerns not so much their power or status as their "transformations." Commenting on a storytelling ritual in a barbershop in which black heroes are extolled, he renders content and occasion in dramatic terms:

> His crimes, his loves, his outrages, his adventures, his *transformations,* his moments of courage, his heroism, buffooneries, defeats and triumphs are recited with each participant joining in. And this catalogue soon becomes a brag, a very exciting chant, celebrating the *metamorphosis* which this individual in question *underwent* within the limited circumstances available to us (italics mine).

Ellison's reference to transformations and metamorphoses recalls the anthropological debate on "liminality" (Victor Turner) and "boundary maintenance" (Frederic Barth). These concepts refer to rites of passage, i.e., to the transformation from youth to adulthood and to that imaginary or real social line which defines the self and the group against others. In America's contradictory self-definitions the frontier, the Mason Dixon line, and the color line have been particularly prominent. Each of them posits a definition of self with implications for mobility and change. And both liminality and boundary maintenance have been particularly pressing concerns for adolescent blacks, Ellison's favorite heroes. Ellison loves rituals in which color and status are at cross purposes; he also pokes fun at the paranoid racist fear that one drop of black blood might soil the mighty white race.

On a more pragmatic level Ellison relates his "positionality" vis-à-vis America and black culture to his place of birth, and to growing up in a very special state of the Union which was then in a state of change. Ellison complained in an address honoring Richard Wright that few of the professional critics engaged in the Wright-Ellison weighing-in contest had paid attention to their respective places of origin—Wright hailed from Mississippi, while he was from Oklahoma City. Oklahoma, which was admitted to the Union only a few years prior to Ellison's birth and was a place on the American margin, was a frontier state defined by a frontier culture and outlook. Within that frontier life, blacks were clearly an "undecided" or marginal issue (Oklahoma had not bothered to "regulate" its laws and attitudes concerning blacks), quite in contrast to Mississippi where their presence *as victims* defined, structured, and *closed* the social system. Ellison's sense of self, place, and time, on the one hand, and his special perspective, on the other, are defined by the frontier paradigm, that transitional space with its options and tensions between freedom and necessity, safety and danger, liberty and restraint, order and disorder.

The frontier paradigm of liminality becomes the central metaphor for those figures who will not be victimized by or surrender to a tight behavioral corset. When the Invisible Man experiences a painful burst of perception after Tod Clifton's death he notices Harlem youngsters who speak "a jived-up transitional language full of country glamour, think transitional thoughts." The much belabored Prologue and Epilogue could be read as an essay on liminality and transition, both in form and content. The protagonist defines his current situation as "hibernation" in a cellar located on the border between white and black neighborhoods. His time and space are liminal. The underground places him at the lower, invisible margin of the vertical social order, with free power from an unwitting power company to light his underground. The underground is Ellison's encompassing metaphor for the locus of black culture in America, both in the sense of providing the "basis" (Marx) or the "mudsill" according to Southern Senators, and also in the sense of the guerilla notion of an invisible underground which may at any moment subvert the mainstream, particularly the mainstream of color. Playing Louis Armstrong in a coal cellar, where he has descended, the protagonist has finally come into possession of his identity and consciousness. Hence his descent, as Ellison reminds us, is also an ascent.

Ellison has often insisted on the importance of the black presence for the American body politic. Writing in "What America Would Be without Blacks," he speculated that in a cleansed state America would probably succumb to a "moral slobbism." Here he merely applies the second law of thermodynamics to social systems, which says that homogeneous, closed systems are incapable of moral and artistic renewal. Creative change rarely issues from the center of a consensus, from the structurally-hard core of a majority or from within hegemonic structures. Closed structures and systems tend to maintain homeostasis, to protect the norm, the habit, the thing done, the boundary. This is why ethnic pluralism and diversity are necessary and why so-called minority groups are essential for the questioning of rigid norms and for activating their renewal. The late Victor Turner writes:

> Members of despised or outlawed ethnic and cultural groups play major roles in myths and popular tales as representatives or expressions of universal human values. Famous among these are the good Samaritan, the Jewish fiddler Rothschild in Chekhov's tale "Rothschild's Fiddle," Mark Twain's fugitive Negro slave Jim in *Huckleberry Finn,* and Dostoevsky's Sonya, the prostitute who redeems the would-be Nietzschean "superman" Raskolnikov, in *Crime and Punishment.*
>
> All these mythic types are structurally inferior or "marginal," yet represent what Henri Bergson would have called "open" as against "closed morality," the latter being essentially the normative system of bounded, structured, particularistic groups.
>
> (*The Ritual Process: Structure and Anti-Structure*)

Such a marginal or transitional position requires a special vision and a special talent for interactions. What Emerson and W. E. B. Du Bois called "double consciousness" Ellison prefers to call a "double vision." This is one such example of turning a social liability into an epistemological asset. Though a double vision may be a symptom of a previous social pathology, it may also lead to a penchant for dialogue. The look across the fence increases sociability and tolerance, whereas a single vision would risk becoming paranoid of the other. Such an artistic "perspective by incongruity" is well known in American ethnic writing. It is the epistemological and moral advantage of an altruistic pluralism, that is, of a pluralism which is not merely a ceasefire among ethnochauvinists. Such a double vision trains the ability and willingness to assume a second self and look at oneself as if from the outside. Double vision implies an acceptance of dialogue and of a plurality of voices. Kenneth Burke talks of the "unending conversation" of culture. In contrast, the characteristic discourse of the master is doctrinal monologue, best expressed in that hierarchical discussion-stopper *Roma locuta, causa finita,* (Rome has spoken, the case is closed). It is a matter of existential survival for Ellison's heroes not to accept centralized monologues whether they come from the church, the union or the brotherhood.

Linkage and Complementarity. Call and Response

An important word in Ellison's vocabulary is the conjunction "and." "I was taken very early with a passion to link together all I loved within the Negro community and all those things I felt in the world which lay beyond." The "and" establishes linkage, but not merely in an additive fashion. It may unite *and* separate, yet it never stops dialogue. It controls and maintains a precarious balance between union and divison, order and disorder. His "ands" are dialectical, combative, antiphonal, and always dialogic. A quick look at his essay titles ought to make this clear: "The Seer *and* the Seen," "Change the Joke *and* Slip the Yoke," "The World *and* the Jug," "Hidden Name *and* Complex Fate," "Some Questions *and* Some Answers," and, ultimately, *Shadow and Act.* Furthermore the blues are described as being "tragic *and* comic" and the protagonist of *Invisible Man* preaches "so I denounce *and* I defend, *and* I love *and* I hate." The novel begins with an "I" and ends with a "You": hence it fills the space of the "and" between protagonist and reader; it provides the narrative linkage. There is no indication that Ellison had intended to quote Martin Buber's philosophy of the "I and Thou," yet there is sympathy for the Talmudic argument in his essays, which caused Irving Howe some dismay. Ellison links black and Jewish culture as being committed to the "word"; and Leslie Fiedler recognizes Ellison: "Oh he's a black Jew." This embrace is unnecessary, for a case could be made for a family resemblance between Ellison and Mikhail Bakhtin, whose understanding of the novel as a "dialogic form" with a polyphony of voices comes to mind. The ground for comparison lies in the anti-hegemonic nature of a dialogic and antiphonal discourse, which is characteristic of black folklore.

Mikhail Bakhtin's theory of the novel was inspired by Russian folklore. Ellison equally draws on black folk sources. Black folk storytelling uses the narrative strategy of signifying the figure embodied in the trickster. The trickster, a prominent character in many folk cultures all over the world, is essentially a figure of ambivalence, openness, and fluidity. Storytelling and the trickster figure are generically involved with each other; one depends on the other. Not only are some of our best stories by and about tricksters, but storytelling itself partakes of the existential ambiguity of this central figure. It is telling that certain stories in black and other folklores are told as "lies." The label "lie" is not only the visa which permits their being told at large with impunity, but also a licensing mechanism and credibility ruse which — on a deep level — inspires both folk stories and fiction. The French call fiction "mentir vrai," lying truthfully. Truth *and* lie.

Is it surprising then that both masterplans of Ellison's first novel were based on such trickster stories. Initially he had planned a novel on flying, but he ended up writing one on invisibility. The topic of flying both as fact and metaphor went into the making of the short story "Flying Home," which may be read as a precursor of *Invisible Man* in the handling of black folklore.

The original folk source is the story of a black man going to heaven. He enjoys his new freedom with that sort of abandon usually attributed to children and blacks. The white power structure, St. Peter to be exact, is irritated by his flying capers and he is asked to wear a harness. Openly defying the handicap and the heavely statutes against speeding the fool flies on and is again called before the authorities. He is told to leave heaven, is provided with a parachute and a map of the state of Alabama and told to jump out from the pearly gates. Before taking that step and "flying home" he "caps" the situation with a brag: "one thing you got to admit, while I was here I was the flyinest sonofabitch that ever hit heaven." Todd, the protagonist on the verge of manhood, to whom this story is told by the old and wise folk-storyteller Jefferson, asks whether he is going to hear one of those lies. And Jefferson "jeffs": "I ain't so sure on account of it took place when I was dead."

This strategy of signifying pervades Ellison's storytelling. It crops up at strategic places in the novel, as when the protagonist addresses the implied reader "Let me be honest with you — a feat which, by the way, I find of the utmost difficulty." Lying or truth, there is also the ambivalent basis of the folk tale about "Sweet the Monkey" who "could make himself invisible." Ellison heard this tale from one Leo Gurley while collecting folklore for the Federal Writers Project (and there is a moral in this as well):

> I hope to God to kill me if this aint the truth. All you got to do is go
> down to Florence, South Carolina, and ask most anybody you meet
> and they'll tell you its the truth.

Legitimation by hearsay, the basis of all legend and rumor, identifies and makes visible *any* narrative construction of reality. In their very presentation such stories constitute *and* deconstruct themselves. Sweet the Monkey, and this is not his real name as the storyteller hastens to inform us, could make himself invisible. He acquired this antinomian talent by "cutting open a black cat, taking out its heart, climbing up a tree backwards and cursing God." These voodoo formulae

tie in with other folk traditions such as European witchcraft or its trickster traditions. This is a world upside down, where fair is foul and foul is fair. Beginning
with Lucifer's reversal of Godhead it invokes the radical "other." Its ambivalence
is at the existential basis of all storytelling magic: "black is . . . and black ain't"
says the preacher. Gurley continues:

> Once they found a place he'd looted with footprints leading away
> from it and they decided to try and trap 'im. This was 'bout sun up
> and they followed his footprints all that day. They followed them till
> sundown when he come partly visible. It was red and the sun was
> shining on the trees and they waited till they saw his shadow. That
> was the last of Sweet the Monkey. They never did find his body and
> right after that I come up here. That was about five years ago. My
> brother was down there last year and they said they think Sweet done
> come back. *But they caint be sho because he wont let hisself be seen*
> (italics mine).

Again we get the typical disclaimer, a withdrawal behind the smokescreen
of fantasy. These lies are well known in other folk traditions, in sailors' yarns or
the tales of Baron Münchhausen. The playful "as if" status carries over from the
folk heritage into fiction. Daniel Defoe attacked the novels of his day as cheap
fictions whereas his *Moll Flanders,* he claimed, was a transcript of actual experience. And the fictional Huckleberry Finn (incidentally, Ellison's nickname for
his younger brother) compliments the real Mark Twain (whose name is actually
Clemens) on his first novel *Tom Sawyer,* though the fictional protagonist repri-
mands the real author for stretching things a bit. Huck's story, as told by himself, will be more truthful. Put-ons, teasing, and mockery pervade the confidence game of fiction and imperceptibly fuse with the folk tradition of signifying in Ellison's work. It would be a moot point to start arguing the question
whether he got this penchant for ambivalence from his understanding of the
craft of fiction or from the craftiness of folklore.

One obvious trickster figure in the novel, Pete Wheatstraw, is both a
manipulator of words and a blues singer, and we should not only pay attention
to what he says, but also to what he does. This street poet from the black folk
tradition is, we are lead to assume, taking blueprints to the shredder. This symbolic act encapsulates his trickster ethos: he destroys paper stories, literate fictions.
Ellison has a bit of fun here. It used to be widely accepted dogma in cultural
theory that literate cultures wipe out oral traditions. Legions of folklorists were
motivated by this fear. Wheatstraw's act turns this theory on its head. Again we
have a play on reversals: it is and it ain't, says the preacher in the dream sequence. Or as Brer Rabbit has it: "Dis am life; some go up and some go down."

The tragic sense of ambivalence in kinship relations is articulated in the dream sequence of the Epilogue. A black mother kills the white father of her sons in order to save him from being more brutally murdered by them. Her comment: "I have learned to live with ambivalence." Or take Trueblood, who is literally true to his blood to the extent of becoming his own son-in-law or father-in-law, whose daughter is his mate and whose wife his mother-in-law. Trueblood ends up singing the blues and accepting that he is who he is. Not surprisingly Ellison has repeatedly defined the blues as an "art of ambiguity." Even the book of history, the rational blueprint for future action, comes into doubt when the protagonist asks rhetorically: "what if history is a gambler," thus echoing the folk formula: "heads you win, tails you lose," (which Ellison quotes in his reply to Howe).

Ellison's pervasive use of what I would call trickster strategies and scenarios which lead to his critique of a simplistic historicism or of blueprints for utopias, and which resist hegemony, flesh out his understanding of human symbolic action. At the bottom of these recurrent strategies is a belief that there is something deeply antirepressive both in the accumulated historical wisdom of black folk and in the African heritage of black culture. In recent years a number of Africanists have taken a closer look at Afro-American culture and have noted a very special handling of patterns and a structuration which, though well known in Europe's antinomian folk traditions, was largely repressed by its high culture. Whereas European high-cultural musicians and artists find satisfaction in the accuracy and structural consistency of patterns, black artists (in Africa or America) will begin with such patterns, but then play with them, deconstruct them into basically open forms. Surely the antimetronomic and antirepressive elements in jazz and black religious music have not escaped scholarly notice. Jazz players are often accused of playing "not quite on the beat" or "dirty" by those who favor a strict adherence to "lines and dots." Born in enforced labor and perfected in the freedom of play, this antirepressive attitude has matured into a full-blown aesthetic, which denies system, closure, purity, abstract design, and which thrives on improvisation, off-beat rhythms, syncopation or what Ellison called "the sudden turns, the shocks, the swift changes of pace (all jazz shaped) that serve to remind us that the *world is ever unexplored*. Clearly the denial of closure is embodied by the very form of the novel which has irritated those readers who, instead of the signifying of the Epilogue and Prologue, wanted a proper beginning, middle, and end. Ellison stands in a tradition established by one of his "relatives," Paul Laurence Dunbar. In his poem "When Malindy Sings," the (presumably), black persona tells her white mistress who tries to sight read Malindy's song:

> G'way an quit dat noise Miss Lucy
> Put dat music book away . . .

In a wonderful ironic inversion of white stereotyping and of the then current, Darwinist racism Dunbar's persona continues:

> You ain't got the nachel o'gans
> fu' to make de soun' come right,
> You ain't got the tu'ns an' twistin's
> Fu' to make it sweet an' light.

Then marking the difference between so-called "literate" white sheet music as opposed to "illiterate" black folk music the persona summarizes:

> Oh, hit's sweetah dan de music
> Of an edicated band;
> When Malindy sings.

Thinly veiled by the plantation dialect, we have here an early declaration of black musical independence, even of black superiority, which heralds the coming jazz revolution—all this is in tune with Ellison's estimate of black creativity. In Dunbar's case the cultural nationalism was undercut by the "jingle in the broken tongue," but when reconstructed as a contemporary jazz number by Abbey Lincoln and Max Roach (*Straight Ahead*) its message rings out clearly. Miss Lucy has to rely on "lines and dots" and cannot get the twistings and turns of black music right. Reversal, off-beat, upside down, denial—these key words mark an aesthetic choice.

The dialogic principle and the trickster ethos come together in the notion of masking or of the second self. In order to enter into different styles, codes, and world views one must be an actor—a changer of roles and a wearer of masks. The theme of masking has two angles: (1) we must be able to wear the mask in order to assume the second self and tolerate the other, and (2) we must be able to manipulate masks for survival. Yeats's much quoted sentences come to mind

> If we cannot imagine ourselves as different from what we are and assume the second self, we cannot impose a discipline upon ourselves, though we may accept one from others. Active virtue, as distinct from the passive acceptance of a current code, is the wearing of a mask.

For Ellison the wearing of a mask is no black monopoly; in fact, the American identity is based on what he calls a "joke." He writes with Yeatsian overtones:

> For the ex-colonials, the declaration of an American identity meant the assumption of a mask, and it imposed not only the discipline of national self-consciousness, it gave Americans an ironic awareness of the joke that always lies between appearances and reality, between

the discontinuity of social tradition and that sense of the past which
clings to the mind. And perhaps even an awareness of the joke that
society is man's creation, not God's.

Those believing in pure authenticity or in the existence of ontological
finality denounce masking as "inauthentic" and as a denial of identity, but they
fall for the joke. On the other hand, if one accepts masking not only as a temporary necessity, but as a constant existential fact, and therefore as a resource,
then even the role playing of Louis Armstrong may hide deeper secrets. We
should go one step further and agree with radical anthropologists that only those
who will assume the second self (or the native point of view), are truly capable of
democracy and humanity (Dürr, Geertz). Role playing and the assumption of
the other mask indicate a political credo, namely an anti-imperialistic and anti-
colonialist willingness to begin to understand the other, though it be in stereotype or in unavoidable initial prejudice. We recall Ellison's evaluation of Faulkner, that he began with the stereotype, but then took pains to discover the
humanity behind it.

It is important to note that the trickster ethos or the notion of masking
should not be misunderstood in the context of ready-made stereotypes which
holds that all blacks are typically tricksters. Though the trickster is a distinct
black folk type, he is clearly a character in a global literary pantheon. The trickster
within America is the characterological distillation of what Ellison called the
"diversity of American life with its extreme fluidity and openness." Many readers
will not share this optimistic evaluation of America's promise; for them Ellison
makes too much of the positive virtues of America's "openness." In fact, Ellison
loves to return to metaphors of fluidity when speaking of American possibilities.

> For the novelist, Proteus stands for both America and the in-
> heritance of illusions through which all men must fight to achieve
> reality; the offended God stands for our sins against those principles
> we all hold sacred. The way home we seek is that condition of man's
> being at home in the world, which is called love, and which we term
> democracy. Our task then is always to challenge the apparent form
> of reality — that is, the fixed manners and values of the few, and to
> struggle with it until it reveals its mad, vari-implicated chaos, its
> false faces and on until it surrenders its insights, its truths.
>
> (*Shadow and Act*)

Where many black American have seen limitations, he sees possibilities, when
others would worship wounds, he would rather explore the not-yet-known, and
see in mere survival enough ground for celebration.

Many of his critics have called this stance a copout—making the best of a bad deal. There is, depending on one's position or ulterior motives, some truth in such criticism. Yet, his detractors ignore the radicalism of his philosophical anthropology which refuses to posit simple utopias of being. Ellison puts more faith in the energy of day to day combat and believes in accumulating wisdom in the here and now. He is a radical American pragmatist, as it were. Others have faulted Ellison's work for the lack of a clear political commitment and have been irritated by his ideological agnosticism, which makes it hard for them to reduce his politics to a platform. Those whose sense of truth is shaped by a simple faith in realism—Nietzsche called this the dogma of immaculate perception—are often bothered by his antimimetic aesthetic which perforates the referentiality of art. Old-fashioned Marxists bridle at his aesthetics. And from a stable ideological center his views may easily be called "conservative." A penchant for mediation, for the reconciliation of opposites, and for the maintenance of an ambivalent state of balance between order and chaos would, according to Karl Mannheim's typology of ideologies, fall into a conservative archetype of thought. But these categories work only if and when there is a firm historicist frame, which according to Ellison—or Levi-Strauss—is merely another transitory myth. "What if history is a gambler," asks the chastened protagonist. Ellison's radicalism is of a different sort: it would doubt the very ideological beliefs on which radical solutions rest. It rejects all closed systems which speak with a single voice. Ellison speaks forcefully against any colonization and against the logocentric hegemony of systems of thought. Yet, Ellison's ideological ambivalence does not lead to mere relativism or to a rejection of any values. In his social philosophy he stands in an American moral tradition which includes Emerson, Whitman, James, Dewey, and Mead. Charles W. Morris characterizes its social ideal:

> This society would not have as its goal the bare sustenance and attainment of any set of existent or authoritatively defined values—this Mead calls the Augustinian philosophy of history. On the contrary, its philosophy of history would be as experimental as the experimental method itself. It would be concerned with the technique for remaking values through the reinterpretation of the situation in terms of the best knowledge available, and that technique, it would appear, could be nothing but morality itself.

Language and Symbolic Action

How do a ritual theory of culture, an interest in transformations, and in the dialogic principle translate into poetic practice? Ellison's understanding of language is not merely instrumental, in the sense of using language to transport meaning or doctrine. For the poet language is both form and content, medium and message. Language is not only in itself a form of reality, but also a way of working through reality, a way of working things out. It is in and by itself a creative force and an agency and repository of wisdom. Language is a special form of artistic production and in the words of Karl Marx "practical consciousness." Poetry is the performance of language, symbolic action. Its smithy is the ongoing vernacular process. Ellison would agree with the great linguist Otto Jespersen, who used to say that grammar and style are the product of generations of illiterate speakers. Ellison is concerned with the American vernacular as just such a working out of social and cultural conflicts; it is also a working out of an American identity. The American vernacular is involved in an unending fight to achieve a better fit between word and thing, between the promise and the reality of its constitution—hence it is a deeply moral agency with particular relevance for the discourse in race relations. Ellison is, with Kenneth Burke, a logological watcher and custodian of American English. As much as Adam Smith believed in the invisible hand of the free market system, Ellison puts much faith in the invisible and collective hand of the vernacular in a free society. But he is not a facile folk enthusiast who would believe that the folk can do no wrong. After all he came to folklore through literature; he discovered its potential, he says, because he had become a literary person by breaking through the horizon of a mere folk consciousness. Ellison insists on the need for transcendence from the unconscious rituals of a folk world to a more generous level of individualistic American freedom. This scenario is not based on a stratified notion of culture. His is a non-hegemonic theory of cultural influence—again a very radical departure from previous assumptions. An earlier theory assumed that folklore had seeped down from the culture bearers to the plebs, and that folksongs were the residue of an operatic or Lied tradition. In the American context this tacit belief translated into George Pullen Jackson's theory that spirituals were essentially white songs, sung badly by blacks. If today black vernacular forms are no longer studied as a pathological offshoot of white culture, we should credit Ellison, who challenged these assumptions long before the cultural nationalism of the sixties. Before him, Sterling Brown and Langston Hughes had discovered the latent creativity and the hidden potential of the vernacular, but their art did not tackle or challenge contemporary Modernist forms. Ellison went one step further in forging a marriage between Modernist narrative techniques (making use of sophisticated notions of the narrative self and its many voices) and the black vernacular (with its pluralism of styles, rituals and rhythms).

In order to make his narrative strategies and his handling of language more apparent let me illustrate certain narrative techniques in his short story "Flying Home." This early story is an excellent vehicle, particularly since it foreshadows his later stylistic virtuosity in *Invisible Man*, to study his handling of voices.

In keeping with the Modernist tradition Ellison chose a central intelligence, named Todd. He is a black pilot in training, whose consciousness controls and reproduces direct speech or reported action and whose feelings and emotions blend freely indirect style and interior monologue. It is telling that Ellison, though principally involved with one character gives him more than one voice with one pitch, one level of intensity or consciousness. Instead he dramatizes internal thought processes by mixing stylistic strategies of address and self-address. This blending of voices is a stylistic means of dramatizing the tension between affective experience and analytical narration, between the biological self and the generalized other, between the private me and the social self. The psychological drama brings to mind W. E. B. Du Bois's notion of a double consciousness; for it consistently underscores the dilemma of having to look at oneself using the linguistic and metaphorical conventions of a deeply racist language. The narrative strategy commonly called free indirect style is particularly suited to dramatize this Modernist notion of the embattled self; for it formalizes the convention of a multiple focus. It is a narrative strategy in which the protagonist describes his inner experience using the narrative conventions of an external narrator. Though feeling as an "I" he refers to himself as a "he." This narrative convention has been largely internalized to the point of being "invisible." But in this instance Ellison takes pains to bring it back into visibility: it allows him to highlight in one consciousness the difference between man and citizen, between the private and the social, between achievement and ascription, thus calling attention to the social construction of the black American self.

This convention creates an ironic distance between the "I" as a central focus of experience and as the controlling narrative voice. This is the formal analogue to the split in human personality much belabored by Modernist psychology, a split which has become sensitized by the color line, namely the split between being a body and having a body.

The irony and ambivalence which is generated by these various tensions work on many levels. The discrepancy develops between Todd's achievement and his ascribed status, between his private identity and his social self. In the present story Todd's preoccupation with his body signals (anguish, panic, dread, sweat, hysteria, pounding blood, shame) highlights this dilemma. As he first comes out of shock, eyes closed, he freezes when he feels the presence of someone, then relaxes when he hears the black idiom. The split between bodily experience, which is a direct and unmediated expression of his anxieties, and analytic, narrative distance, which tries to control or rationalize these anxieties by explanation, is particularly obvious in the following passage:

> *That buzzard knocked me back a hundred years*, he thought. Irony danced within him like the gnats circling the old man's head. *With*

> *all I've learned I'm dependent upon this "peasant's" sense of time and space.* His leg throbbed. In the plane, instead of time being measured by the rhythms of pain and a kid's legs, the instruments would have told him at a glance. Twisting upon his elbows he saw where dust had powdered the plane's fuselage, feeling the lump form in his throat that was always there when he thought of flight. *It's crouched there,* he thought, *like the abandoned shell of a locust. I'm naked without it.* Not a machine, a suit of clothes you wear. And with a sudden embarrassment and wonder he whispered, *"It's the only dignity I have . . . ."* (italics mine, indicating direct speech).

The shift from unmediated experience rendered dramatically as interior monologue or direct speech (dependence, nakedness, dignity) and the ironic distance of free indirect style (irony, lump in his throat, embarrassment, wonder) permits Ellison to contrast *in one* consciousness intimacy and distance without interfering as author. This antiphonal style in the dramatization of a consciousness would be continued in the novel.

Apart from his own thought processes Todd's consciousness registers and echoes other voices. Ellison introduces all sorts of different levels of discourse: Jefferson's warm, ironic black idiom (a precursor of Trueblood's vernacular gift), Todd's own meticulously neutral diction, and Graves' aggressively racist discourse. All these buttress or assail his self and dramatize intimacy and isolation. At all times, one might say, Ellison follows the Jamesian dictum to dramatize, to show rather than to tell; hence minds and bodies undergo perpetual change. Todd has lost the safety of objective, physical time (his instruments & time piece) and is now thrown back on a more primitive sense of time marked by pain and anxiety. His panic and impatience are structural stimuli for the flashbacks in the tale. Pain drives him back into his personal time. These flashbacks are not merely ways of passing the time (though they are these, too) but provide an occasion to work out what doctors call "anamnesia," i.e. the forgotten history of one's pathology. We find out that he has simply suppressed certain types of experience from his youth. He did learn about racism but he buried his knowledge under his social ambition, which in turn forced him into the straightjacket of bourgeois attitudes. The bodily pain interrupts the controlled narrative of the current experience and drives him back into chaos of his past. All these conflicting strains and motives are choreographed by his language over which there hovers a mocking sense of irony. This is how language as a symbolic action incorporates the social and cultural complexity of black existence in a racist society. The protagonist of this tale is in many ways a precursor of the nameless hero of *Invisible Man*, who goes through similar agonies and changes.

II. MODERNISM

Modernism loosely describes a period of heightened aesthetic consciousness (and self-consciousness) which gathers in its fold many of the authors Ellison names as his ancestors: Eliot, Hemingway, Joyce and Malraux. "In or about December 1910 human character changed," wrote Virginia Woolf somewhat apodictically, and Ezra Pound, everybody's literary coach, pep talked his artist friends into "making it new." With aesthetic changes came a new social role for art: it is seen by the artists themselves partly as a diagnosis of crisis, partly as a new transcendence. Diagnosis in the sense of Marx, Freud and Nietzsche, laying bare the invisible deep structures beneath the visible surface of things. Transcendence in the sense of T. S. Eliot, who advocated the return to older myths and rituals (and folklore) to combat the "chaos of modern history." Crisis and diagnosis inform the logic of discovery inherent in Modernism; therapy and transcendence inform the logic of demonstration. Art is a kind of writing cure: the imagination is itself a utopian sphere and the poetic imagination helps to liberate text and reader from the bondage of history. Belief systems in general collapse, their centers no longer hold. The self becomes unhinged and is in perpetual search of alternatives, new frontiers, other worlds. Hence "change itself" is the hero of Modernism and time is its keeper. In formal terms this translates into a sophisticated handling of narrative, into a metaphorical complexity and a play of paradoxes, and the general absence of security results in a new intimacy between author and protagonist on the one, and hero and reader on the other hand. All this applies to Ellison—who is a "Spaetling," a latecomer to Modernism—and yet it doesn't.

Ellison is no mere follower of Modernism, but reconstructs its general purpose within a black historical consciousness and structure of feeling. Surely the inner history of black literature has followed its own logic — in counterpoint to the mainstream of American literature. While nineteenth century white heroes such as Huck Finn or Ishmael were in flight of the body politic, lighting out for the territory or going in search for the primitive, Frederick Douglass fought against the primitive ascription and for a place within that very body politic. Much later Claude McKay protested against exclusion from the "white house." The structure of black experience generates its own desires, topics, themes, and formal conventions, which, in comparison with the dominant American literary trends, seem traditional simply because blacks had to fight older American battles of self-liberation all over again. Heinrich Heine spoke of it as the traditionalism of the excluded.

Hence Ellison's Modernism is certainly not one of white alienation or anomie caused by a disgust with the world. "I'm not a separatist. The imagination is integrative. That's how you make the new — by putting something else with what you've got. And I'm unashamedly an American integrationist." This is indeed hard to swallow for critics driven either by white angst or black anger. Ellison's insistence on linkage, dialogue and complementarity and his pragmatic American optimism are not quite on the beat and not in tune with the Modernist theme song. Using Ellison mocking metaphors, one might say that he was inspired by his Modernist ancestors, but that his and his relatives' cultural experience runs on its own, black track.

Like his ancestors, however, Ellison practices a literature of consciousness, and he treats consciousness as a value which deserves to be maximized. Indeed consciousness gives value to unconsciously lived lives. "It might sound arrogant to say so, but writers, poets, help create or reveal hidden realities by asserting their existence" ("A Very Stern Discipline"). "I do not find it a strain to point to the heroic component of our experience, for these seem to me truths which we have long lived by but which we must not recognize consciously." Art, in his words, represents not only a special form of creation but it constitutes a realm of liberation. Therefore he criticized Wright for excluding from his work the possibility of his own self-creation as a successful writer, and for denying his characters the chances of the consciousness which he had. Literature is seen as a radical alternative to artlessness and chaos (in Eliot's sense of that word), or to confusion which issues from ignorance. Whereas Wright's chief curse was the evil of racism, Ellison's pet peeve is ignorance, particularly when it is self-imposed and self-perpetuated. The appropriate generic choices were therefore in Wright's case tragedy, in Ellison's case comedy.

The *telos* of comedy is peace. Surely Ellison, as was said before, embraces democracy, pluralism, and tolerance as ultimate values which shine out from his work. This basic attitude carries a concept of culture in its wake which is partly Modernist, partly black. Ellison has a deep commitment to the invisible hand of culture as a symbolic system of checks and balances and a way of honing and shaping experience, all of which works itself out in language. He writes a very conscious Modernist prose, i.e., he brings the poet's care to "naming" and to language. Craft consciousness inspires and directs his work which aims for an almost hypertrophied literariness and for a self-conscious network of *literary* quotation and *folk* allusion. Those who tire of his literary signifying may call him an overachiever, for he would cross semantic wires wherever possible and he delights in confusing those readers who want the strong authorial hand. He cannot bypass a potential pun which lies buried in language and would rather let his protagonist have a "bad one" than none at all (outhouse–Wrestrum). The richness and pliability of the black code which the history of linguistic subterfuge (putting on Massa) has resulted in is for Ellison not a cause for abolitionist outrage, but possibility for a Joycean field day. Rather than avoid the politically freighted black sociolects and dialects, be they minstrel or ghetto English, Ellison exploits the code precisely for its playfulness and for its rich ambiguities. What for many bourgeois or political activists is a badge of inferiority—black folk culture—becomes a resource for this Modernist. He attempts to recreate the full range of black talk in terms of Modernist contextuality which amounts to what Roman Jakobson called the strengthening of the "poetic function" of such language. Whereas Eliot and Joyce achieved poetic contextuality by using myth as a structural scaffolding and as a way of ordering the "chaos of modern history," Ellison mockingly invites the country cousin of myth—black folklore—into the salon of Modernist intertextuality. For him the black vernacular holds a store of repressed values which need to be made conscious through literacy. "Oh yes, I was involved with folklore, but this was the end result of certain sorts of conscious experience based upon literature. I discovered the folklore because I had become a literary person." Folklore then in the sense of Foucault is the "invisible deep structure" of black life, invisible because it is unconsciously lived and has not become "cultural" as a text. So a belief in the positive virtue of the irrepressible wisdom of the folk is matched with a belief in consciousness through literacy. Immersion into the folk and ascent from the folk are his goal. "When I listen to a folk story, I'm looking for what it conceals as well as what it states."

Ellison's understanding of black folklore and what it conceals or reveals ties in with Clifford Geertz's notion of "thick description." Culture is seen as a complex and thick web in which people enmesh themselves; they are, as a German philosopher said, "entangled in stories." While for those who favor dogmatic simplicities such a state is aggravating and sets in motion strategies of repression, Ellison seeks out these complex webs, makes connections and unites the heterogeneous elements of black and white culture. Therefore he is irritated by stereotyping and simple formulas whether advanced by white sociologists or black radicals. "I don't deny that these sociological formulas are drawn from life, but I do deny that they define the complexity of Harlem." There is something else and "it is 'that something else' that challenges the sociologist who ignores it." Ellison's complex notion of white-black interaction does not find favor with white liberals or black radicals; he is in the Nietzschean sense "untimely," and therefore without a constituency, in advocating a reading of American history which denies simple genealogies but insists on a mutual, complex fate. He would perhaps approve of Diderot's understanding of the counterproductive nature of all hegemonic relations. Surely in the area of culture (if not everywhere), Ellison says, the black folk have subverted white America. Black culture seeped up into the mainstream while those who embraced it, strenuously denied any such influence. White Americans to this day become very uneasy when Europeans tell them "how black" their cultural styles are. C. G. Jung committed this *faux pas* as early as 1929.

Conversely, black Americans are surprised, on going abroad, that often their being Americans means more to others than their being black. This is particularly true in Africa. Many white American kids who love popular music are quite ignorant of the black origins of most American music. Conversely, Amiri Baraka's history of jazz studiously ignores the open borrowing and exchanging between black and white musicians. Ellison, who started out as a jazz trumpeter, has little sympathy for myths of purism or strategies of avoidance.

Modernist craft and Modernist aesthetics permit Ellison to achieve two strategic goals (1) to legitimate and rescue a hitherto invisible or suppressed black language, culture, and folklore by translating it into high Modernist forms; and (2) to make visible the complex hidden linkages between blacks and whites in creating an American vernacular culture. His insistence on one cultural history does not imply that there is no cultural difference based on color. Yet, in long range terms, processes of ethnogenesis and cultural creation are integrative. Cultures live by borrowing and exchanging.

> If white and black
> blend soften and unite
> a thousand ways
> is there no black and white

asked Alexander Pope in his *Essay on Man*.

III. JAZZ AESTHETICS: MAKE IT NEW, BUT NOT QUITE ON THE BEAT

Ellison's Modernism, as was said before, is not one of crisis and despair, but of innovation and hope. He accepts the discipline implied in the slogan "make it new," but rejects the cultural pessimism of his ancestors. One explanation for his special optic lies, I believe, in his understanding of jazz as more than a form of musical entertainment. Eliot in his notorious essay "Ulysses, Order and Myth" had called for myth to replace moribund historical frames of reference. For Ellison there is no need for therapy or replacement. Jazz, blues, spiritual, and black folk religion have provided the rituals which give order to the "chaos" of black experience. The problem is that these forms, though crucial to black American and general American culture, were denied, rejected, and suppressed — invisible. In the history of jazz the tangle of black-white relations is particularly complex, but also paradigmatic for an understanding of what makes American culture what it is. Jazz also represents a testimony to a black coming-of-age in American culture, it announces the break into audibility and visibility, and marks a black appropriation not only of the instruments, techniques and strategies of music making, but also of the public sphere and the marketplace. Jazz also represents a break through the mask of Stephen Foster minstrelsy. It constitutes an act of what Robert Stepto in a felicitous phrase calls "self-authentication." All this may sound as if Ellison considers jazz to be a purely black creation. It is, in his view, rather a hybrid, a creole, a fusion of heterogeneous dialogues from the folk traditions of blacks and whites. The marching bands of the German Turnverein in New Orleans, society orchestras, honky-tonk and ragtime went into its making; and many of the first jazz artists received instruction from French or German music teachers, as Ellison did from Dr. Ludwig Hebestreit. Jazz therefore is a fitting paradigm for Ellison's understanding of the multi-ethnic American musical vernacular. Though not a friend of current jazz radicals, he would probably agree with jazz saxophonist and scholar Archie Shepp, who told Amiri Baraka:

> But jazz is American reality. Total reality. The jazz musician is like a reporter, an aesthetic journalist of America. Those white people who used to go to those bistros in New Orleans etc., thought they were listening to nigger music, but they weren't, they were listening to American music. Even today those white people who go slumming on the Lower East Side may not know it, but they are listening to American music . . . the Negro contribution, his gift to America.

Jazz is the only purely *American* cultural creation which, shortly after its birth, became America's most important cultural export. The Army newspaper *Stars and Stripes* featured an article during the Korean war which told the story of a North Korean, i.e., Communist, soldier who had a record of Charlie Parker's "Bird of Paradise" among his possessions. This may be human interest blarney, but it rings true. Despite its international success jazz has not received the official recognition at home which it deserves, precisely because it is so inescapably American in its shameless fusion of heterogeneous elements.

Attempts to trivialize or whiten it have failed; as have black cultural nationalists claims of a black monopoly in jazz. It is a mulatto, a bastard, a creole — and, most important for Ellison's self-assessment as a black American, jazz wouldn't have happened *without* blacks. It is, in the words of Richard Wright, a social system of artistic communication in which whites and blacks cannot deny each other's presence. Though to this day European classical music ranks higher in America in status and prestige than jazz, it was Europeans primarily who urged Americans to treat their own cultural product more seriously. Jazz then is a most complicated product of cultural antagonistic cooperation between black and white, a true American hybrid; and it has subverted global musical culture. One reason for its success, it seems to me, is that jazz is the true idiom of an American Modernism. Let me elaborate this assumption which, I submit, is also Ellison's. Jazz emerged as a distinct type of music in that period of innovation from about 1890 to 1920 which Paul Valéry heralded—and his words fit jazz very well: "We should be ready for such great innovations in all of art that invention itself will be changed and perhaps lead to a magic transformation of the concept of art itself." America was in a privileged situation at this moment in time to observe not only the meeting of many European vernacular cultures, but to witness their contact with the Afro-American, mostly rural, traditions in America's frontier cities: New Orleans, Kansas, Oklahoma City, and Chicago. Jazz emerged in this quotidian space of social license; it arose not in structurally strong cultural centers, such as Boston and Philadelphia, but in such cities which allowed a maximum of fluidity and contact. Marginality, normally seen as a social evil, may, in art, turn into advantage, particularly in the urban context. Here an eclecticism is made possible which means not only artistic or existential, but also social freedom, a situation in which the son of an Italian laborer could learn to sing the blues. To wit, blues and spirituals are central black traditions which, though distinct from jazz, have revitalized and blackened the jazz tradition in the cities. Jazz, and this is of central importance, emerged in cities and developed with increasing distance from the cotton fields—it is therefore essentially a city culture. It flowered in cities where a number of classes and cultures merged and meshed, cities which did not have an old cultural profile but were, like America, brand new and wide open. Jazz arose in this setting and its first name "novelty music" called attention to the slogan of Modernism, make it new. Modernism gave jazz its penchant for innovation; yet, jazz like many products of the new capitalism could easily have ended in sterile commodification, if it weren't for an irrepressible "African" element in it, a disruptive, antinomian vitality. Therefore we ought to expand the slogan: "Make It New," and add "But Not Quite on the Beat."

With Louis Armstrong in the twenties jazz stops being a collective folk music, and becomes a Modernist art whose hallmark is originality and innovation. In a perpetual contest with his peers the jazz musician must assert his individuality by enlarging the collective grammar of jazz expression. Learning from tradition by copying masters the jazz artist's goal is to overcome his peers in the so-called "cutting contests." The progress from copying to ironic quoting to critical travesty to reconstruction is a path of increasing self-discipline. Characteristic of jazz are improvisation, open-ended innovation and versatility, a constant negotiation between travesty, quotation, and masking, and a perpetual making it new as a principle of composition as improvisation. It is dialogic, combative, antiphonal. And it connects with what Eliot wrote in his statement "Tradition and the Individual Talent." Here is Ellison running jazz through Eliot's changes:

> For true jazz is an art of individual assertion within and against the group. Each true jazz moment (as distinct from the uninspired commercial performance) springs from a contest in which each artist challenges all the rest; each solo flight, or improvisation, represents (like successive canvasses of a painter) a definition of his identity: as individual, as member of the collectivity and as a link in the chain of tradition.
>
> (*Shadow and Act*)

The true jazz moment could be defined as ecstatic creativity in transience. The jazz session is an ephemeral happening, in which creation, reception, composition, and performance become one. This explains why jazz was so attractive for the Modernist avant-garde in literature and art. The drive for innovation which is so characteristic of jazz identifies it as a truly Western child of Modernism. There is that discipline of making it new. Yet, jazz is not exclusively Western. The ritual and the nature of the jazz event owes much to an older, Afro-American, perhaps even African tradition. While in Western music there is a division of labor between composer and musician, the jazz musician is both. Such performance requires a new creative spontaneity which Charles Mingus describes in the following manner:

> Each musician when he takes a horn in his hand — trumpet, bass, saxophone, drums — whatever instrument he plays — each soloist, that is, when he begins to adlib on a given composition with a title and improvise a new creative melody, this man is taking the place of a composer. He is saying, "Listen, I am going to give you a new melodic conception on a tune you are familiar with. I am a composer." That's what he is saying. I, myself, came to enjoy the players who didn't only swing, but who invented new rhythmic patterns, along with new melodic concepts. And those people are: Art Tatum, Bud Powell, Max Roach, Sonny Rollins, Lester Young, Dizzy Gillespie and Charles Parker, who is the greatest genius of all to me because he changed the whole era around. But there is no need to compare

composers. If you like Beethoven, Bach or Brahms, that's okay. They were all pencil composers. I always wanted to be a spontaneous composer.

The performing composer radicalizes the act of composition. It is imperative that he "innovate" and this in a seemingly spontaneous fashion. The worst put down of a jazz musician is that he repeats himself. Bill Evans, pianist of the famous Miles Davis Quintet of the late fifties, expressed the dual tension in his liner notes to *Kind of Blue:*

> There is a Japanese visual art in which the artist is *forced* to be *spontaneous*. He must paint on a thin stretched parchment with a special brush and black water paint in such a way that an unnatural or interrupted stroke will destroy the line or break through the parchment. Erasures or changes are impossible. These artists must practice a particular *discipline,* that of allowing the idea to express itself in communication with their hands in such a direct way that deliberation cannot interfere.
>
> The resulting pictures lack the complex composition and texture of ordinary painting, but it is said that those who see well find something captured that escapes explanation.
>
> This conviction that *direct deed* is the most meaningful reflection, I believe, has prompted the evolution of the extremely severe and unique *disciplines* of the jazz or improvising musician.
>
> Group improvisation is a further challenge. Aside from the weighty technical problem of collective coherent thinking, there is the very, human, even *social* need for sympathy from all members to *bend for the common result* (italics mine).

The Modernist drive for innovation appears in song titles: "Things to Come," "Now's The Time," "Tempus Fugit." in short, the essence of jazz is a constant overcoming, a transcendence in art of the limitations of the *status quo.* Jazz lives in a perpetual opposition to existing systems of musical expression. Hence it expresses for Ellison the central drive and function of art. Protest, he argues, should not be the content, but the essence of art "as technical assault against the styles which have gone before."

The language of jazz is expressive of this deep desire for progression. Those unwilling to swing through the changes are known as "squares," "lames," or "moldy figs," all words expressing stasis and paralysis, whereas jazz musicians have referred to themselves as hepcats, hipsters, swingers, etc. Consider also the terms for the music itself: Jazz, Boogie-Woogie, Rock'n'Roll, and Jive are words connoting movement and sexual activity. Dance and sex are the subtext of these names. Linguists have traced down the etymology of "jazz" as a creole word meaning "to speed up," implying, of course, orgasm. Radical critics have worried about this sexual "mortgage" of jazz. There has been many a Mr. Clean in black cultural nationalism movements who wanted to excise this libidinal aura of jazz. But there is no easy or ideological way out of history: jazz arose as an antirepressive freedom zone in a basically prohibitive society, a society which for a long stretch of its history was hostile to dance, song, and sex. Jazz articulates those experiences which do not conform easily to ideology or to attempts at colonization. It is essentially anarchistic, though never undisciplined. This is one reason why jazz has not fared well in totalitarian systems: Nazis and Stalinists rejected it violently. In fact it is a sort of litmus test for exposing authoritarianism and fundamentalism and therefore it comes as no surprise that not only the KGB, but also the FBI and religious fundamentalists are equally determined to combat it, each of them calling it an invention of the enemy. Christian Crusade Publications, Tulsa, Oklahoma, believes that Jazz is part of a Communist master music plan; conversely, Stalinists called it a form of capitalist depravity, and Nazis referred to it as "degenerate art." The totalitarian international clearly did not like it for its liberating potential, its subtly subversive and seductive nature, and its antidogmatic stance.

Ellison called jazz "that embodiment of a superior democracy in which each individual cultivated his uniqueness and yet did not clash with his neighbors." Jazz is by no means "democratic" in the sense of being noncompetitive; however, its main goal is not to just cut the other player, but to cut him by conquering one's own limitations and by becoming better than before. Improvisation is not "free" in the sense of being arbitrary. It follows the difficult discipline of searching out the inherent curve of language as collective consciousness, in finding the inherent rhythms and rituals of the vernacular. Neither free verse nor improvisation are free, but they are similar in that they overcome straitjackets and blueprints. Ellison mentions that he heard the sound of jazz in Eliot's *The Waste Land*, the flagship of Modernist poetry. Despite the bowler hat and a banker's attitude Eliot did not forget the sounds of his home town, St. Louis, one of the most important thoroughfares of the sounds of the Mississippi. "Under the Bamboo Tree" in *Sweeney Agonistes* quotes a composition by Bob Cole, the partner of Rosamond Johnson, whose brother, James Weldon, wrote the first major novel of black musicality, *The Autobiography of an Ex-Colored Man*. The ironic title refers to a cultural fact: the passing of black music into the white mainstream. The history of ragtime is indeed one such case of cultural passing. Scott Joplin, the black composer, put ragtime on paper, and it instantly became a national craze. Around 1896, Ben Harney wrote what amounts to the

first ragtime-inspired popular hit, which caught the country by storm. When
Alec Wilder in preparing his book *American Popular Song* (1972) interviewed
Eubie Blake, the veteran black pianist, about Ben Harney's knack for the black
idiom in music, Blake said: "Of course, you knew that Harney was black."
Harney had passed for white and only then could he become a *national*, popular
songwriter. He did in fact what James Weldon Johnson's "Ex-Colored" protagonist had initially wanted to do: to bring black music into the American mainstream. In *Invisible Man* those ten drops of a black substance which make "Optic
White" the Right White are not only a whimsical invention of Ellison's, but have
a basis in historical fact. Those ten drops gave us a Paul Whiteman (mark his
monniker), the famous "King of Jazz" who would write a book entitled *Jazz*
(1928) without acknowledging one black musician. We are told that Whiteman
actually got his start in jazz through the help of a black musician. Lest we forget.

The Politics of Being Ellison

Sadly most discussions of Ellison's politics are cluttered by questionable assumptions, yet he undeniably inspires political controversies. Briefly then, let me
rehearse these and speculate on their deeper causes.

For one who values improvisation, dialogue, and innovation Ellison does
not have much tolerance for black writers who practice an unfinished, improvisational style. For Ellison much of the writing of Zora Neale Hurston or Langston
Hughes is not good enough, not up to Modernist standards. His love of folklore
and of a freewheeling anthropology is disciplined by a high-Modernist value
system. While folklore is his freedom, Modernism his necessity. He urges a
greater freedom in the discovery of a rich cultural heritage, but curtails and
domesticates it by his Modernist dictates. The contradiction extends into his
political philosophy. Whereas his political ideal seems to tend towards an anti-
hegemonic notion of grass roots egalitarian democracy (i.e. the antinomian
American tradition from Emerson to Whitman), his aesthetic choice of Modernism is tied into a hierarchical, even aristocratic notion of cultural excellence.
Modernism as a program implies an evolutionary fiction of poetic improvement;
it sets in motion an unending spiral of maximizing poetic profit, a development
which tends towards elitism, alienation, and isolation. These are indeed labels
Ellison has to live with. His group-centered anthropology battles (and perhaps
looses) against an individualistic aesthetic. When the chips are down, individual
talent beats tradition.

Behind this conflict there lurk two notions of culture: one is egalitarian and
loose — inspired by a black and general American vernacular tradition; the other
is hierarchical and tight — beholden to a Western aristocracy of values. The division splits his kin: his relatives belong to the first, his ancestors to the second
cultural definition.

This conflict is at the bottom of all discussions about the role of black intellectuals: whether to remain loyal to the group at the price of self-marginalization or wether to "whup the game" (and join it) at the price of loosing one's group. Ellison cannot be accused of ignoring the problem, it is in fact his central theme. The lame ending of "Flying Home" may be an indication that he doesn't have the answer. In the story, the protagonist Tod is "reconciled" with the black folk. But perhaps Ellison is putting us on, who knows?

How can one square the circle of intellectual excellence and group loyalty, of individuation through art and loyalty to collective vernacular traditions, of effective group politics and cosmopolitanism? It has been argued that by lifting folklore out of the folk horizon and by giving it the high seriousness of Modernism Ellison has pulled its political teeth and has robbed it of its antinomian power. Joel Chandler Harris turned the basically malevolent Brer Rabbit into a domestic pet. Did not Ellison turn the antinomianism of folklore into "celebration?" To be sure, Zora Neale Hurston, whom Ellison does not particularly like for her low comedy, remains closer to the black experience from which she came. For her the living culture was like a skin, difficult to shed or to escape from. Ellison, who did not grow up within southern black folklore but came to it through literature, stands in a different relationship to it, one more pastoral than political. Yet, when all this is said Ellison did the best job in bringing folklore into the *power* of literacy. He must be credited for giving it "cultural power" within the mainstream.

The fact that his Modernist aesthetic tends toward isolation and ultimate silence weighs more heavily. Modernism (perhaps all great art) rejects the common reader and is punished by ever-decreasing audiences and continued misunderstanding. On a very pragmatic level, therefore, the stern discipline of Modernism has tended to undo Ellison's liberating folk ethos, or has given it the lie.

In this seemingly insoluble situation jazz becomes his political solution. Jazz indeed is a squaring of the circle: it is deeply rooted in the black folk and its music (Charlie Parker and Ornette Coleman played in jump bands) and it has repeatedly been revitalized by black folk energy, such as the blues and gospel. At the same time it is a global, Modernist idiom. It transcends or simply ignores ethnic boundaries, and that makes it suspect to all sorts of cultural nationalists. And it is a musical creole which is neither purely African nor purely Euro-American, yet which is inconceivable without black participation in a key role. Whereas one could easily envisage the rise rise of jazz without the "Spanish tinge" (Jelly Roll Morton's word) or without the French input, it would be inconceivable without its African base. Jazz mediates a cultural contradiction: though socially a subculture, it has been an aesthetic avant-garde since Armstrong's Hot Five.

Jazz then encapsulates best the contradictions which went into the making of a black-inspired American culture. Its very existence and resilience is Ellison's proof of the pudding. Declared dead many times, it has, like the novel, ignored its obituaries. And it has made possible some of the highest achievements in American art, Charlie Parker's "Koko" and "Lover Man" or Bud Powell's "Un Poco Loco." Last, but not least, it has added character to American culture.

One needs to make known these ramifications of the jazz phenomenon as part of a truly American vernacular in order to understand Ellison's deep commitment to jazz — not only as a form of music making, but also as a paradigm for the manifold processes of historical give and take, or borrowing and exchanging, misunderstanding and misappropriation, and also of celebration. Jazz embodies — in its very substance — the complex fate and the stern discipline of an American art. What indeed would America be like without blacks?

Chronology

1914 Ralph Waldo Ellison is born in Oklahoma City, Oklahoma, on March 1. He is the son of Lewis Alfred, a construction foreman and later a peddler of ice and coal, and Ida Millsap Ellison, a stewardess at the Avery Chapel Afro-Methodist Episcopal Church.

1917 His father dies.

1920 Enters the Frederick Douglass School in Oklahoma City.

1933 Attends Tuskegee Institute as a scholarship student to study music.

1936 Leaves Tuskegee for New York City, intending to study sculpture. Free-lances at various occupations to support himself. Meets Langston Hughes and Richard Wright.

1937 Ellison's mother dies in February, in Dayton, Ohio, where Ellison spends the winter. His first published work appears in the fall—a review of Waters Edward Turpin's novel *These Low Grounds* in *New Challenge*.

1938–42 Ellison is hired by the Federal Writer's Project, for which he participates in oral-history research. Writes book reviews for *New Challenge, Direction, The Negro Quarterly,* and *New Masses.* Publishes several short stories: "Slick Gonna Learn," "The Birthmark," "Afternoon," and "Mister Toussan."

1942 Resigns from the Federal Writer's Project, becoming managing editor of the short-lived *Negro Quarterly.*

1943–45 Joins Merchant Marine.

1945   Awarded a Rosenwald Fellowship to write a novel. Begins work on *Invisible Man* while staying with a friend in Wakesfield, Vermont.

1946   Marries Fanny McConnell.

1952   *Invisible Man* published, for which he receives National Book Award and Russwurm Award.

1958–61   Teaches Russian and American literature at Bard College.

1964   *Shadow and Act* published, containing essays from 1942 to 1964. Teaches creative writing at Rutgers. Fellow in American Studies at Yale.

1968   A fire in his summer house in Massachusetts destroys 365 pages of his second novel.

1975   Ellison elected to the American Academy of the Arts and Letters in December.

1981   "Ralph Ellison's Long Tongue," a mixed-media theater piece with the composer Julius Hemphill performing, is staged in New York.

1984   Awarded Langston Hughes medallion by City College in New York for contributions to arts and letters.

1986   Publishes *Going to the Territory,* containing essays from 1957 to 1980.

Contributors

HAROLD BLOOM, Sterling Professor of the Humanities at Yale University, is the author of *The Anxiety of Influence, Poetry and Repression,* and many other volumes of literary criticism. His forthcoming study, *Freud: Transference and Authority,* attempts a full-scale reading of all of Freud's major writings. A MacArthur Prize Fellow, he is general editor of five series of literary criticism published by Chelsea House.

R. W. B. LEWIS is Neil Gray Professor of Rhetoric at Yale University. He is the author of *The American Adam, The Picaresque Saint, The Poetry of Hart Crane, Trials of the Word,* and *Edith Wharton: A Biography,* for which he received a Pulitzer Prize.

JONATHAN BAUMBACH is Professor of English at the City University of New York, Brooklyn College, where he has directed the M.F.A. Program in creative writing since 1974. His books include *The Language of Nightmare, Reruns, Babble, The Return of Service,* and *My Father, More or Less.*

ALLEN GUTTMANN is Professor of English and American Studies at Amherst College and is the author of *The Conservative Tradition in America, The Jewish Writer in America,* and *From Ritual to Record: The Nature of Modern Sports.*

TONY TANNER is a Fellow of King's College, Cambridge. His books include *The Reign of Wonder: Naivety and Reality in American Literature, City of Words, Saul Bellow,* and *Adultery in the Novel.*

ROBERT B. STEPTO is Professor of English, American Studies, and African and Afro-American Studies at Yale University and the author of *Beyond the Veil.*

SUSAN L. BLAKE is Associate Professor of English at Lafayette College.

CHARLES T. DAVIS was Professor of English and Afro-American Studies at Yale University. He is the author of *Black Is the Color of the Cosmos.*

175

HOUSTON A. BAKER, JR., is the Albert M. Greenfield Professor of Human Relations at the University of Pennsylvania. He is the author of two volumes of poetry and many critical works, including *Long Black Song, The Journey Back,* and *Blues, Ideology, and Afro-American Literature.*

MICHAEL G. COOKE is Professor of English at Yale University. His books include *Acts of Inclusion, The Blind Man Traces the Circle, The Romantic Will,* and *Afro-American Literature in the Twentieth Century: The Achievement of Intimacy.*

DOUGLAS ROBINSON is Professor of English Philology at the University of Tampere in Finland. His books include a study of John Barth and *American Apocalypses.*

BERNDT OSTENDORF is Professor of Afro-American Studies at the Amerika Institut, University of Munich. He has published extensively on modern American black writers and on the history of jazz.

Bibliography

Allen, Michael. "Some Examples of Faulknerian Rhetoric in Ellison's *Invisible Man.*" In *The Black American Writer,* edited by C. W. E. Bigsby, Jr., 143–51. Deland, Fla.: Everett / Edwards, Inc., 1969.

Anderson, Jervis. "Going to the Territory." *The New Yorker* 52 (November 22, 1976): 55–108.

Baker, Houston A., Jr. *Long Black Song: Essays in Black American Literature and Culture.* Charlottesville: University Press of Virginia, 1972.

Bell, J. D. "Ellison's *Invisible Man.*" *Explicator* 29 (1970): item 19.

Benston, Kimberly W. "Ellison, Baraka, and the Faces of Tradition." *boundary 2* 6 (Winter 1978): 333–54.

Bloch, Alice. "Sight Imagery in *Invisible Man.*" *English Journal* 55 (1966): 1019.

Bluestein, Gene. "The Blues as a Literary Theme." *Massachusetts Review* 8 (1967): 593–617.

Bone, Robert A. *The Negro Novel in America.* New Haven: Yale University Press, 1965.

———. "Ralph Ellison and the Uses of Imagination." In *Anger and Beyond,* edited by Herbert Hill, 86–111. New York: Harper and Row, 1969.

CLA Journal 13, no. 3 (1970). Special Ralph Ellison issue.

Callahan, John F. "The Historical Frequencies of Ralph Waldo Ellison." In *Chant of Saints,* edited by Michael S. Harper and Robert B. Stepto, 33–52. Urbana: University of Illinois Press, 1979.

Clarke, John H. "The Visible Dimensions of *Invisible Man.*" *Black World* 20, no. 2 (1970): 27–30.

Collier, Eugenia W. "The Nightmare Truth of an Invisible Man." *Black World* 20, no. 2 (1970): 12–19.

Covo, Jacqueline. *The Blinking Eye: Ralph Waldo Ellison and His American, French, and Italian Critics, 1952–1971.* Metuchen, N. J.: Scarecrow Press, 1974.

Davis, Arthur P. *From the Dark Tower.* Washington, D.C.: Howard University Press, 1974.

Emanuel, James A. "The Invisible Men of American Literature." *Books Abroad* 26 (1963): 391–94.

Fass, Barbara. "Rejection of Paternalism: Hawthorne's 'My Kinsman Major Molineux' and Ellison's *Invisible Man.*" *CLA Journal* 24 (1971): 317–24.

Ford, Nick A. "The Ambivalence of Ralph Ellison." *Black World* 20, no. 2 (1970): 5–9.

Gayle, Addison, Jr. *The Way of the New World: The Black Novel in America.* Garden City, N.Y.: Anchor Press / Doubleday, 1975.

Gibson, Donald B., ed. *Five Black Writers: Essays on Wright, Ellison, Baldwin, Hughes, and Le Roi Jones.* New York: New York University Press, 1970.

Glicksberg, Charles I. "The Symbolism of Vision." *Southwest Review* 39 (1954): 259–65.

Greene, Maxine. "Against Invisibility." *College English* 30 (1969): 430–36.

Griffin, Edward M. "Notes from a Clean, Well-Lighted Place: Ralph Ellison's *Invisible Man.*" *Twentieth Century Literature* 24 (1969): 129–44.

Hassan, Ihab. "The Novel of Outrage: A Minority Voice in Postwar American Fiction." *American Scholar* 34 (1965): 219–53.

————. *Radical Innocence.* Princeton: Princeton University Press, 1961.

Hayes, Peter L. "The Incest Theme in *Invisible Man.*" *Western Humanities Review* 23 (1969): 335–39.

Hersey, John, ed. *Ralph Ellison: A Collection of Critical Essays.* Englewood Cliffs, N. J.: Prentice-Hall, 1974.

Horowitz, Floyd Ross. "The Enigma of Ralph Ellison's Intellectual Man." *CLA Journal* 7 (1963): 126–32.

Howard, David C. "Points in Defense of Ellison's *Invisible Man.*" *Notes on Contemporary Literature* 2 (1971): 13–14.

Howe, Irving. "A Reply to Ralph Ellison." *The New Leader* 47 (1964): 12–22.

Hyman, Stanley Edgar. "American Negro Literature and the Folk Tradition." In *The Promised End: Essays and Reviews 1942–1962,* 295–315. Freeport, N.Y.: Books for Libraries Press, 1963.

————. "The Negro Writer in America: An Exchange." *Partisan Review* 25 (1958): 197–211.

Isaacs, Harold R. "Five Black Writers and Their African Ancestors." *Phylon* 21 (1960): 317–36.

Kaiser, Ernest. "A Critical Look at Ellison's Fiction and at Social and Literary Criticism by and about the Author." *Black World* 20, no. 2 (1970): 53–59.

Kazin, Alfred. *Bright Book of Life.* New York: Dell, 1971.

Kent, George. *Blackness and the Adventure of American Culture.* Chicago: Third World, 1972.

Kist, E. M. "A Laingian Analysis of Blackness in Ralph Ellison's *Invisible Man.*" *Studies in Black Literature* 7 (Spring 1976): 19–23.

Klein, Marcus. *After Alienation.* Cleveland: World Publishing Company, 1964.

Kostelanetz, Richard. "Ralph Ellison: Novelist as Brown Skinned Aristocrat." *Shenandoah* 20, no. 4 (Summer 1969): 56–77.

————. "The Politics of Ellison's Booker: *Invisible Man* as Symbolic History." *Chicago Review* 19, no. 2 (1967): 5–26.

Lee, Robert A. "Sight and Mask: Ralph Ellison's *Invisible Man.*" *Negro American Literature Forum* 4 (1970): 22–23.

Lewis, R. W. B. "Days of Wrath and Laughter." In *Trials of the Word,* 184–235. New Haven: Yale University Press, 1965.

Lieber, Todd M. "Ralph Ellison and the Metaphor of Invisibility in Black Literary Tradition." *American Quarterly* 24, no. 1 (March 1972): 86–100.

Ludington, Charles T., Jr. "Protest and Anti-protest: Ralph Ellison." *Southern Humanities Review* 4 (1970): 31–39.

Margolies, Edward. *Native Sons: A Critical Study of Twentieth-Century Negro American Authors.* Philadelphia: J. B. Lippincott Company, 1968.

Margolies, Edward and David Bakish, eds. *Afro-American Fiction, Eighteen Fifty-Three to Nineteen Seventy-Six: A Guide to Information Sources.* Detroit: Gale, 1979.

Murray, Albert. *The Omni-Americans.* New York: Outerbridge and Dienstfrey, 1970.

Nash, Russell W. "Stereotypes and Social Types in Ellison's *Invisible Man.*" *Sociological Quarterly* 6 (Autumn 1965): 349–60.

Neal, Larry. "Ellison's Zoot Suit." *Black World* 20, no. 2 (1970): 31–52.

O'Daniel, Therman B. "The Image of Man as Portrayed by Ralph Ellison." *CLA Journal* 10 (1967): 277–84.

O'Meally, Robert G. *The Craft of Ralph Ellison.* Cambridge: Harvard University Press, 1980.

Radford, Frederick L. "The Journey towards Castration: Interracial Sexual Stereotypes in Ellison's *Invisible Man.*" *Journal of American Studies* 4 (1970): 227–31.

Reilly, John M., ed. *Twentieth-Century Interpretations of* Invisible Man: *A Collection of Essays.* Englewood Cliffs, N. J.: Prentice-Hall, 1970.

Rovit, Earl H. "Ralph Ellison and the American Comic Tradition." *Wisconsin Studies in Contemporary Literature* 1 (1960): 34–42.

Schafer, William J. "Ralph Ellison and the Birth of the Anti-Hero." *Critique: Studies in Modern Fiction* 10, no. 2 (1968): 81–93.

Schwartz, Delmore. "Fiction Chronicle: The Wrongs of Innocence and Experience." *Partisan Review* 29 (May–June 1952): 354–59.

Skerrett, Joseph T. "The Wright Interpretation: Ralph Ellison and the Anxiety of Influence." *Massachusetts Review* 21, no. 1 (1980): 196–212.

Stepto, Robert B. *From Behind the Veil: A Study of Afro-American Narrative.* Urbana: University of Illinois Press, 1979.

Tischler, Nancy M. "Negro Literature and Classic Form." *Contemporary Literature* 10 (Summer 1969): 352–65.

Trimmer, Joseph A. *A Casebook on Ralph Ellison's* Invisible Man. New York: Thomas Y. Crowell, Co., 1972.

Warren, Robert Penn. "The Unity of Experience." *Commentary* 34 (1965): 91–96.

Waughmare, J. M. "Invisibility and the American Negro: Ralph Ellison's *Invisible Man.*" *Quest* 49 (1968): 29–30.

Werner, Craig Hansen. *Paradoxical Resolutions: American Fiction since James Joyce.* Urbana: University of Illinois Press, 1982.

Acknowledgments

"Ellison's Essays" by R. W. B. Lewis from *The New York Review of Books* (January 28, 1965), © 1965 by Nyrev, Inc. Reprinted by permission.

"Nightmare of a Native Son" (originally entitled "Nightmare of a Native Son: *Invisible Man* by Ralph Ellison") by Jonathan Baumbach from *Five Black Writers: Essays on Wright, Ellison, Baldwin, Hughes, and Le Roi Jones,* edited by Donald B. Gibson, © 1970 by New York University. Reprinted by permission of New York University Press and the author. An earlier version of this essay appeared in *The Landscape of Nightmare* by Jonathan Baumbach (New York University Press, 1965).

"American Nightmare" (originally entitled "Focus on Ralph Ellison's *Invisible Man:* American Nightmare") by Allen Guttmann from *American Dreams, American Nightmare,* edited by David Madden, © 1970 by Southern Illinois University Press. Reprinted by permission of the author.

"The Music of Invisibility" by Tony Tanner from *City of Words: American Fiction 1950–1970* by Tony Tanner, © 1971 by Tony Tanner. Reprinted by permission of the author, Harper & Row Publishers, and Jonathan Cape Ltd.

"Literacy and Hibernation: Ralph Ellison's *Invisible Man*" by Robert B. Stepto from *From Behind the Veil: A Study of Afro-American Narrative* by Robert B. Stepto, © 1979 by the Board of Trustees of the University of Illinois. Reprinted by permission of the University of Illinois Press and the author.

"Ritual and Rationalization: Black Folklore in the Works of Ralph Ellison" by Susan L. Blake from *PMLA* 94, no. 1 (January 1979), © 1979 by the Modern Language Association of America. Reprinted by permission.

"The Mixed Heritage of the Modern Black Novel" (originally entitled "The Mixed Heritage of the Modern Black Novel: Ralph Ellison and Friends") by Charles T. Davis from *Black Is the Color of the Cosmos: Essays on Afro-American Literature and Culture, 1942–1981,* edited by Henry Louis Gates, Jr., © 1982 by The Estate of Charles T. Davis. Reprinted by permission of Garland Publishing Inc.

"Creativity and Commerce in the Trueblood Episode" (excerpted from a chapter entitled "A Dream of American Form") by Houston A. Baker, Jr., from *Blues, Ideology, and*

Afro-American Literature by Houston A. Baker, Jr., © 1984 by The University of Chicago. Reprinted by permission of The University of Chicago Press.

"Solitude" (originally entitled "Solitude: The Beginnings of Self-Realization in Zora Neale Hurston, Richard Wright, and Ralph Ellison") by Michael G. Cooke from *Afro-American Literature in the Twentieth Century* by Michael G. Cooke, © 1984 by Michael G. Cooke. Reprinted by permission of the author and Yale University Press.

"Call Me Jonah" by Douglas Robinson from *American Apocalypses: The Image of the End of the World in American Literature* by Douglas Robinson, © 1985 by The Johns Hopkins University Press. Reprinted by permission of the publisher.

"Anthropology, Modernism, and Jazz" by Berndt Ostendorf, © 1986 by Berndt Ostendorf. Published for the first time in this volume.

Index